SOLDIERS OF THE CROSS

Pioneers of Social Change

Susie Swift
and
David Lamb

By Norman H. Murdoch

D1057289

CREST BOOKS

The Salvation Army National Publications

Alexandria, Virginia

Published by Crest Books, Salvation Army National Headquarters
615 Slaters Lane, Alexandria, Virginia 22314
(703) 684-5518 Fax: (703) 684-5539
http: //www.salvationarmyusa.org

Printed in the United States of America

Book design and layout by ATLIS Graphics & Design

Library of Congress Control Number: 2006920102

ISBN-10: 0-9740940-7-2
ISBN-13: 978-0-9740940-7-6

Special thanks to the following: The Salvation Army International Heritage
Centre; The Salvation Army Archives, Australia Southern Territory; The
Salvation Army Archives, Canada and Bermuda Territory; The Salvation
Army Archives, New Zealand; The Salvation Army Archives, National
Headquarters; and Sinsinawa Dominican Archives

Contents

General Acknowledgments

I have incurred many debts during the fifteen years I have been working on the biography of Susie F. Swift. I am indebted to The Salvation Army's former National Editor in Chief of Crest Books, Lt. Colonel Marlene Chase, and her staff for choosing to publish and circulate this work and for guiding me through the process.

Most of my research support has come from the University College, where I was a faculty member, and the Research Department of the University of Cincinnati. I first sought a grant in March 1990 from the university's Research Council to go to the Sinsinawa Dominican Convent in Wisconsin where Susie Swift is buried and where she left her papers in the Archives. While I was at Sinsinawa Archivist Sister Marjorie Buttner copied Swift's papers for me—I am most grateful to her. In that post–Vatican II era she even invited me to receive the Eucharist at the community's mass. It was my first experience of the opening windows of the Catholic Church that occurred as a result of John XXIII's papacy.

I dedicate this Susie F. Swift biography to my father, Brigadier Walter H. Murdoch, who was raised a Roman Catholic by his mother, Agnes Bridget Fitzgerald Murdoch. Subsequent to Vatican II, my father's sister Alice asked him to pray at the funeral mass of his brother–in–law, George McNamara, where he received the Eucharist for the first time since his teen years when he converted to Methodism. My father later became a Salvationist through the influence of Commissioner Samuel Logan Brengle, Susie Swift's brother–in–law. He had met Brengle at Asbury College in the late 1920s, while he was still a Methodist. Thus Susie Swift's story of crossing boundaries caught my eye.

*****

The University of Cincinnati and The Salvation Army have supported my David C. Lamb research at three of the Army's Archives: in Alexandria, Virginia; London, England; and Toronto, Ontario. Their research grants also made it possible for me to visit the British Library and Public Records Office in London. I am grateful to these institutions for their suggestions and patience. For the Lamb material I am particularly in the debt of David Pitcher at the Army's Toronto Archives, to Scott Bedio in Alexandria, and George Hazell in Sydney, Australia.

In London in September 2003, Commissioner Dr. Paul du Plessis and Major Christine Clements arranged for me to present an address at The Salvation Army William Booth College on the three steps that lead to a history: "From an idea, to an investigation, to the invention of a history." Participants in the discussion included the faculty of the college and the staff of the Army's International Headquarters. In June 2003, I had given a paper on "The Life and Work of Susie Forrest Swift (Sr. Terese Imelda),"[1] on a panel on "Women Religious from Multiple Faith Traditions: Crossing Boundaries, Comparative Perspectives on the History of Women Religious," at the Benedictine Sisters of Mount St. Scholastica, in Atchison, Kansas. In London and Kansas I was challenged and enlightened by questions and points of agreement and disagreement made by those present.

*****

For years I have tested research ideas on colleagues of the Humanities Faculty of the University College, University of Cincinatti. Professors Janine C. Hartman, Mark A. Lause, L. J. Andrew Villalon, Charles A. Seibert, and Blasco Sabrinho have helped me look at my work from outside the parameters of my own thinking. Professor R. G. Moyles of the University of Alberta has read my work and made helpful comments. Other experts in Salvation Army organization and history who commented on the work were: Dr. John Coutts, Mr. Tom Aitken, Commissioners Drs. Paul du Plessis and Harry Williams, and General John Larsson in Britain; Major Dr. Harold Hill in New Zealand and Envoy Dr. George Hazell in Australia. Illustrations have come from the Toronto, Alexandria, Sydney and the Sinsinawa Archives.

For the patience and support of my wife, Professor Grace M. A. Murdoch, I am most grateful. While others deserve praise for lending their time and ideas to this study, the mistakes are my own. Since history is in the end a result of taking an idea, giving it careful consideration through the investigation of a multitude of dry facts, and then applying a personal interpretation to the meaning of those facts, I take total responsibility and invite reactions and rejoinders from all quarters.

---

[1] Abbreviation Sr. denotes a Catholic sister or nun.

General Introduction

Biographies of Susie Forrest Swift and David Crichton Lamb

To combine biographical studies of Commissioner David C. Lamb and Brigadier–Sister Susie F. Swift may seem a strange marriage indeed. It appeared to be just that to me when the editor first proposed I combine the two biographies in one book. My friend, Harry Williams, endorsed the marriage.

I began research on Susie Swift two decades ago, and began a study of David Lamb in 2004. To the naked eye these are contrasting personalities who took life in what seemed to be completely divergent directions after touching down in London at the Salvation Army's International Headquarters in the 1880s. Both Swift and Lamb claimed divine guidance in the roads they took. But for Swift there were several spiritual and vocational by–ways on the road to London in 1883 and then to Rome in 1897. Lamb's journey took what appears to be a more or less straight line.

David C. Lamb was for most of his life a Salvation Army commissioner and a member of the Army's International Headquarters staff in London during the first half of the twentieth century. He was the Army's third and longest serving international social commissioner, responsible for all of its social enterprises under the Darkest England program of social redemption. He was a family man, with a wife who was prominent in England's courts and poor law administration; they had six children. In 1934 he was a candidate for general and a recipient of high honors from the British government, professional societies, and the University of Aberdeen in his native Scotland. Almost certainly he was a candidate for a knighthood and a seat in the House of Lords. He was at the center of the Army's most horrendous internal battle, the 1929 removal of Bramwell Booth as general. He continued to be a supporter of change in the Army's constitution that followed in 1930–31. He was a highly visible public figure as he toured the world after World War II to proclaim his personal agenda for peace and the social improvement of the masses.

Susie F. Swift was another matter altogether. Unlike Lamb's well-focused thoughts and life, she was a life–long seeker who only occasionally fulfilled her dreams for sanctity, romance, and childbearing. Her best friends saw her as a troubled personality, prone to suspect the worst. She was a Salvation Army officer for only a decade and a half at the end of the nineteenth century. She resigned in 1897 in New York City, where the Army had sent her to organize an association to find financial contributors to support its work. Beginning in 1883 she served the Army in London in the rescue of "fallen women," and later as an initiator of a program for boys termed "waifs and strays." Because of her Vassar College B.A. degree, the Army employed her wit and wisdom at its Training Home for Women and as editor of *All the World*, a missionary journal. She was well–connected. Her brother–in–law, Commissioner Samuel Logan Brengle, was a leading officer—as was her sister, Elizabeth Swift Brengle. The Army has eulogized them in biographies. At one point, according to a newspaper report, Swift was tentatively engaged to wed General and Mrs. William Booth's third son Herbert. About seven years after this alleged broken engagement she "left the work," converted to Roman Catholicism and accepted the veil of a Dominican nun.

These biographies, joined at the hip if you please, provide vivid examples of the contrasting lives of the thousands of men and women who became Salvation Army officers after its inception in 1878. While many remained in what the Army refers to as "the work" for a lifetime, thousands of others, for personal or spiritual reasons, left the Army to continue their lives in other realms. Which is the superior of the two groups? It would be well to honor the work of both, since no one can fully discern the hand of God in human affairs, particularly as God intervenes in personal choices that are mostly hidden from our view.

Soldier of the Cross

Pioneer of Social Change

Susie Swift

Brigadier Susie Forrest Swift–Sister Mary Imelda Teresa
(1862–1916):

From Sisterhood to Sisterhood
Vassar College to Salvation Army to Dominican Orders

Dedication

Brigadier Walter H. Murdoch (1906–1985)
Roman Catholic to Methodist to Salvation Army
His Life Went in the Opposite Direction
from that of Susie F. Swift
But He Shared Her Christian Faith

Acknowledgments—
Susie F. Swift Research

I owe many debts to those who have assisted me in the research and writing of this biography of Susie Forrest Swift. First, my father taught me, from his personal search for salvation, that Christian faith is not the property of any denomination, but is the lifetime search of an individual soul. When our family visited his Roman Catholic mother, Agnes Bridget Fitzgerald Murdoch and the family of his sister Alice MacNamara, we worshipped at St. James Church in Royal Oak, Michigan and acknowledged their faith. My father's Roman Catholic baptismal certificate from Oil City, Pennsylvania, was in his papers when he died in Asbury Park, New Jersey in 1985.

Walter H. Murdoch, spent his life from 1906 to his teens as a Roman Catholic. Then he experienced conversion in a Methodist revival in Oil City, Pennsylvania, and attended Asbury College in Wilmore, Kentucky. He then served with my mother as an officer in The Salvation Army from 1933 to 1985. His life and faith indirectly led to my curiosity about the religious journey of Susie Swift. My father met Swift's brother–in–law, Commissioner Samuel Logan Brengle, at Asbury College during his undergraduate years in 1927–31. Brengle used the college as a retreat from his evangelistic work. Dad's friendship with Brengle led to his desire to become a Salvation Army officer.

Archivists and librarians are an historian's best friends. Most of the primary material for this work is in the archives of the Dominican Convent at Sinsinawa, Wisconsin, where the archivist made Swift's work available to me. I had the same privilege at The Salvation Army Archives in Alexandria, Virginia and London, England. Sr. Librarians Les Vuylsteke at Langsam Library, University of Cincinnati, were generous with his time and wisdom.

Introduction to Susie Forrest Swift

Herringshaw's American Blue Book of Biography: Men of 1913, states that Sister Mary Imelda Teresa (Susie Forrest Swift), O.P.[1], claimed that as a Salvation Army officer in 1890 she "gave General Booth the first outline of his Darkest England social scheme."[2] Beyond that reference, which she likely gave to *Herringshaw* when they requested biographical information, there may be no other report of her role in producing the Army's premier social reform program.[3] The proposal of the Darkest England program was that the Salvation Army would move vast numbers of urban England's unemployed "back to the land," both in England and in what the British saw as the "wastelands" in their vast overseas empire.

As an 1883 graduate of Vassar College, America's first elite "Ivy–league" women's college in Poughkeepsie, New York, Susie Swift was an exceptional find for The Salvation Army in 1887. William and Catherine Booth, like leaders of other social and religious agencies, were pleased to attract a small group of women of Swift's social class and talent to manage social settlements for "fallen" women and poor children and to write for and edit their journals and books.

There is no reason to doubt Swift's word that she wrote the first outline of the Salvation Army social reform plan. Published in October 1890 as a book, *In Darkest England and the Way Out,* William Booth is listed on the title page as the author. There is nothing in the preface to the book to indicate her role, but it was not unusual in 1890, nor is it unusual today, to have research assistants do the grunt work for a distinguished "author."

It is also reasonable to surmise that Swift received the material from which she wrote the first outline of the scheme from Frank Smith, the first commissioner of the Salvation Army's Social Wing. Smith had been the principal exponent of a social reform program in the Army. He had been intrigued with Anglo–American and European social reform ideas since 1884, the year he read Henry George's seminal work, *Progress and Poverty*, on his way to take charge of the Army in the United States. General Booth likely asked Swift to organize Smith's notes into an outline of how the program would work before he decided to pass the outline to W. T. Stead who put the work into a narrative book form. While Swift was composing the outline, Smith was setting up factories of the City Colony in London's impoverished East End, the first step in the program that proposed to move Britain's unemployed from city slums "back to the land."

At some point the Booths, William and Bramwell, with the approval of William's wife Catherine, had decided to ask W. T. Stead, one of Britain's leading journalists, to provide a final pre–publication text of the book. Once Stead turned Swift's outline and Smith's research into a book, the Booths put their final touch on the copy that went to press in October 1890, as Catherine lay dying of cancer.

So who was this anonymous woman writer of the first outline of the social reform plan that evolved into the book, *In Darkest England and the Way Out*, that became the foundation of the Salvation Army international social program? And why did the Army hide her role, as well as that of Frank Smith, behind a veil of anonymity?

Susie F. Swift's Early Life and First Sisterhood: Education & Methodist Conversion

Susie Forrest Swift was born on June 10, 1862 in the village of Amenia, New York, to George Henry and Camelia Forrest Paine Swift. Writers variously describe George Swift as a banker and lawyer. He may have been both, since these were days before graduate schools and formal credentialing existed in either profession. Both of Susie's parents traced their American lineage to the first arrivals in Plymouth, Massachusetts. Camelia's line of Boston Paines traced their pedigree to Plymouth Colony in 1624, four years after Pilgrims disembarked from the Mayflower.[1]

At age fourteen Susie experienced her first "conversion" experience under the guidance of the Rev. George A. Halls, a Methodist preacher, although the family had earlier attended a Presbyterian church. Thus the Swifts had moved from Calvinist–Puritan to Wesleyan–Arminian doctrinal sympathies. Susie was sufficiently devoted to Wesleyanism to have memorized four volumes of Methodist catechism and to have studied the Berean confirmation course for five years.

But later, after she converted to Roman Catholicism, she claimed that she had always been "wholly Catholic in instinct, though destitute of any dogmatic basis for my intuition." This was the testimony of a new convert. There are no clues to support such instincts in her early diary or letters. She also later claimed that her family was "not overly devout but fairly 'orthodox,'" a seemingly contradictory analysis that she shared with her sister Elizabeth.

Susie wrote that she attended "Methodist, Presbyterian and Episcopal churches by turns," to which she added Universalist and Congregational churches while she was at Hillside Seminary, a girl's boarding school in Bridgeport, Connecticut. As a girl she read *Barnes' Sermons for the Young*, a little of *Clarke's Commentaries*, Dwight L. Moody's *Sermons*, and "snatches of Butler and Hooper."[2] For a girl from a not particularly devout family that was quite a theological bundle of books.

In 1883, when Swift received her B.A. from Vassar College, she described her college faith as "agnostic," a late 19th century Greek construction that indicated that a person claimed not to "know" and not to claim a creed. This was her position until she accepted baptism and confirmation at Christ Church, Episcopal, Poughkeepsie, rituals she referred to as "a scientific experiment."

After graduation she signed a contract to teach in Morristown, New Jersey at a "fashionable boarding school" in 1883–84. When a horse ran away and she was thrown from a carriage, her parents decided to send her to Europe to recuperate. Susie later recalled her thoughts as she "spun through the air" from the carriage: "I'm glad that here is the end of the miserable mess I'm making of my life."[3] Such morbid thoughts are not uncommon to young minds. Susie's sister Elizabeth, called Lil or Lilly by the family, and Vassar friend Ella Leonard, later the business editor of *Kate Field's Washington*, accompanied her to Britain. Lil had dropped out of Vassar due to poor health.

Susie was unhappy that her parents insisted that she break her school contract. She recalled stopping to look at New York's St. Patrick's Cathedral while the trip was still being discussed. An idea seized her to ask a priest to help settle her dilemma. The sacristan (priest on duty) sent her to a Madison Avenue address to see "Fr. McD.,"[4] possibly her later spiritual advisor, Fr. McDermot, a 22–year–old secretary to Archbishop Corrigan at the time. McDermot did not deal with the question of conscience she raised, but "leaped at once to the fact that my religious system gave me no basis from which to settle my ethical difficulties."

In 1897, after her Catholic conversion, Swift recalled that Mc-Dermot, the future "Bishop of B.," had impressed her with his grasp of theology. He told her she was more than a creature of "ignorance or error [since she] admitted the existence of a Creator [and] tacitly admitted duties toward Him, and that the doctrine of the Trinity was not necessarily unreasonable because it transcended reason." Swift observed that eighteen years later, "I put the book *Faith of Our Fathers,* which he gave me that day into the library of the Dominican Convent where I was Mistress of Novices. Fourteen years later Susie recalled that on her voyage to Britain she had read Catholic literature, Newman's *Poems* and the *Dream of Gerontius that* "gave me a brief, strong creed."[5]

As with any memory that recalls early impressions we must note the timeline of Swift's accounts of her four "conversions." When did she write each account? How do the later accounts fit with early letters and diaries. Swift's movement from Methodism, to agnosticism, to Salvationism, to Catholicism, are best understood from what she wrote at the time each conversion occurred. Her later recollection of earlier premonitions must be set in the context of her new mindset as a believer in a new faith. For a person writing autobiography, memory is a convenient, but often a faulty means of explaining the later development of new beliefs and circumstances. Diaries and letters that existed at the time of the conversion are a far stronger indication of rationale for the change of heart and mind.

Primary documents are a more reliable support for a biographer's history than the fragile memory of a mature convert's later claim to what she experienced fourteen years in the past. By that time memory is colored by years of experiences of a new faith and myth clouds reality. Fortunately for this biographer, Susie Swift kept a diary which is available at the Sinsinawa Dominican archives in Wisconsin. The diary is particularly helpful for Swift's two decades in The Salvation Army. Dominican and Salvation Army archives also contain many letters she received from friends. Letters she wrote are not available except in rare cases when friends cited them in their responses. These are also in the Sinsinawa archives.

Susie Swift's 2nd Conversion—
The Salvation Army, Glasgow,
Scotland, 1884

On her recuperative journey to Britain, Susie Swift wrote a first person narrative in her diary. Their first stop was in Glasgow, Scotland where two members of the trio of girls "poked their inquisitive heads" into the second floor hall of the Salvation Army Glasgow V. Corps on Sauchehall Street. Ella Leonard had asked Susie, "What is the Salvation Army?" Susie answered, "I don't exactly know ... but I think they are something like Mormons; they act very queerly, and they believe in perfection." There were only fifteen soldiers at the afternoon meeting that Susie and Ella attended. They returned for the evening service. Susie recalled in her 1893 account of her Salvationist conversion that she and Ellen had cared little for the prayers or for the singing, but when the testimonies began, they "were most interested."

> The spiritual ... experiences of these people seemed so much above the language in which they were able to describe them! The doubts, the conflicts, the complications, which we had been wont to set down as peculiar to people of a certain amount of culture, seemed to have been theirs as well as ours. Could it be that the acts of surrender and faith by which they claimed to have broken through all their entanglements, were possible for us?[1]

Susie wrote that her sister Lil went with them on Sunday evening to see what there was about the Salvationists that made

Susie and Ellen so "crazy about them." When the meeting closed with an invitation to pray, Ella went to the front of the hall and knelt at the "penitent form," a Methodist "mourner's bench"[2] where penitents sought forgiveness for their sins and faith for their salvation. Susie followed, but sensed that her elder sister Lil was watching her with disapproval.

Ten years later, as a Salvation Army officer, Swift described this conversion experience to readers of an Army journal with emotional enthusiasm. I "flung myself upon the last chance which Protestantism held. I had never been at enough Methodist meetings to understand the etiquette of the 'Mourner's Bench.'" Susie wrote that at the "penitent form" a Salvationist "sister adjured me to 'let go all the little things and slide down the hill.'" Susie asked her to go away and let her think. Then Lieutenant Mrs. Downing came and told her: "you must be willing to do whatever God wants you to do. For instance, I never dreamed that He could ask me to join the Salvation Army." Susie responded "serenely, 'No, oh no!'" and Downing apologized:

> "I don't suppose He could. Of course, you are different. But what I meant was, that you must be willing for even that, if such a thing could be as that He should want you." "Oh, yes," I answered, "I shouldn't mind. Only He couldn't, you see." She suggested that I should pray, and I shut my eyes and tried; but all I could think of to say was: "Oh, God, I don't believe as these people do, but I believe they have a power that enables them to live up to their ideas of right and wrong. I give myself all up to Thee. I will do right! Give me the power." ... It was no process of reasoning. I just saw Jesus with my soul, and I saw Him as the working man of Nazareth, who had come down from heaven to earth, which had been tired and cold and hard worked, and roughly clad, and who called me now to follow Him to the poorest and the lowest.

Susie recalled that her sister Lil "swept up to me, notebook in hand." Lil was "the self–constituted chaparone of our party." Susie, who seldom spoke well of her sister, noticed Lil's outrage and recalled her charge:

> "Well, you have done it now!" "I sympathize with you in your search for literary material, but I think you have carried it too far this time.

*I don't think its right." "What?" [Susie] asked meekly. [Lil contin-
ued] "To come out here and kneel down, just to see what these people
will say to you, and to write them up more in detail. I consider it absolutely irreverent."*

As Susie put it later, she "felt for [Lil] nothing but pity, because
she had not found what I had found. I knew that work the soldiers had spoken about was done in me."[3]

These were Susie's recollections of her 1883 Salvation Army
conversion in 1893 while she was still an officer in its ranks serving as a writer, teacher and social worker. But after she became a
Dominican Roman Catholic nun in 1897 she never renounced
the faith she received in 1883. But she did denounce the Protestant dogma on which it was based.

She wrote of her Salvationist conversion in an 1897 account
of her conversion to Roman Catholicism: "It seems to me as if all
my life long, I had been looking for a religion which should be
strong enough to do something for me, although very few people suspected it." As she recalled her childhood influences, she
noted they had led her to see "all religions as equally false and
all equally true." At Vassar College she had embraced Herbert
Spencer's agnostic dogma: "Soul of good in all things evil, soul
of truth in all things false." This was to her "a condensation of
the utmost attainable wisdom on the subject" of religion. She
wrote: "I think by nature I was a born skeptic."[4]

In the Salvation Army's early years as a home mission society in London's East End in the 1860s and 1870s, it had been
common for members to paint dark pictures of their sinful past
so as to make their conversion experiences appear quite remarkable. It was not easy for middle–class converts like Susie Swift to
vie with prostitutes and drunkards for a testimony that renounced sins of intemperance or sexual promiscuity. But Swift,
writing as a Salvationist in 1893, did her best to find a compara-
ble sin. She unearthed skepticism at the tender age of eight over
whether or not the Bible was true.

In 1897, after her Roman Catholic conversion, she once again
looked back and recalled that as a child she had seen beyond the
mountains "the Eucharistic God of Whom I had never even heard
in all my ten years of life. But He waked in my heart that night

the hunger which was never stilled till the hour of my First Communion—the hunger which was to make me bold enough to cut loose, bit by bit, from all convention and from all tradition."[5]

Always an introspective soul, while she was a Salvationist Susie Swift wrote a penitent's hymn that remains in the *Salvation Army Song Book*. The hymn might just as well have been written when she was a soul–searching young Methodist, or Salvationist, or a Roman Catholic penitent and nun:

Mine to rise when Thou dost call me, Lifelong though the journey be;
Thine to measure all its windings, Leading step by step to Thee
Mine to follow, even blindly, Thine, O Christ, to go before;
Mine to try and scale the barrier, Thine to fling an open door.

Mine to smile in face of failure, Thine to gladden my defeat;
Mine to kneel and drink of Marah, Thine to make its waters sweet.
Thine the sealing and revealing all the outcome of my vow.
As I give Thee soul and body, Mine no longer, Thine just now.

[Refrain:] I am Thine, O Lord and Master, Thine to follow to the end.
Thou art mine, O Christ my Savior, Guide and Helper, Lover, Friend![6]

Following Swift's 1883 conversion in the Salvation Army's Glasgow V. corps, the Vassar–trio drifted into Army meetings around England. As Susie put it, they were "getting mixed up with Salvationists from sheer love of them." They "studied the Army's workings in 33 corps and in more than a hundred meetings" before she and Lil joined its ranks as "soldiers."

For Lil, the future Mrs. Samuel Logan Brengle, conversion came later in the trip when they went to the Army's International Headquarters in London, and met "a cultured, sincere young man," Percy Clibborn. Her conversion is recorded in her future husband's biography. Clibborn asked Lil, "Are you a Christian?" When Lil said no, he asked if he could tell her "how God saved me." He explained how he had been "an infidel, a reckless man who had sown his wild oats at home and abroad; but God touched that hard, cold, proud heart, and in obedience to the call he had left all and followed." Biographer Clarence Hall wrote that, "Then and there, Lily Swift was converted."[7]

After Ella Leonard returned to Vassar in September the Swift sisters stayed in London and met Catherine Booth, wife of Army founder General William Booth. Canadian Historian Pamela J. Walker observed that Catherine's "particular class and social status were exceedingly important to her interpretation of women's preaching as well as providing opportunities for her to establish a preaching career."[8] The Swifts were from a class of converts that Catherine relished as potential leaders for the hundreds of working–class women the Army was attracting to its ministry.

The Swift sisters moved to the Clapton Training Garrison in London, where the principal, Emma Booth, Catherine's second daughter, asked them to teach. Susie also worked on the Army's new missionary magazine, *All the World*, as an assistant to the editor, Staff Captain Keith. She would spend most of her Army career in the publications department that was located first at 96 and 56 Southwark Street and later at the Army's Trade headquarters.

In 1893 Susie wrote in her own words that her call to become a Salvation Army officer had come to her:

> *as distinct and as transforming as my conversion—through the hearing of my experience told by somebody else's lips at the old Grecian Theatre, while I listened, never knowing till the end of the story that the speaker's words were of myself, and saying in my mind, 'How can that girl hesitate one instant? [Susie said that it became] quite clear what God wants of her. She was made for the Salvation Army!" [Of herself Swift said]: "In eight years and five months I have never but once doubted that I was where God wanted me to be." [Signed]: "Yours in Army bonds, Susie F. Swift."*[9]

In May 1885 Susie and Lil returned to Amenia, New York to visit their parents. They were not yet officers in the Army. But at the end of the summer Miss Susie Swift, as she was called at the time, returned to London and her editorial work on *All the World*. Meanwhile Major Frank Smith, the Salvation Army's commander in New York, heard about Lil's evangelistic work near Amenia and asked her to go to Boston to do Army work. In Boston she met Samuel Logan Brengle, a Methodist pastor who was studying at Boston Theological Seminary. On one of her trips she gave him a copy of a book she had written in London, *A Cradle of Empire* (the Army had not put her name on the cover).

That fall Brengle met William Booth on his first visit to America and was drawn to the Army.[10] After a lengthy romance, Sam and Lil married. Brengle went to the Men's Training Garrison in London in 1887 to be trained in Army tactics and be commissioned as an officer. He gave up a career as a Methodist minister to become a corps officer, divisional commander, writer and international evangelist in the Army.

Nearly all of Susie Swift's years in the Salvation Army were spent in its London literary department where she became friends with Eileen Douglas, Mildred Duff,[11] and other middle–class women who were drawn to the Army's life of selfless social service. Swift wrote hundreds of stories, poems and biographical sketches for Army journals. Like her Army sisters she also worked in social services in East End London slums. She wrote *Receiving House Girls Statements* at a home of rest on Gore Road, overlooking Victoria Park, between Bethnal Green and Hackney.[12] She worked with wayward boys at London's "waifs and strays" home. And she founded a home for newspaper boys on Fleet Street.

Soon after Lil's marriage in 1887, Susie became an "adoptive parent," something her friend and successor as editor of *All the World* Mildred Duff would do eight years later. On October 18, Swift adopted Eliza Madeley, born on December 9, 1882 to George and Mary Madeley of Manchester. A 4–page adoption agreement, witnessed in London at the office of Salvation Army solicitor Dr. A. W. G. Ranger, provided that Swift, as "adopting parent," would pay £25 to the parents, who lacked "pecuniary means" to care for Eliza. The money would help them open a china and earthenware shop and find a home. If they wanted Eliza to be returned they would have to give six months notice and pay Swift £10 per annum for the first four years and £15 for each additional year. For as long as she had custody of Eliza, Swift would benefit from the child's earnings. Most interesting, Swift promised not to "place or exhibit the said child on any public platform as a child rescued from degradation and immorality in connection with the names of the parents."

That phrase almost certainly represented the Madeley's reaction to a public uproar that had occurred in 1885 when The Salvation Army had played a role in W. T. Stead's "Maiden Tribute

Crusade" against child prostitution. With the Booths' aid Stead had arranged for the abduction of 14–year–old Eliza Armstrong in order to prove that purchasing a child from a parent for money, with their knowledge that the child might engage in prostitution, was possible in England. A London prosecutor tried Stead, Bramwell Booth, Rebecca Jarrett, and others at the Old Bailey for Eliza's abduction, which they had done to prove that England had a "white slave trade." The Madeleys refused to suffer the public ridicule that would surely come if their child became a second "Eliza." Under the adoption agreement, Swift would take Eliza from her "disadvantageous surroundings" and see that she grew to womanhood with a healthy body and mind, and became a worthy citizen and sincere Christian.

For reasons not explained in the agreement, Swift changed Eliza's Roman Catholic baptismal name of "Eliza" to "Christobel." Parties to the agreement stated the hope that Eliza would, in time, "serve as a Soldier in the Holy War against sin and Satan and for the spread of the Gospel of Our Savior Jesus Christ in this or other lands in which service the adopting Parent is herself devotedly laboring." Florence Booth, wife of the Army's Chief of Staff Bramwell Booth, eldest son of William and Catherine, arranged the adoption. The agreement named her to arbitrate disputes over the settlement if they arose. If she was unavailable Dr. Ranger, the Army solicitor, would arbitrate.[13]

The agreement was in force until September 29, 1897, when Susie converted to Roman Catholicism and became a Dominican nun. In The Salvation Army, family matters, including adoptions of children by officers, had to be approved under strict *Orders & Regulations* drawn up and enforced by the Booths. This one and several others may have been a concession by the Booths to a friend and a woman of class.[14] Susie Swift carefully recorded the process in her diary, including the role of Florence Booth.[15]

3

Submission to Authority: Grace, Healing and Spiritual Discipline

Throughout her adult life Susie Forrest Swift struggled with depression. At various times its symptoms could be physical or psychological pain. But she herself and friends or superiors in The Salvation Army, and later in the Roman Catholic Church, often saw the depression as a spiritual malady. It was a constant theme in her diary and in letters she exchanged with friends and advisors. When dealing with mental and physical maladies of the Victorians, one must remember that life was not easy and that medical solutions were still quite primitive.

In early December 1887, Swift attended a Salvation Army "Two Days with God" at Exeter Hall, London's principal auditorium for evangelical conclaves. In her diary she referred to the "Two Days" of spiritual retreat as among the worst days of her "whole spiritual life." She had written an "impertinent and unsoldierly letter" to a fellow–Salvationist and had not "assumed a proper attitude toward the general [William Booth]." The general's son, Chief of Staff Bramwell Booth, triggered her anxiety when he had not invited her to attend a meeting of the Staff Council. This was a sort of Army discipline by exclusion, a sort of shunning.[1] When she sent an apology to her superiors for her offense and spiritual pride it brought her to a "last surrender. Hallelujah!" She went home singing a hymn:

Show Thyself, O God of power, my unchanging, faithful friend;
Keep me till in death's glad hour, faith in sight shall end.

She wrote to her diary that "pride was taken out of my heart."
After a meeting for a "Half Night of Prayer" General Booth sent
her a "loving message" and a ticket to the Staff Council meeting
from which she had been excluded. This experience led to a further struggle with the devil and, at the end of the month, a
"frightful cold ... and my whole mucous membrane [was an] in-
strument of torture, but, thank God, my clean heart isn't lined
with mucous membrane!" She decided that the devil was trying
to convince her that her health would "break down in the old
way," while the devil made "desperate assaults on his old
stronghold." But Susie also saw her problem as "interesting literary material." It was evidence that Jesus "does keep me little"
and "it is so nice to be just *a clean baby* like Christobel!"

On December 30 Swift attended the General's Staff Tea. On
New Year's Day 1888, she did her annual spiritual assessment.
This time everything was right with her world. She could even
welcome the possibility of an unhappy death. "Life is such a
very practical thing to me this New Year's Day." The previous
Saturday night she had gone to bed with a fever and ached all
over. Mrs. H. had asked her if it was "scarlatina." Susie thought
that:

> *some day, anyway, I shall lie down to die in a dingy–bright, grubby–*
> *glorious cheap–texted–all over room like this—it doesn't matter*
> *when—God chooses. I have given up expecting to be happy. That is*
> *a great thing. In 1888, I look for no happiness; I expect much joy. I*
> *expect changes; I look for no rest; I know I shall have peace. I love*
> *God; I love the Army; I love my commanders. Life holds no more sur-*
> *prises for me. I know my own weakness. I am leaning on God's*
> *strength.*[2]

But by August 1888 her diary entries shifted from spiritual
joy back to physical exhaustion and mental depression. On August 8 she wrote: "Did I know my own weakness? No. I was a
fool when I said it. But He [God] had kept me." Lonely, she saw
herself as "frowned on and pillied [sic]." As a result she trusted
"my God alone in a fresher sense every day. O, hallelujah!" On the

practical side, the General's article was late and her journal, *All the World*, was "standing still." The Cardinal[?] wasn't speaking to or looking at her. Her friends the Carletons were away, and her adopted sister and co–editor of *All the World*, Eileen Douglas, had taken Christobel to Dublin. Susie and Eileen lived together. Although she felt that "more than the Channel rolls between us," she claimed to be content. But two days later she wrote—"Life is such a grind!" She had rejected invitations from friends to visit Lily Wells at Croydon on Sunday or to go to Mrs. Major Keates, the wife of her supervisor. By September 6th she once again complained of spiritual malaise.

4

Romance, Maternity, Independence

Possibly most revealing of Susie Swift's general state of mind in 1888—she craved romance. Was the cause of her spiritual funk a hoped–for romance in the fall of 1888? Her diary describes her mental state, but reveals virtually none of the details of how the romance began. But she laments that when romance did not bring the desired end, for "weeks it has been so hard to *realize* God or to *feel* anything! And the grind of routine growing hollow seems to have sapped my strength." She wrote in her diary that she was ready "for excitement—for *romance*—for passion in life. Dear God, calm me! There is little to do. Life and work stand still. I want to write a novel!"[1]

We may assume, although we cannot conclusively prove, that the romance and passion she craved was physical. But since she refuses to describe it in her diary we can only speculate. At some point in the late 1880s we know she had some sort of romance with Herbert Booth, William and Catherine Booth's fifth child and third son. But Salvation Army histories and Herbert's biographer do not mention it. The Booth children lived public, yet protected lives. On occasion historians revealed their trysts, and how the senior Booths managed to place the fault on the other party when they failed to end in marriage.[2] Possibly Herbert's interest in Susie took place early in the summer of 1888. Maybe he proposed marriage and then rescinded the engagement. Or possibly William and Catherine Booth intervened and called it off. By October, following Susie's period of agony,

William Booth dispatched Herbert on a "world tour" on the premise that getting away would help him recover his health, an excuse the Booths often used for a stressful period for family members and a troublesome time for their mission.

On September 17 Susie reminded herself that she had asked God to give her a "new cross" for 1888. To her a "new cross" meant new suffering. She realized that "God does not let such prayers go unanswered." She wrote in her diary: "I trust Him from the grave where all my human life lies buried. I do not even ask Him to give me a wonderful spiritual nearness to make up for *my losses* [her emphasis]." She did not explain what she meant by her "losses," but a diary one writes to one's self does not need to explain. She underlined the word *losses*, as she had previously underlined *romantic*. Her hurt gave way to a brief verse: "I am not eager, strong nor bold; All that is past. I am willing *not* to do—at last, at last!"[3]

By November 9, 1888, Swift had emerged from "that awful fog" after a "scolding" from Commissioner John Carleton, leader of her department at the headquarters, and Major Keates, her immediate supervisor. Together with Bramwell Booth, they served as her male spiritual advisors. Carleton and Keates had taken her to tea at the Neller Room to give her an hour and a half of spiritual counsel in which Keates told her that she was letting herself "drift into hell." Carleton's advice was that 999 times out of 1,000, when people could not realize God's guidance "the fault was in hidden wrong in their own heart." Thus Swift needed to confess her sin. Although she violently objected to their remarks, she later submitted to the idea that "there must be something in it *for me*."[4]

During most of 1888 she experienced depression that led her to introspection. She recalled that in 1883, when she had started teaching at the elite New Jersey girls' school after graduating from Vassar, she had been "restless, unhappy, dissatisfied." As a result she had considered entering an Episcopal Church Sisterhood. At that time she used sarcasm as a weapon when she was angry. She also recalled that when her parents insisted that she go on a tour of Europe she had resisted and had sought advice from a Catholic priest, "Fr. McD." She recalled his comment that: "You are always wanting to know about God and you wish to know the will of God." But "what you ought to pray for is grace to do it." Susie remembered that he "made me admit to myself at last, if not to him, that in God's sight I was a sinner."[5]

In each of her sisterhoods, at Vassar, in the Salvation Army, and in two Dominican convents, Susie expected religious or intellectual men to provide her with a rudder for her mental and spiritual stability. This reliance on men had likely begun at home with her father, George Swift, and had continued at Vassar with male professors (she never mentioned women professors). While teaching at a private girls' school in New Jersey, while writing and doing social work in the Salvation Army, or praying, teaching, and doing social work in Roman Catholic convents, she turned to men for spiritual and vocational direction.

But these men were either married to other women or married to the church. There is scant record of only one single male who offered her romance that would requite her craving for passion. And that romance, so far as we know, only lasted for a relatively brief period in 1888. Male spiritual directors acted to mediate for her in the female sphere of sisterhoods, but they were in no position to satisfy her romantic cravings. The man who could have satisfied her, Herbert Booth, removed himself, or was pulled away from her by his parents. And his romantic passion turned toward another. The blow to Susie devastated her and may well have drawn her away from the Booth–run Salvation Army. We are largely in the dark as to why she "left the work," as The Salvation Army would have put it. We only have her statement to rely on.

5

After Herbert Booth's Failed Marriage
Proposal, 1889–97

On March 23, 1889, *The War Cry* announced that General Booth was promoting Miss S. F. Swift, heretofore a Salvationist without rank, to Staff Captain. Was this a sign of the Booth family's pleasure with Swift's work or a gesture to sooth a troubled mind over their rejection of her as a member of the Army's royal family and their third daughter–in–law? Her assignment was as the editor of *All the World*, the Army's international missionary magazine,[1] as she had already been without an officer's rank. Swift acknowledged this appointment in her last diary entry for 1889.

On January 29, 1890, Swift belatedly wrote her annual diary check–up for 1888. It was a sad account—she had once again experienced a fall from grace, but she only vaguely points to the cause. "I don't know where I slipped out of God's hold again. But I did, bit by bit; now trusting to people and work and diversion of thought, probably, rather than to Him. The New Year came in with a fearful battle. I felt He had been hard and cruel and I could not love Him. I could only *work on—'Dogged as does it.'* ride the General." In the end she arrived at a stage where she:

> felt I must have missed my way; knew I needed more grace, although
> I had not enough channels for it. When J. A. C. [John A. Carleton]

told me he didn't believe I put my past [was he referring to Herbert?]
*on the altar—I said, "Oh God, **Thou** hast permitted this and I accept*
it, if I never see the reason for it in this life!"

She had turned against the Booths. She was *"almost hating the
Chief [Bramwell Booth],"* at which point *"Mrs. Bramwell attacked
me* as being *bitter* ... and [for] blaming God for letting things
come on me. I have. I almost do. And I daren't trust Him not to
let me do it again!"

But Susie claimed that she would trust God, although she
was "too stupefied" to work out her spiritual problems in an
Army meeting. She would not *"dare* to let myself go. I've cried
myself sick as it is. I've fought. I *have* rebelled. Oh now as if in-
numerable devils tare [sic] me. And Mrs. Florence Booth said no
one was to blame but—that *she'd* rather I blamed Him than
blamed God." Whom did Bramwell Booth's wife mean by
"Him"? And for what should Susie blame him? Surely it must
have been Herbert or those who pulled Herbert back from marriage to her.

We know that the romance with Herbert was a serious affair
for Susie. Her continuing depression, sense of spiritual failure,
and moroseness over life in general may well point to Herbert as
the culprit. Could it have been this frustration that in the next
decade led her away from The Salvation Army? She said that she
could no longer attend Army meetings. Just more than seven
years later she would make a public conversion to Roman
Catholicism and be baptized. Did a private conversion take
place prior to the 1897 public one? There are indications that
may have been the case and that her road to Rome began early
in 1890, or even sooner.

In her only diary entry for 1890, possibly the busiest year in
her life, Swift wrote: "The General asked me to go to Japan." She
had responded: "If you like, general." Was this a chance to do
missionary work for which she had longed, or was it the Army's
way of disposing of a problem by moving an officer to a distant
foreign assignment, away from its London headquarters? The
Booths were known to use this device. Susie anguished over the
appointment:

What if God means Japan and you are not fit or the fate of a nation hangs on the perversity of a child who cannot give up her people ... her playhouse of a home, her plans for the game of human life? The eternities are beyond! I must be good! I must be fit for God's "next thing"— I have disappointed Him often enough![2]

There is no evidence that Swift went to Japan. Rather, in 1890 she continued to edit *All the World.* It must have been that spring and summer that she wrote the first outline of the Salvation Army's new social program that in October led to the publication of *In Darkest England and the Way Out* as W. T. Stead took her outline and Frank Smith's notes and prepared the manuscript for the Booths' approval. Since Catherine Booth was dying of cancer, the Booths needed its best and brightest officers in London to carry on the new social service plan and extensive editorial work.

Was it Herbert's marriage proposal that troubled Susie and led to the general's idea of sending her to Japan? Did the Booths have other plans for Herbert? Or was it Masahisa Uemura's 1890 interview with William Booth? Uemura was a Protestant evangelical leader from Japan who had met the Army at its training garrison in San Francisco. He hoped that the Army would extend its work to his homeland. Did Booth want Swift to prepare Japan for a Salvation Army invasion? He often sent his best officers on exploratory missions to assess fields for expansion. At the time the Japanese government was becoming increasingly nationalistic, endangering Christianity's future on the islands. Whatever the case, Swift did not go and the Army did not open operations in Japan until September 4, 1895.[3]

Possibly removing Susie from London was important for another reason. In 1889 Herbert had returned from his world tour, apparently with better health and ready to take another post that would require exhausting work. Herbert's father made him the Salvation Army commandant for the British Isles. More surprising was an announcement on September 18, 1890, with no prior notice, that Herbert was engaged to Cornelie Ida Ernestine Schoch. The marriage would take place almost immediately since Herbert's mother, Catherine Booth, wanted her youngest son to marry before she died. Cornelie was of Swiss–Dutch descent with impeccable lineage, the sort of marriage that would join the Booths to a European evangelical elite, much as monarchs sought diplomatic marriages for their children.[4] Swift's reaction to the marriage appears in the spiritual and mental angst of her 1888–90 diary. But only after her conversion to Catholicism in 1897 did she publicly reveal her romantic tie to Herbert Booth.

6

Susie Swift's Role in Writing the Salvation Army Social Reform Plan—In Darkest England and the Way Out, 1889–90

S usie Swift's most important contribution to The Salvation Army as an organization may have been her 1890 preparation of the outline for the Army's social plan, published as *In Darkest England and the Way Out*. Swift's diary does not cover this period, but her *War Cry* and *All the World* articles show that she was busy promoting social reforms.[1] One can reasonably surmise that Frank Smith, who did the research on a reform agenda in North America and Europe, turned over his notes to Swift for her to produce an outline for a possible book. As a result of his work Smith became the Army's first social commissioner in 1889. Since 1884 he had read social reform literature, talked with reformers in the United States and Britain, and visited farm colonies, likely including those on the European continent.

Smith was particularly impressed by Henry George's proposal for a single tax on the value of uncultivated land owned by the rich. Land vacated by the rich due to taxes would be offered to the landless urban poor and rural peasant. The Darkest England land and emigration plan derived from Henry George's ideas. The migration program would move the urban unemployed to the land in stages, from urban colony (workshops), to an English farm for training in farming skills, and in its last stage the unemployed whom the Army had trained as farmers would move to empty lands of the British Empire in Africa, India, Canada, Australia, and New Zealand.

Swift organized Smith's research into Darkest England's first outline, while William and Bramwell Booth looked after Catherine, who was dying of cancer at Clacton–on–Sea, Essex, and ran their international Christian imperium.[2] W. T. Stead, with three stenographers, wrote the book from Swift's outline of Smith's research notes. As the editor of the *Review of Reviews*, Stead declared the book to be Britain's "Book of the Year."[3] William and Bramwell Booth had read the manuscript and put their imprimatur on it.[4] Catherine also lent her support to the plan prior to her death.

William Booth was primarily a revivalist, not a social reformer. He had given social issues some thought in his early life as an assistant pawnbroker working in poor neighborhoods of Nottingham and South London, when Chartism, a political movement in the mid–19th century, was appealing to England's working poor. But by 1886 Booth's work as an urban missionary was endangered as his Salvation Army was losing membership in England's largest cities, while it grew in England's midlands and on the outskirts of Britain's colonial empire. Journalists and clerics who monitored Booth's claims that the Army was converting the poorest of the poor to Christianity challenged his statistics in such public forums as the *Times* of London. That his work was being labeled a "unique failure" led Booth to disclaim the notion that he was only interested in the poorest of England's social classes. When Anglican vicars charged that most Army converts had come from the working classes rather than the destitute and that they had been members of other churches, particularly Methodists, the Booths gave defensive responses.[5]

So by the late 1880s the Booths were looking for an idea that would stimulate the Army's troops to recoup its reputation as a mission to the poor of the slums. According to W. T. Stead, the social reform ideas, often secular ones, came to the Booths from Frank Smith, an evangelical socialist in the Army's ranks. As for Swift, her diaries and letters give no clue as to her political persuasion, but as a well–educated woman she must have been acquainted with social reform ideas of her time in both the religious and secular media. In her home state of New York, the

Rev. Walter Rauschenbush was raising the level of evangelical Protestant social thinking after reading Henry George's *Progress and Poverty*, the same book that influenced Frank Smith and other religious leaders. In 1886 reformers had supported George's run for mayor of New York City and his surprising second place finish, ahead of Theodore Roosevelt. In 1891 Rauschenbush, on a European tour, met William Booth.[6] After Pope Leo XIII issued his 1891 encyclical *Rerum novarum*, Jesuits began social reform programs in the Catholic Church.[7] Social reform ideas were in the air.

The Salvation Army nearly always gave William Booth complete credit for what it accomplished. Authorship of its literature was, in most cases, either credited to Booth personally or to "the authority of the general," rather than to Salvationists or even secular friends who actually wrote it. *In Darkest England and the Way Out* was no different. Thus the contributions of Swift, Smith, and Stead must be construed from external evidence— provided by their friends, their biographers, and by their own claims. Due to their loyalty to Booth, they rarely made such claims themselves.

Susie Swift, from her earliest Salvation Army experiences in 1883 to her resignation in 1897, was involved in social programs aimed at rescuing women from prostitution and street children from hunger and homelessness. Frank Smith, after his resignation from the Army at the end of 1890, gave his life to socialist politics in Britain's Independent Labour Party, trade unions, the London County Council, political journalism, and even to a seat in the House of Commons in 1929–31. A "spiritualist" during his later life, Smith did not enter a cloistered life or engage in doctrinal speculation as Swift did. When his social activism in the Army ended, he moved into fields of secular social activity, although he took his Salvation Army terminology and his loyalty to the Booths with him.

Around this time now Major Susie Swift entertained her Vassar College sisters in what she termed the "queer corners of London slumdom." She took Mrs. Ray on an inspection tour of "the piggeries of a social farm," no doubt the Army's farm colony at Hadleigh, Essex, the second step in the Darkest England program, where the Army was preparing urban workers for farm life. Swift traveled extensively and often found an "old Vassar girl" along the way.[8] In January and March of 1890 she wrote articles on "Sociology and Salvation," to introduce the Army's new social emphasis. Commissioner Smith and General Booth also wrote articles on sociology, as did secular journalists.[9]

But Susie Swift ultimately rebelled against the Salvation Army's "secular" trends to which the Booths were giving an increasing amount of their energy. She was not alone. Many officers felt that their first call was to minister to souls, and they at least mildly disapproved of amelioration of social distress as too indirect a means to the goal of soul salvation. The Booths straddled this fence by referring to social work as "wholesale salvation." The general was finding it difficult to hold the two wings of his Army, the social and the spiritual, together.[10] Booth pushed the social enterprise to the end of his life in 1912, but he also continued spiritual campaigns to save lost souls while he was lobbying Parliament and wealthy donors for support of his emigration program to move England's poor to what he termed the "wastelands" of the Empire. When Bramwell became general in 1912 upon William Booth's death, he continued the Army's aggressive social programs, as did his sister Eva in America.[11]

Susie Swift noticed on January 17, 1891 that there was a "gap of a year" in her diary entries. This was apparently due to her 1890 work load, including the *In Darkest England and the Way Out* outline, writing social articles, and editing *All the World,* a magazine that was chronicling the Army's progress in spiritual and social work in Africa and South Asia. She launched into her annual diary introspective with a question: "Have I grown?" She began with her 1890 itinerary. She had visited the United States, Canada, Norway and curiously, "Brighton and all it meant."

Without comment she wrote that she had seen the "happy gates of death opening before me." Was she referring to her failed engagement to Herbert Booth? In her only diary reference to her romance with Herbert Booth, now the Salvation Army's British Commander, she did not mention his name, but she left no mystery as to his identity. She lamented that in 1890 Herbert had given "Corrie [Schoch] the gold he didn't dig for her, and here I sit tonight."

Susie was fatigued by "the same old [*All the World*] editor's chasing grind." Nevertheless, on December 31, 1890, she wrote, uncharacteristically, that she had "grown in my soul very much this past year."[12] John Carleton had written her a "personal" note on New Years Day that assured her that in her 28th year she had indeed grown in "steadfastness and solidity," but she was "very little better so far as brashness of speech and spirit went." She did not agree with this assessment, quite reasonably, and attributed her "brashness" to "tired nerves and physical torture" more than "vexation." She knew her limits and tried not to see people when she was tired. She confessed: "I do so need more prayer and Bible! And yes I creep to bed so worn out that I can't get up in the mornings. And there is more to do all the while and more it seems as if *I* must do! And the General and the Chief seem to want so much *secular* information got at for 'A.W.' [*All the World*]—such as demands *specialists*."

The Army's secular emphasis was taking an increasing toll on its leaders and staff. After Frank Smith's departure and prior to David Lamb's appointment as the Director of Migration in 1903 and then as Social Commissioner in 1912, they lacked social reform specialists to advise them on how to run the new enterprises.

From her discussion of Army work Susie moved to an appraisal of her physical and marital situation, and to her "fits of such *awful* depression when I am tired. They frighten me. Surely, my soul ought to rule this miserable ... body of mine that seems as if it could never rest or let me rest just because its humanity cries out so for maternity." Christobel could not satisfy her desire for a complete family life. Surely that was what she meant by "maternity?"

Swift complained that "only Elizabeth Stuart Phelps seems ever to have understood—Jesus doesn't seem to have taken things into account!" Phelps (1844–1911), a Victorian feminist author of 57 volumes of fiction, poetry and essays, focused on the rights and problems of women. Her fictional focus was on Arthurian legends. In her third Arthurian poem, "Guinevere," Arthur's queen who was placed in a convent because of her betrayal of her husband, Phelps reinvents Tennyson's interpretation of a guilty queen groveling before her moral king, and alters the sign of her failings to weakness caused by a desire to repress her natural instincts.[13] This, Swift saw as a parallel to her own situation.

In response to John Carleton's New Year's note Swift wrote that she had begun the New Year with a proclamation, "I shall try." Carleton answered "All right." She prayed for "off–hand goodness ... healthy goodness" to take the place of "off hand sentences." She saw herself as "a morbid thing that could sit and cry tonight for my lost youth and the yellow out of my hair! Is anybody so noble as they want to be?" Gena had told her that her photo was "a constant inspiration." But she wished "stupidly for somebody ... to pet me, and to think I'm nice even when I'm nasty." She wanted "a baby all my own at any price as if I'd never had a 'call.'" A "baby" of her own she held as the trophy that exceeded her "call." But as always she ended her wishes with a call to God for "His goodness day by day," goodness she had not always seen.

In the clearest inkling of her leaning toward Rome as early as 1890, Swift wrote that she was "going away to pray and let Faber scold me." In reading Frederick William Faber (1814–64) she was immersing herself in devotional writings of "an ardent propagandist for the Roman Catholic Church."[14] In 1845 Faber had left the Church of England to join John Henry Newman as a Catholic convert. Swift wrote in her diary that she had been used by God in 1890 to help other souls "as never before." Was she finding her spiritual sustenance in the Army or in the Church? She does not enlighten us, but she concluded with a prayer: "What ought to be enough. God make it so!"[15]

In February of 1891 she had an in interesting conversation with herself in her diary and for a change she acted as her own spiritual director:

> I wish I could be of help to you. But I am so satisfied that these strug-glings and wrestlings must be conquered by yourself that I have no faith in anything done by me being an effectual cure. You have the light and won't walk in it.

She felt better in her soul. "God is in His universe! And so I shall find my 'way out.' And I can, at least, bring others along the path I have come."[16]

Ten months later, on the first Sunday of 1892, she discussed her personal relationships in The Salvation Army in her diary. The two focal points of her life outside her home were at her editorial office and at the Penge Corps [church]. And she often spoke of interactions with the Booths at times of spiritual crisis. Her stock taking generally began with yet another admission of spiritual failure, followed by the manner in which the Booths or other senior male Army officers led her to confession and spiritual regeneration. But in the spring of 1891 she wrote that she had "lost the blessing distinctly."

> *It leaked a little. Then I let all go in a fury at Mac over nothing at all. I agonized for weeks before I would admit the fact. I asked God for my lost grace at Penge [corps], where I knew I ought. I did at last and He was very, very good to me.*

God had told her to talk to Emma Booth and she had agreed, but put it off. She went to America and had a restful time and good meetings, "but never felt *right inside* or *sure of my state*." She was upset over a discussion about Kathleen [?] moving in with her and Eileen Douglas and Christobel. She had been *"selfish"* and knew that she had lost her "clean heart." She "lacked *faith* for it," but "tugged on." She "had a row" with Bramwell Booth and then apologized. He had told her that she "puzzled and discouraged him. But he believed the whole trouble was that I didn't really *give up my own way*." The "Comr [Commissioner Carleton] said I was trying to save myself." Swift went to see Emma Booth, her friend from her Training Home days, but with little result spiritually. During a holiness meeting, a service where Salvationists examine their lives and pray for deeper spiritual experience, Swift wrote in her diary:

> *I was angry—went out [to the Penge Corps] because I had to—then flung myself on God at home and am trusting Him now. But I feel a lack. I am tired and crowded. But that is not all—I've not something I once had. I have no power. I'm not equal to my silver stamps of full salvation. God must give me more—more for the corps, more for my home, more for the office. I am asking Him to do it today, to do it now. I'm not so sharp tempered—and I don't let myself be selfish. But I could be. I mustn't lose my zeal for God! For **God**—!*

On New Year's Eve General Booth gave an impromptu lecture about being *trustworthy* and not distrusting Headquarters and "flying off at tangents." He told Susie to learn in 1892 to lean on *him*, when necessary. Swift described the lecture as "not nice. But it was good for me and good for my pride and sensitiveness." She took even a "not nice" admonition from William Booth as "good" for her soul. She willingly submitted to male authority. She ended her 1891 review with a list of 16 questions and New Year's resolves, some of which derived from a personal insult. Was the insult the break–up with Herbert Booth, a rising star in the Army that Swift may have seen as her only long–term hope for personal security?

In 1890 Herbert Booth had led the Army in Britain and had married Cornelie, the daughter of a former Royal Army colonel who was the Salvation Army's chief secretary, second in command, in Belgium. But twelve years later, on February 3, 1902, Herbert and Cornelie would resign from the Army while he commanded its branch in Australia.[17] But Susie was searching her soul in January 1892. Was it still a smothered heartache for Herbert that bothered her, or was there something new? She asked herself with cautious confidence:

1) *Have I—do I freely forgive injury? So far as I can rule my own heart I will do ... [she would] try never to think of him [Herbert?] except as Jesus Christ's property and servant, not to be judged by me—and God keeps me now.*

2) *Do I try to reconcile those who have aught against me? Yes— I do.*

3) *Do I know how to lead souls to Jesus better than I did a year ago? I fear not.*

4) *Do I improve opportunities? Not as eagerly as sometimes before.*

5) *Do I truly long to see sinners saved? Not so much as sometimes before*

6) *Do I make reproof a Christian duty? So far as I dare—I have not been fit to look after others!*

7) *How do I take reproof or warning? God gives me grace to take both thankfully, even when they hurt and from people I don't care for.*

8) *Do I provoke my comrades to love and good works? I try to. But I know I ought to go to 12:30 [prayer meeting] and I will.*

9) *Am I faithful in my home? So far as I have time and strength.*

10) *Do I speak of others as I would like to be spoken of? Not yet—God help me. He has and He will!*

11) *Does my light shine steadily? It has not. I trust for it to do so now.*

12) *Am I anxious to know God's will? From my soul—Yes.*

13) *Do I in any way resist the Sprit? Not consciously—please Lord, make & keep my spirit sensitive!*

14) *Am I consciously filled with the Spirit? I believe just now! God has blessed my stock taking!*

15) *Do I want, above all things, to be like my Lord?* **Yes**—*at any cost.*

16) *Do I think first of the Kingdom or the King? The King, I am sure.*[18]

7

Susie Swift's Decision to Leave The Salvation Army, 1895–97

In July 1895, Major Swift was in the United States for two months on personal leave to visit her sick mother. When she returned to London she worked as director of a social program for "Waifs and Strays." Mildred Duff replaced her as editor of *All the World.* In December, General Booth sent her to New York to take charge of the Auxiliary League, a position in which she worked with supporters of the Army's work. In February 1896, the Booths' second son, Marshall Ballington and his wife Maud, the Army's American commanders, rejected orders from General Booth sent through Chief of Staff Bramwell Booth to move to South Africa. This refusal to obey orders led to their resignation and a decision to start the Volunteers of America, an evangelical–social service organization much like the Army, but based on a more American type of governance system. Commissioner Eva Booth, William's third daughter, filled in until her sister Emma (the Consul) and husband Commissioner Frederick Booth–Tucker arrived to take command.[1]

Swift's job with the Auxiliary League during this turmoil was to raise funds by contacting wealthy donors, discussing the Army's work with them, and inviting them to join the League. Thinking back on this period Swift noted that contacts with ministers of other churches and others outside the Army had led her to think about the nature of the church and its sacraments.[2]

On January 4, 1896, Swift wrote her annual spiritual and personal assessment for 1895.[3] She had been mulling over a possible change in her life. Frustration with the Army was leading her to migrate toward a new vocation. The year 1896 came in "with a rush!" God held her "quiescent, scarcely allowing me to look on before all this strange year and a half [when] the man of sorrows ... showed me that I was to break my life *again* sharply in two."

She had spent an afternoon with Mrs. Rose Hawthorne–Lathrop, daughter of the writer Nathaniel Hawthorne, and a Roman Catholic, who had opened a cancer clinic in New York City's slums. Hawthorne–Lathrop indicated that they could have "friendship and fellowship in the deep things of God," offering her hand in sisterhood. She introduced Swift to Father Van Rensselaer.

Looking back on her first encounter with the priest, Swift later recalled that "God forced the words from my mouth. Father, I am so far convinced of Catholic truth that if I were a private woman, I should have but one thing to ask of you." The "one thing [was] to ask [for] reception into the true fold," which she called "the highest and the best and the One." She saw it as "the helps and the comfort and the unity." But she would wait for God's revelation. She wrote that she was "ridiculously, fantastically, absurdly, light–heartedly happy!" But she knew that her Catholic conversion would "grieve my dearest and alienate my best friends." And she would be alone in finding a "way to earn my own living."

While still a Salvation Army officer Swift wrote about her new–found faith in her diary. She was convinced that "the Church of Christ *must* be based on Christian tradition as well as the written word," a point on which Protestants had disagreed with the Church of Rome since Martin Luther held out for *sola Scriptura*, only Scripture, as the guide to faith.

Susie believed that her mother's recent death had helped bring a "longing for the communion of the Body and Blood" as a means of comfort. The Salvation Army had not practiced the sacraments of baptism and communion since 1883, soon after the Booths had discussed a possible merger of the Army into the Church of England as its urban evangelistic branch.[4] The first Sunday in July she felt a desire for "the Real Presence." But she did not yield in order to commit herself to being "a Salvationist more entirely than ever" and to work for God as such.

She began to think that her new work in America was causing her to see weaknesses in the Army system. She wrote that despite the Army's ability to bring sinners to repentance, it lacked the ability to "make *saints*." Due to the absence of the sacrament of penance, she held that the Army's officers' soul–lives failed and died, our holiest men fall into fanaticism "as I have done myself," for a substitute to sacramental sustenance.

In her work as Auxiliary Director, the recently promoted Brigadier Swift met two Protestant ministers, Dr. John Hall and Dr. Abbott, who challenged Salvationist doctrine as it concerned sacraments, and also pressed her on the authority for sacraments in Scripture and in church tradition in the 1500 years before Luther. In 1884 she had concluded that there was no logical theological position between the doctrines of the non–sacramental Quakers and the sacerdotal "doctrines of the Catholic Church." She had "accepted the former," the Quaker position, in 1884, but she had since changed her mind.

Father Searle, a Paulist—the first priest that she had spoken to since she spoke with Father McD. in 1883—told her on December 30, 1895, that she was well informed on theology and did not need to read his book. Neither he nor Father Van Rensselaer asked her to repudiate what she knew about scripture or faith. For her part, Swift was ready to accept the teachings of the Roman Catholic Church. Her struggle against the idea of the Church Visible came to an end on New Year's Eve 1895 as she prayed quietly in her room.

Sunday morning, as she considered conversion to Roman Catholicism, Brigadier Swift recalled the *"anguish"* she had felt in Glasgow that day in 1883 before she went to the Salvation Army meeting. As she read her soul, she sensed that "the God whose Spirit led me into the Army, leads me on and out *in the same way."* But she doubted that the Archbishop would find a way for her to tell her father. Yet she wrote that every day that she kept the secret was a kind of "bondage."

Father Van Rensselaer recited a few Bible verses that she had often used in speaking to others about their souls. "Christ says, 'He that professeth me *before men* will I profess before my Father which is in Heaven.'" He credited her Salvationist profession as belief in a "*partial* Christ." Above all, she had "helped souls because you were in good faith." But now she was "*not* in good faith any more." He gave her no books, but urged her to attend the "Mission." He told her that she was "convinced. All you want is *action*."

The only question in Swift's mind was whether the Archbishop would permit her not to tell her father, since she felt that the only thing that held her back from Roman Catholic conversion was a decision concerning when to tell her father and Consul Emma Booth–Tucker. She wrote in her diary: "Their *lives* seem at stake."[5]

Emma Booth, now Booth–Tucker, William and Catherine's second daughter, had been the women's training home principal in London in 1882–88 during the time the Swift sisters were becoming Salvationists and teaching at the school. Emma and her husband were now Susie's commanders in the United States. Emma had likely been the first person to explain the Army way to Susie, both its doctrines and its polity.[6] And Susie could not torment her father in his last years with yet another trauma after the passing of his wife.

When Swift had returned to London after caring for her mother in mid–1895 to work with "Waifs and Strays," in times of personal crisis she had read Catholic devotional literature. That summer and winter, she later wrote to the Army's Chief of Staff Bramwell Booth: "after every ray of human happiness faded out of my life, my mode of religion failed me, too." She did not explain what she meant by "every ray of human happiness" that left her devoid of religion as well, but Bramwell surely knew her meaning. It was at that time that she claimed that Faber's *Spiritual Conferences* and *Growth in Holiness* had helped her recover her faith.

Swift found that "C.C." [Commissioner Carleton's] counsel matched Faber's. But when she told him so, he had warned her to end her contacts with the Church and he tried to keep her so busy at the office and at the Penge corps that she had little time to read Catholic books. Carleton was a Northern Irish Protestant who had joined The Salvation Army in the village of Ligoniel, near Belfast, and had risen to its highest rank.[7] He and his wife were no friends of Romanism.

At this time Swift was claiming particular comfort in the "Catholic doctrine of impetration," procuring grace by entreaty,[8] offering prayers "in act and will for his soul," an idea she took from a poem by Adelaide Proctor, and from a sermon at the Church of the Holy Name, Manchester, England. She had gone to the church in 1893 on a free Sunday evening when she was too tired to go to an Army meeting. It was the only Catholic sermon she had heard, except one while on a rest leave in England in 1895. She attended none between then and her 1897 conversion.

Swift told Bramwell Booth in her 1897 letter of resignation as a Salvation Army officer that she had been concerned about what she saw as the Army's lack of provisions for the "saint–i–fying and keeping in real self–knowledge of our own people." Others had commented on the Army's inability to hold its members, how it had been kept from becoming a nurturing church by focusing its attention on being a home mission society that passed its converts on to churches for nurture in the faith. Swift held that confession and communion, as she saw them at high Anglican (Anglo–Catholic) church parishes like St. Peter's of the Docks, seemed "to supply a want" that the Army's "peni-tent–forms" and "personals" (spiritual interviews) met less well.

Swift recalled for Bramwell Booth her three months of soul "darkness" in 1895 when she could not sense God's presence. One day God had seemed to say to her: "Will you come out from the Army and be a Catholic, if I ask it?" "Yes, Lord," she had an-swered. She wrote that peace came, but God said, "Not yet," and she came to see the episode as a test of obedience. Sometime that same year she had read the *Life of St. Teresa*. A book of Teresa's "prayers for me" stirred her to ask questions. But Mrs. Drum-mond, who was a Salvationist at the time, but later became a Catholic, told Swift not to be perplexed.

About that time Swift "was horrified" when her sister Lil (now Mrs. Colonel Brengle) told General Booth that Susie was "a Catholic at heart," a tale that Susie considered to be cruelly in-correct. She thought that she held only Catholic doctrines that were the foundations of Christianity that the Church and the Army held in common, except that they were obscured by Protestant beliefs."[9] Lil was still misrepresenting her motives and actions, as she had in 1883, or so Susie thought.

In 1896, the Salvation Army in New York added to Brigadier Swift's auxiliary job work as Eva Booth's secretary. Eva, a field commissioner in England, was the Army's acting American commander after her brother Ballington's resignation. That was until her sister Emma and brother–in–law Booth–Tucker arrived. In April *The War Cry* belatedly announced Swift's added assignment.[10]

That winter, as she later told Bramwell in a face–to–face meeting, she studied Salvation Army principles of "internationalism," "unity in faith," and "surrender of individualism for the sake of membership in a Spirit–guided body." She valued the Army's officers for their "good disposition and intention," but she was "horrified" by what she held was "their shallowness" and "spiritual ignorance." They needed "the confessional even without absolution." Indeed, on a trip to Chicago, she and Eva Booth and Brigadier Evans had done little but "sit in the confessional." Was Swift seeing working–class officers from the perch of her middle–class education and training? Or was there a spiritual deficit in the Army's nonsacramental practices and theology?

As Swift looked back from 1897, every event in her life from 1895 on seemed to have led her to Rome and sacrament–based faith. When her mother died on June 20, 1896, her passing was "not like a Salvationist, but like a Catholic saint." Swift saw her mother's soul as craving "in its last extremity for strong, sacramental help." Her sister Lil told Susie after their mother's death that she felt "a strange separation of soul from me over Mamma's deathbed."

When Swift returned to New York in December 1896, she was conflicted over sacramental ministry. The Army, like the Quakers, practiced no sacraments apart from those it substituted for baptism (dedication) and communion (a love feast).[11] Roman Catholics had seven. After studying Barclay's *Apology* by a Quaker scholar, and the Bible, Swift concluded that the New Testament offered no grounds for a Protestant view of the sacraments. In fact, she decided that the New Testament, when "interpreted by tradition," taught Roman Catholic doctrine on baptism and communion, the two sacraments that Protestants practiced. She told Bramwell: "As I said to the General [William Booth]; 'There is nothing for me between Salvationism and

Catholicism.'"[12] On a Sunday evening she had gone to St. Francis Xavier Church for Benediction and had felt "for the first time" that it was possible to believe that Christ was present there in a way that his spirit makes him present with his people everywhere. Transubstantiation of the body and blood of Christ in the mass she now saw as no more difficult to believe than Jesus' Incarnation as the God–man.[13]

Around this time Mrs. Drummond, Swift's Protestant "anchor," wrote to tell her that she had joined "the Holy Catholic Apostolic Roman Church." She proposed that Swift seek an interview with Father Searle, a convert, Harvard Man, and Professor of Astronomy at Catholic University in Washington. Searle told Swift in a "cool, mathematical way," that prayer could answer her question: "Did our Lord intend to establish a visible Church as well as an invisible kingdom?" By New Year's Day 1897, Swift claimed to know that the Catholic Church was Christ's creation. She read Cardinal Manning's biography and the next day, "prostrated with mental pain," she went to Rose Lathrop's tenement house to "look into a Catholic woman's eyes" and ask her to "pray for me." Hawthorne–Lathrop had known Swift through press reports and had introduced her to Father Van Rensselaer.

Swift later recalled that she told Van Rensselaer that she "was convinced." "Light came, joy, rapture" that lasted for "thirty–one days of a heaven upon earth." But she told Bramwell Booth that she was troubled by the thought of him, her father, John Carleton., Emma Booth–Tucker, and American comrades, whose souls "will not follow me out of dawn into noonday." She realized that she would again be "friendless, homeless, penniless, professionless, and cut off from all public work for Our Lord."[14] She saw Archbishop Corrigan as a "sufficiently broad–minded Christian gentleman" who might "see the Army's side as well as his own." While Corrigan did not sanction "silent Catholicism," he did permit Swift to keep working for The Salvation Army until June, the delay she asked for, "especially since I needed instruction."

Swift wrote to Bramwell Booth that although she could manage public meetings, she could not do "hand–to–hand work with souls" as a representative of both The Salvation Army and the Church. She assured him that she would spend much of her life praying for him, but she asked that her resignation take effect the first of June unless he wished to have it sooner. She mentioned Eva Booth, Eileen Douglas, John Carleton, and R [?], as her "dearest earthly friendships," and wondered if Bramwell could keep her as an "employee," since the Army had Catholic employees.

But she knew that this would be difficult since she wanted to tell her Salvationist comrades what she felt and believed. Despite the many things of faith they had in common, Bramwell Booth "could not sanction that." Yet she asked to keep his friendship, and wanted to see him when he visited the States. She signed her resignation letter, "Yours, soldier and servant of Christ, Susie Swift, Brigadier," and asked Father A. P. Doyle to mail it. She went to her father's home "to breathe and pray for a week," and to find an opportunity to tell him about her conversion.[15]

A Salvation Army friend wrote to ask her about "a strange something" she detected in her letters. When Swift responded, the friend turned the letter over to Bramwell Booth despite Susie's request for "secrecy." Bramwell cabled her to "Come to London at once. Inform no one. B. has told me all. Cunard Company will furnish passage." American leaders, Emma and Frederick Booth–Tucker, Bramwell's sister and brother–in–law, insisted that Swift should not go to London until they had been officially informed of the reasons for her "recall." Fathers Searle and Doyle also asked her not to go. But Swift wrote, "At this last moment, a strange unwillingness to be baptized 'in a hurry' seized upon me."[16] She arranged to go to London.

Thursday, March 4, 1897 was Brigadier Swift's last day at New York's Salvation Army headquarters. In two days she would sail for London. She saw Captain Madelle Wilson, a young officer and daughter of a former canon at the Church of England's cathedral of St. George, at Kingston. Wilson asked Swift: "Do you think baptism is absolutely necessary?" Swift put her off. She said that she would answer after she returned from England and asked her not to tell anyone about the conversation. As Wilson left Swift's office Rose Hawthorne–Lathrop entered "in an agony" that Swift "failed to comprehend." Fr. Doyle had told her that he doubted that Swift would be baptized before she sailed to England on Saturday. Lathrop, who lived at the Samuel Street House cancer home, told Swift that if she had no place to go, "half of all I have is yours." But she must not delay "the receiving of Our Lord." Doyle had assured Lathrop that if Swift's ship went down she would have "the baptism of desire." Swift asked Lathrop to "go away. I can't have any more." But she added, "I may go up to be baptized this afternoon." Lathrop went away, but asked her cancer patients to say the Rosary for Susie.

8

Susie Forrest Swift's Roman Catholic Baptism on March 4, 1897 Final Interview with Bramwell Booth[1]

At 3:00 on March 4, 1897, as Brigadier Susie F. Swift left her Salvation Army office in New York for the last time she passed a room where six "girl officers" worked and noticed a 17–year old stenographer who had been baptized Catholic a few weeks earlier and had feared that Swift would fire her. Today Swift had no feelings but affection as she walked past the girl and out the front door on her way to her flat. When she entered her quarters she prayed, "Oh God, I can think nothing, remember nothing, feel nothing of all I have thought and felt in these weeks. I stand alone with Thee in the universe. God of Abraham, God of Adam in the garden, help me to act as I should act as if there were only Thee and me existing." She wrote that her "fog lifted." That morning she had made an appointment for baptism, the door out of The Salvation Army and into the Roman Catholic Church.

When Swift arrived at Fr. Alexander P. Doyle, C.S.P.'s[2] church he was reading his afternoon mail. He had arranged for a godmother, "Miss McG," and Swift had chosen a saint's name, Teresa of Avila, whose "friendship" she claimed was as real as that of her Catholic friends, Rose Hawthorne–Lathrop or Mrs. Drummond. She recalled that she had felt Teresa's presence on a wintry London morning in 1895 when the saint "had spoken to me through the gray London daylight and said: 'I shall never leave you till you too are a child of the Church.'"

Swift told Father Doyle that she felt numb. Doyle assured her that she'd done her part, "I'll attend to the rest." Susie later wrote that in Doyle's office, "at that blessed font, the peace of God, which passeth all understanding and which had visited me so blissfully during those trying months, settled down on my soul and the long, winding, dusty Road to Rome ended."[3]

In her 1909 autobiography, Swift told of her meeting with Bramwell Booth, her Salvation Army "spiritual director," in London after her Roman Catholic baptism. He had guided her as a woman who "presented some difficulties to his father," General William Booth, but he "never failed to understand or to manipulate [her] with ease." Previously she had presented herself to him with "fear and trembling." Now she claimed that she was surprised to find that "he was absolutely powerless against a soul armored in sacramental grace."

In this March 1897 meeting, the last she would have with a Salvation Army leader, Susie said that she was "perfectly frank." She recalled "the overwrought rhetoric of Salvationism," which bothered her most when her religious testimony had been "cold." She had found expressing her experiences in public to be torture "until I poured them out in the only safe place—behind the dear confessional curtain."[4] She had addressed a resignation letter to Bramwell Booth, the Army's Chief of Staff: "My dear Chief, I am a Catholic." She realized that she had chosen "no easier path." "Rome has no prizes for women" and offers "no inducements to converts." She told him that in her time in The Salvation Army "I have learned to love our Lord Jesus Christ supremely." Yet she said that she:

> would rather die in the Charity Hospital on Blackwell's Island, free to worship my Savior in His own appointed way for me, than to have the wealth of a Helen Gould or the opportunities of your own mother [Catherine Booth] and stand in spirit where I did three months ago. I love the Army. I love you all. I suffer far more in leaving you all than I did in leaving friends and home and country to come to you … I have not a Catholic friend on this side of the water [England] whom I ever saw before December 29th and only fragile old Mrs. [Adelaide] Drummond.[5]

But as a Catholic convert she praised God for calling her, since January 3, 1897, to the Via Dolorosa.[6] She asked Bramwell to show her letter to his father, General William Booth, and to Commissioner John A. Carleton, the head of her department for whom she had worked as editor of *All the World,* the Army's missionary magazine. But Army leaders were unable to dissuade her from her decision to convert. As she later put it in a letter to her Vassar College reunion class in 1903, conversion to Roman Catholicism was no hasty decision on her part:

> *I came to the Church slowly, after years of study and reading which filled many a night after a toilsome day, any of my friends who care for its chart as I drew it six years ago, can find it in a little book called the* City of Peace, *published by Benzinger Bros., Barclay Street, New York.*

During her interview with Bramwell Booth, Swift said that she thought about the sacraments of confession and communion as the Catholic and High Anglican churches practiced them. Lena Bostwick had told her that "Our Lord seemed to know the need of the world even better than Mr. Booth."[7] But Swift looked back with appreciation on The Salvation Army of 1883, the year of her Salvationist conversion in Glasgow, Scotland. As she recalled:

> *The Army taught in those days that it was **"not a church but a mission"** and placed no obstacle in the way of my receiving the "sacraments" on my own[8] or any other denomination ... To those who do not see how an educated person can work with the Salvationists, I simply say that they do not know the Army's leaders, or the freedom of thought and mental activity permitted to those officers who show that they can make a wise use of liberty.[9]*

Brigadier Swift's Roman Catholic baptism on March 4, 1897, shocked Salvation Army leaders. Her Catholic friends and mentors hailed it as a great victory for their church. Yet, as she told fellow–Vassarians in 1903, she continued to think well of the Army: "the S.A. was the best man–made organization of the century for dealing with the lowest strata of humanity." The Army had given her a "thin basis of Catholic doctrine and unlimited philanthropy," a claim to which her first Catholic confessors attested. She continued to correspond with Army friends, including her "adopted sister" Eileen Douglas and Eva Booth, as well as with her sister Lil, who was, with her husband Samuel Logan Brengle, a ranking officer in the Army.

When Swift returned to New York in March 1897, after her meeting with Salvation Army leaders in London, she plunged into an editorial and social service life similar to what she had left in the Army in London. She became associate editor of the *Catholic World Magazine,* editor of *The Young Catholic,* and a contributor to the *Sunday Companion.* In the evenings Rose Hawthorne–Lathrop, Swift's closest Catholic friend, taught her how to dress cancer patients' wounds in the slums.

While Swift's vocations in journalism and social work were little changed from her Salvation Army postings, her Protestant and Wesleyan theology drastically altered to adhere to Roman Catholic dogma. She now professed to belong to Christ's visible church whose sacraments brought grace and faith that were unavailable in any Protestant Christian denomination. Yet as a Catholic she continued to rely on male intellectual and spiritual directors as she had done in the Army—albeit in a new sisterhood. Male authority figures had ruled her life in the elite Vassar College female environment, in the Salvation Army's mixed social sisterhood of middle and working–class women, and Swift would soon experience male domination in the sisterhoods of two Roman Catholic Dominican convents.

On June 18, 1897, Fr. McDermot, who replaced Chief of Staff Bramwell Booth and Commissioner John A. Carlton as Susie Swift's principal "spiritual director," wrote a long letter to tell her that he felt it likely that "God might give you a vocation to some religious Order." McDermot said that thinking about the matter of a religious vocation for her had cost him "anxiety." He criticized her problem of submission to authority, just as John Carleton had done in The Salvation Army. He was unsure of how to be a spiritual "father" to a 35–year–old "child." He had thought of her entering an established, enclosed order, but decided that he must advise her on the disadvantages of that life. She had been accustomed to having a life of "great activity and of much authority." He observed that she had "soul scars—of pride, of disinclination to submit." He would need God's help to find the right place for Swift and how to fit her for it. But as a priest he was certain that God had made him fit for the task:

> *You will give me your confidence. You cannot know, my child, how a spiritual director feels about his penitents! I could die easily for the safety of the soul of any one of them, and I should be bound to."* [She must not] *"take any step toward the religious life except with my knowledge."*

He told her that it was possible to stay in the world and become a saint, but in "religious orders, it is almost hard not to attain a high degree of sanctity, the helps are so great." Nevertheless, "if we decide that God wills you to stay in the world, you will have courage, will you not?"

McDermot reasoned that Swift might work in the Catholic press, in which she was already engaged, and this would free him from many anxieties. But then he would insist that her life be hedged "with all that has safe–guarded the old orders—a very strict rule, many community exercises, above all for you, subjection to a Superior." It would be "safer to be under rule, my child."

He was mostly inclined toward her entering an old, enclosed order that he believed "would be a refuge after the truly terrible trials" of her past life. She needed a shelter of "rest and peace." Swift agreed that converts ought to go to the old orders "to have their crudities hedged." New orders were for born Catholics. McDermot had found so much sense in his advice "that it could only come from the Spirit of God." But to be settled in a proper convent was crucial. An uncongenial sisterhood would be hell on earth, "worse than purgatory," since in purgatory we are free from our human weaknesses.[10] In fact this "worse than purgatory" convent turned out to be Swift's lot in her first Dominican congregation.

9

Sister Mary Imelda Teresa, O.P.: Congregation of St. Catherine de Ricci, 1897–1913

On August 23, 1897, Susie Swift joined her third sisterhood. Like Vassar and the Salvation Army, a Roman Catholic sisterhood would make discipline and submission requisites of life. After consultation with several male spiritual directors and female friends, on August 24, 1898, Swift entered a convent of Dominican nuns of the congregation of St. Catharine de Ricci, with the Bishop of Albany's permission. Mother M. Loyola of Jesus was prioress at Albany, New York, and supervisor of a branch house at Saratoga Springs. The order, directed by the Albany diocese, was known as the Monastery of Our Lady of the Sacred Heart.

The 1899 *Catholic Directory* gave as its resident population: 24 sisters, 5 novices, and 3 postulants. Its mission was "a life of reparation, adoration and thanksgiving" devoted to "love and worship of the Sacred Heart." It claimed affiliation with a Dominican order led by the Very Reverend Father Larocca, Master General of the Order of Preachers. The *Directory* claimed that it enjoyed "all the privileges and indulgences accorded to the Conventual Sisters of the Order." Its program was to set up private retreats for ladies and monthly retreats for working girls. A resident chaplain led the retreats.[1] Swift did not discover until later that the order did not offer perpetual (final) vows, which put its claims in doubt.

Swift "entered religion" with the name Mary Imelda Teresa, O.D., from Teresa d'Ahumada, better known as Teresa of Avila (1515–82).[2] St. Teresa had founded a discalced Carmelite reform order that attracted violent opposition to its strict rule of an enclosed community of nuns. Swift had read St. Teresa's *Autobiography* (1565); *The Way of Perfection* (1573), and *Interior Castle* (1577). St. Teresa had combined hardheaded intelligence and deep spirituality in an active life of contemplation. Pope Gregory XV canonized her in 1622 and in 1970 Paul VI made her the first woman to be acclaimed a doctor of the Church.

That Swift chose Teresa's name was appropriate. Like the saint, she craved spiritual perfection and a life of service and writing.[3] On September 8, 1898, she received her postulant's cap. A year after her Catholic baptism she wrote in her diary that she had committed her life to a cloistered community: Mother de Ricci's book on the congregation "is *wonderful.*"

> *I flung myself down with more tears than I have shed in all this year (except once, for sin) ... But this does seem like the home of my soul. I can see absolutely nothing against this house for me. What their constitution may have against me, I don't know yet.*[4]

If Fr. McDermot led Swift to the Albany convent he made a serious mistake. He said that he was looking for an established order, which Albany was not. Fifteen years later Fr. John T. McNicholas, who was advising Swift on what she needed to do to leave Albany in 1913, said that Fr. Pardon, S.J.[5] had given her the bad advice. Did she know that the order was not recognized by Rome and thus could not give her perpetual vows as a Dominican nun? Not likely. She had agreed with McDermott that converts should enter established orders; new orders were more appropriate for birthright Catholics.

And what about Christobel, Swift's daughter? The October 18, 1887 adoption agreement was to have expired on September 29, 1897. But Swift had brought Christobel to New York. In 1898, when Swift entered the convent she gave the care of Christobel to Sr. Rose (Rose Hawthorne–Lathrop), head of the Home for Incurables, who agreed to raise the girl who was entering her teen years. Swift kept in touch with Christobel, who now referred to her as "auntie." Christobel later joined Swift in

Cuba on missionary service, and was an "acolyte" in an "Italian circle."

On April 30, 1899, Swift took her first vows, received a white reception veil, and donned the habit. Mary Stevens represented her 1883 Vassar class at the ceremony. The press was intrigued at the idea of a "Salvationist nun." In July 1898 the *New York Herald* named Swift's earlier sisterhoods: Vassar graduate; teacher of higher mathematics and English at a Morristown, New Jersey school for girls; and "Brigadier in General Booth's Army." And now she officially entered the sisterhood of the congregation of St. Catherine de Ricci of the Third Order of St. Dominic.

In a press interview Swift said that while she worked with the Salvation Army Auxiliary League she had inquiries from ministers and others that led her to reexamine the Army. She claimed that she had always seen it as a "mission," not a "church" or "denomination." Now she said that she realized that Christ "did establish a visible church on earth ... the Church of Rome." For that reason she had "embraced the Catholic faith." Christobel, now 15 and at school in New Jersey, would be looked after by Mrs. Lathrop.[6]

The World observed that a Vassar graduate had become a Salvation Army brigadier and now a Dominican nun. It published her picture in Army uniform and Dominican habit. Besides noting Swift's work with waifs and strays of London, and her opening of a home for newsboys on Fleet Street, the reporter made public that she was "at one time reported to be engaged to Herbert Booth." But the reporter pointed out, "Gen. Booth, who regulates the matrimonial affairs of his soldiers (as well as his children), refused his consent to the union." Surely Swift was the source of this previously unpublished scoop. *The World* also noted that Christobel had been baptized in infancy as a Catholic.[7]

In 1899 Susie's father, George Henry Swift, made a will "in which he left all" to Susie's sister Lil, a Salvation Army officer. He provided for a dowry for Susie, something the Albany convent required. He promised Susie "orally" that the dowry would be "paid at his death." In fact his will called for the dowry to be paid in April 1910. George Swift had died in 1908. Susie attended his funeral and heard the will read. At Lil's request and, according to Susie, at "the disgust of the notary," Susie signed a "quit claim and promised not to litigate." Lil wrote to Susie in January 1909 that her father was "thousands in debt." Even the "grocer couldn't trust her" to pay his bills. As a result of the debt, Susie asked the Bishop of Albany to allow her to "give her dowry to her sister." He agreed. So in November 1909 Susie made out a "deed of gift" to Lil. Lil believed, as Susie later learned, that their father had already paid the $1,500 dowry to Albany, but Albany denied it. The evidence is unclear.

Susie later held that Lil's hatred of Catholicism influenced her to deny her money from the will that she wanted to give to Christobel. Lil had by then given Susie $200 to pay her board in New York when she left the Albany Convent in 1912 and $50 for her reception at the Sinsinawa convent in 1913. Since there are no copies of Lil's letters, there is no way to determine her views in this affair that was upsetting Susie at the time of her death in 1916.[8]

In 1900, at age 38, Sr. Teresa took the black veil (first profession vow of obedience) at Albany. She wrote that the "reforming" congregation was "one of the most apostolic in the church," devoted to prayer, penance, good works and salvation of souls, one of the "most progressive" and "strictest as to cloister and austerities." Its focus was women's mental and moral uplift, especially the "miserable rich" who were "most neglected spiritually." These middle–class women were closer to Susie's own class than were most Salvation Army women or the poor they served. Teresa's retreats included spiritual readings, instruction for converts, and Exercises of St. Ignatius. Since "study is a law of Dominican life," Teresa proudly told her Vassar classmates that candidates for admission to the community had met educational standards.[9]

An Albany newspaper article that called attention to Teresa's moves from sisterhood to sisterhood stated that in five years she would take "perpetual vows that will make her a bride of the church."[10] But in fact, the Albany Convent was not recognized by Rome to offer final vows. Teresa seems to have been unaware of this problem. The convent, founded in 1880, was still awaiting Vatican acceptance of its constitutions. When this approval did not come by 1913, Teresa sought a convent with full credentials.

Swift's work at Albany in 1898 was translating Latin and French publications and scrubbing and painting a Novitiate in Saratoga Springs. On September 27, 1900 she went with Mother Loyola (Isabel Smith), the 2nd Prioress, and Sr. Henry to found a convent in Havana, Cuba. Teresa became ill with yellow fever, but quickly recovered. In Havana she established an orphanage and a Free School for black children left homeless by the Spanish–American War. Since students knew no English and the nuns knew no Spanish, the nuns took their first Spanish lessons the day school opened.

After three months, the bishop asked them to open an academy for white families in a fashionable suburb. Swift became Directress of the Convent School of Our Lady Help of Christians. She found little Cuban good will toward Americans who had helped oust Spanish rule in the brief Spanish–American war. And the "children were utterly spoiled and undisciplined." The school year ran a hectic 13 months without intermission. Nuns taught 13 classes a day. But the school prospered as the only English–speaking Catholic school in Cuba, the only school where girls could study for the Institute of Havana examinations. Teresa wrote to her 15th Vassar reunion that her diploma was "the bulwark of the school." The American Secretary of War assured the Cuban government that a Vassar diploma was of value in America.[11]

In November 1902, the Order moved Swift to Philadelphia's Dominican House of Retreats and Catholic Guild. The slum institution was much like those she had administered as a Salvationist in London's East End. It was a settlement and a young ladies Christian association. As a home for self–supporting girls it offered training in millinery, stenography, kitchen gardening and sewing. Nuns visited and nursed the sick and ran workrooms for old women. They also offered retreats, Bible classes, and classes for Sunday School teachers. It had an advice bureau and employment agency.

Swift's Vassar friend Lena Bostwick visited the settlement where sisters worked in a crowded space between a mortuary, a Consumptives' Home, and a cemetery. But Archbishop Ryan found a better house for their 75 girls for whom Swift was "Secretary and Educational Directress." With a full head, heart and hands she wrote to her 20th Vassar reunion that she was "far healthier and immeasurably happier than on the day I graduated." In the summer of 1903 she returned to Albany for three months as secretary to the Mother Prioress and remained there as Sub–Mistress of Novices and Secretary to the Council in 1904.[12]

The 1904 to 1910 period for Swift appears to have been devoid of work or achievement. In February 1905 the convent received her "for life," but she had to renew her vows annually due to the unrecognized status of the Order. She worked at convents in Newport, Rhode Island and Albany, apparently teaching the novices.[13] In 1907, her sister Lil Brengle sent Susie *Red Flowers of Martyrdom*, written by her adopted–sister Brigadier Eileen Douglas, which included a chapter on St. Benedict from a series The Salvation Army was publishing on Christian saints.[14]

On June 28, 1910, Dr. Mayo diagnosed Teresa as having appendix and gall bladder trouble.[15] He took out the appendix and emptied the bladder of "a mass of stones." An undated letter from Sr. M. Celestine states that in Mayo's opinion Teresa "would never have regained health or energy" if the bladder problem had persisted.[16]

10

Another Sisterhood—Transition to Sinsinawa Dominicans, 1911–16

By late 1911, Susie Swift (Teresa) wrote to Dominican priests to seek advice on how to move to another sisterhood. Fr. M. Thuente had written a letter that she had not received, in spite of the fact that Mother Bertrand had given him "permission to write to you and receive letters from you unopened." Bertrand blamed an unnamed (apparently male) "superior" who had not known of the "concession." Thuente was responding to Swift's plea for advice by telling her that established Dominican orders would not likely accept her due to her age, she was over 50, or because convents did not approve of transfers. Her options were unattractive. At Albany she would not be able to take perpetual vows, or join a "hopelessly struggling community." He gave two alternatives: 1) stay at Albany or 2) "return to the world." To stay at Albany she would have to "change the conditions of your soul sufficient to carry your cross." This would mean:

> Keep your mind busy with your God, your inner self and intellectual work, and shun all thought and conversations about superiors and sisters ... Change the heart by praying for your enemies ... If you can begin to accomplish that, remain where you are.

If not, and it is clear that Thuente did not think that Swift could accomplish such change, she would have to give up the "habit of

St. Dominic, but not the Dominican spirit." He advised her to leave in a peaceful way and find a place where she could rest and pray until her mind was calm, and her nerves were in good working condition.[1]

Since Swift's departure from The Salvation Army had been widely publicized, Thuente did not want a noisy departure from the Dominicans. He responded to a letter from Swift that he was relieved that her "mind seems more peaceful." He advised her to renew her vows on the feast of St. Catherine and work on her translations of important Spanish and French texts.[2] Teresa had returned to the translating work she had done as a novice in 1898, a job that allowed little interaction with the other nuns or superiors. Thuente advised her to "make a real inner retreat."

For her "inner retreat" Teresa left Albany to stay with friends in Brooklyn in September 1912.[3] As she contemplated transition to another convent or to the world, she renewed ties to earlier sisterhoods. On August 18, her sister Lil wrote that Susie should not worry about the heart condition of her adopted sister, Brigadier Eileen Douglas. In November The Salvation Army's U.S. Commander, Evangeline Booth, responded to a letter from "Susie," who had written to console her on the death of her father, General William Booth, on August 20, 1912.

> *It was just like your old Dearness to write me and your words dropped into their old preserved place in my changeless heart. The loss of my precious father has almost shattered me. I can't yet realize it, as ... he was everything to me. After God I lived for him, thought for him, worked for him.*

At the end Eva asked Susie: "*How are you*! I would love to see you. You were always so good to me. I wish I had you helping me ... my burdens are *very heavy*. In prayer and love unchanging, Evangeline Booth."[4] There is no indication that Swift tried to renew her ties with The Salvation Army as Booth suggested she might.

On New Years Day 1913, the nun that Teresa held most dear at Albany, Mary Innocent of Jesus, wrote a tender note from Cienfuegos, Cuba, with her picture enclosed. Innocent expressed "love too deep and too pure for human expression" from a "little sister" whose love had "its source in the tender Heart of our Spouse." Innocent referred to her as her *mater* and big sister.

Fr. John T. McNicholas, later Archbishop of Cincinnati, was Swift's second male advisor. He interceded for her with a friend, Mother Samuel of the Dominican Convent in Sinsinawa, Wisconsin. He told Samuel that he and Swift had corresponded for four years. In the fall of 1912 he had advised her to leave Albany. In December, Mother Bertrand had questioned the purpose of his correspondence. She thought Swift was blaming her convent for her situation. Bertrand protested: "I cannot conceive why she persists in this distorted and perverse view which makes her the victim and scapegoat instead of the deserter and offending individual." The Booths had used "deserter" to describe officers who "left the work" in their mission's early days. Bertrand asked McNicholas why he had asked for information about Swift. "Does she authorize you to collect these data for a biography or what?" She feared that "Sister is trying to throw the responsibility of her present status on me and her community. In this she does us injustice, for her present situation she alone is to blame. She is absent [in Brooklyn] by permission of her Bishop Superior for reasons best known to herself and not because of any action taken by her community... but because of her distorted and perverse views."

McNicholas sent what Bertrand termed a "spirited reply." She responded that she "regretted the effect of her letter on him." Writing to Samuel, McNicholas stated that Bertrand's "letter was probably written by Mgr. Walsh and given to Mother for her signature." Thus men on both sides of the issue were interceding for a woman whom the church expected to submit to priestly authority. Sensing that Bertrand might "open the case of her letters again with me," McNicholas wanted to make sure that Samuel did not destroy the correspondence. His frank opinion of Bertrand and her Convent[5] was that:

> *Mother is an ignorant woman. Her letters are written, so I am told, by a Fr. Walsh of Troy, N.Y. I have told her in the most unmistakable language what I think of this. I do not wish to be unjust to the Congregation, but it is a very strange expression of the Dominican Spirit. Founded by a convert, the government continued by her sister, a Convent without a Constitution, away from Dominican influence, with what the Fathers have interpreted as hostility to them, gives some idea of their present status!*

McNicholas concluded that Swift "has not had a fair chance to be an active useful Dominican," but she deserved to be "fully tested."[6]

McNicholas suggested to Mother Samuel that Swift apply to the Sinsinawa Dominicans. He thought Samuel might recall "Miss Swift of The Salvation Army," well known "in England and the U.S." He described Swift as thoughtful on theological issues with an "A.M. [sic] from Vasar [sic]." Her exceptional teaching ability would be an asset at Sinsinawa, as there was "no Dominican Congregation in the country where her educational acquirements could find their full measure of usefulness." If Samuel agreed Swift could take a course at Columbia University, with or without her habit, with permission of Bishop Burke of Albany. McNicholas assured Samuel that he had no interest in Swift as "a friend," and did not want to become her spiritual director. He said that he had refused that responsibility "until it seemed to me that God wished it."

In McNicholas' opinion Fr. Pardon, S.J., yet another male advisor, had made the great mistake of sending Swift to Albany. For years Swift "has had either no duties (for her natural activity) or those of a boarding mistress." The convent aimed "at the contemplative state, but of course fails because of no organization or Constitution." Swift wanted perpetual vows. Bishop Burke had allowed her to move to Brooklyn until her vows expired. Bertrand had said that she "would have no part" in Swift leaving Albany. Swift would have to enter Sinsinawa as a postulant. This would permit Samuel to judge her suitability and for Swift to become acquainted with the community.[7]

On September 4, 1912, Swift had left Albany to live with Mrs. Russell in Brooklyn. McNicholas had changed his mind on her taking a course at Columbia. He wrote to Samuel that he "had no fixed views on Sisters attending university courses, but I have actually delt [sic] with loss of faith at Columbia University owing to the teaching of some of its professors. Thus I advised against Columbia for Sister Imelda." McNicholas had two other congregations in mind if Mother Samuel rejected her, but he had told Swift that "if she wishes to follow my advice she must first have a refusal from you. She seems to me a Dominican at heart and if she be humble enough to be a good religious I think she can do untold good for your Congregation."[8]

Mother Samuel promised to interview Swift in New York at the end of January. On January 10, 1913, Bertrand sent Swift $100 to buy clothes for her trip to Sinsinawa. Bertrand was packing Swift's letters and books and a sister returning from Havana would bring books she had left there.[9] In February Bertrand sent her report on Swift to Mother Samuel. In the 14 years Teresa had been at Albany she had "never seemed happy with us, but if she was content she would do good work for God." Bertrand would not come to New York City to meet Samuel or McNicholas.[10]

McNicholas gave Swift his high estimate of Mother Samuel, a perfect nun or female Salvationist, and an ideal model for Teresa:

> *She is indeed a very able woman. Her ability is surely supernatural-ized. In a community room one would never suppose Mother S. [to be] either the Superior or a woman of intellectual parts and great ac-complishments. She never talks of herself. I trust that it may be God's will to receive you at the Mound and I pray that you can be a truly humble religious enjoying peace and spreading peace while giving valuable service to God in the interest of souls."*[11]

Sister Imelda Therese Swift, O.S.D., 1913–16

On January 25, 1913, Mother Samuel wrote to her Council at Sinsinawa from New York, where she had met Susie Swift. Samuel described Swift as "prepossessing—a nice–looking, re-fined woman, 44 years old [actually 49], with a New York ac-cent." Samuel explained that when Swift had joined the Albany convent as a convert she understood that they would soon be al-lowed to offer perpetual vows, but 14 years later the sisters were only allowed to take annual vows. Swift's vows would expire on February 15. Uncertainty around taking the perpetual vow, and without definite work, led her to want to leave Albany.

Samuel explained that Albany's mission was to give women's retreats, but they were doing little of this. Swift was living with Mrs. Russell of Brooklyn with the bishop's permis-sion to wear her habit in a secular house. Samuel commended Swift's "frankness near simplicity, a tenderness of heart yet very keen sense," and willingness to become a postulant and novice and accept any employment. Her deficiencies were "her convert attitude," her age, and "our little knowledge of her."[12] It is unclear what Samuel meant by "convert attitude," but her Council likely saw this as a common problem among those who came from "outside" to join the Catholic Church.

Samuel sent a letter of welcome to Swift two weeks before her vows expired, and Swift had a phone conversation with McNicholas. She sent Mother Samuel her travel plans and thanked her for her offer of fare and clothing, but her sister Lil (Mrs. Brengle) would provide these "within reasonable limits." Lil held their father's dowry for her use after he died on November 17, 1908. Swift told Samuel that she was "grateful to God and to His servants, who are willing to give me the opportunity of proving His will fully in respect to my Dominican vocation."[13]

Swift needed to meet relatives before leaving and thus could not travel with Mother Samuel and Sr. Vincentia. She would travel alone. Lil assured Susie during a "kindly visit" that she would provide whatever was necessary for her entry into the convent. Susie claimed that Lil saw the sisterhood as "a trade or profession," and had "no religious scruple against aiding and abetting it!" Lil furnished clothing as a novice, and if Susie gained the white habit again, Lil would pay "a hundred or so dollars at my profession," or Lil would pay the cost of returning to New York if Susie did not pass the test. Susie bought plain black dresses, a dark ulster and a hat. She would buy capes, veils and other postulant wear at Sinsinawa. Her hair was "rather a desperate proposition. I'm afraid it won't grow!" McNicholas told her to write personal letters to Bishop Burke and Mother Bertram. Mother Samuel would handle formal correspondence.[14]

On February 3 Samuel responded to Swift's letter accepting the conditions of transfer, signing as "Sister M. Samuel." She hoped that "all will be well, and that you will be content and able to do much for God's glory and your own perfection at Sinsinawa." She suggested that when Swift was ready to leave New York, she should write or wire Mother Clara—of 1431 North Park Ave., Chicago—who would meet her train. From Chicago Samuel told her to board the East Dubuque train of the

Burlington line.[15] From Dubuque, a six–mile carriage ride would take her to Sinsinawa, Wisconsin.

Bertrand wrote Swift a note: "Begging God and St. Dominic to bless the step you are about to take, and may you persevere to the end, is the prayer of yours in Xto[16]. God has been good to you to open more than one door into another Congregation. I pray that you may find the happiness you are seeking, but remember the words of the Invitation, 'there is no place so holy or so retired but we will find the Cross.'"[17]

Throughout this transition to a new sisterhood Swift was in contact with her family, and with sisters from her previous sisterhoods at Vassar, The Salvation Army, and Albany Convent. On February 26, her sister Lil wrote of family matters, but never mentioned Susie's move to Sinsinawa. She had sent a book to Susie's Catholic friend Miss Jeffrey at her request. Susie's "adopted sister" Brigadier Eileen Douglas, was choosing furnishings for her cottage at "OG" [Ocean Grove].

Lil's husband, Colonel Samuel Brengle, was physically worn out from his work as an evangelist and "promised to cut out his afternoon meetings." His diet was "educator crackers, olive oil, honey, and raisins!" The Brengle's daughter, Elizabeth, was doing the cooking and their son George was "having great fun" with a chum's cousins, "sweet girls and 'easy to look at,' if you know what that means!" Lil was thrilled "to see him trolling after a girl ... Better yet, two girls!" The summer before he had "fooled around with that Vassar girl" that Lil did not care for.[18]

When Swift arrived at Sinsinawa, possibly her first letter came from Mrs. Russell, her friend in Brooklyn, signed "Your devoted child, Belle Katherine." She was anxious about the "first few days of meeting strange sisters. It is so hard for you to meet new people after these years." She said that Swift was "doing what you had done all your life—following God's will. May He give you much consolation on the fresh path!"[19]

Florence Jeffrey, a Vassar and Catholic friend who called Swift "mi muy querida amiga," mentioned the kindness of Mr. and Mrs. Byles and the Russells, Swift's Brooklyn hosts. Jeffrey taught in New York and was fitting herself for "greater service for God" by attending Fr. Martin's lectures and Fr. Maturin's sermons and prayers at the Altar of the Blessed Sacrament in the Cathedral. She wanted to freshen up her languages: Latin, French, and Spanish, and become less insular, less Eastern. She wanted to give her life to God "in the service of children." Florence adored her sister in the faith.[20]

Belle Katherine Russell had discovered a "strangely significant row" back in 1884," when Susie's family had sent her to England and she joined the Salvation Army. Why had God broken Susie's life in two so often? Russell argued that it was "because the accepting of that offering made your life as near a crucifixion as any human life could be." She saw the cross and suffering as a regular focal point of life in Susie's various sisterhoods.[21]

Letters from other women asked Swift to maintain a sisterly connection.[22] In May she received what may have been a last direct letter from her dearest spiritual friend, Innocent of Jesus, who was still in Cienfuegos, Cuba. Mother Bertrand had prohibited correspondence between the two for reasons not clear in their letters. Innocent wrote, "My God, how painful it is to say it! ... this must be my last letter 'at least for the present.'" It did not occur to her to circumvent an order from a superior. But of course she knew that Bertrand read her mail. Of all the sentimental correspondence between Teresa and her secular and religious sisters, Innocent's letter is the most convincing and tortured.

> *Innocent wrote her last missive from May 4th to the 16th, to a "spouse"–"mother"–"friend." Only God knows what our love for each other has been, is, and always will be; and so, He alone knows what such a sacrifice means to His and Your little one! ... But I have His help and your love and prayers, as well as the privilege of having a confessor.*

Fr. Laston, who heard confessions on Wednesdays, Innocent saw as a friend and "a judge who inspires love, not fear ... a tender Father. She realized "what the Communion of Saints ought to mean to those who love each other, and I cannot understand how people can live and not believe in this consoling article of our Holy Faith!" God, being the same as the church, had "only for the present" asked of her "the sacrifice of separation from those I so tenderly love."

As with many Victorian–era letters, Innocent's missive reports the illness of each member of her family, ending with her mission "to suffer through love and to love through suffering!" She was in no hurry to complete her letter—and prayed that Mother Bertrand would realize "that only good can come from our corresponding to each other." But her submission did not inhibit her plotting with God and the saints. She proposed that she and Teresa:

> *speak to each other through our love and prayers, channels of corresponding to each other over which no one but God has control ... and it is our, not my, Holy Father St. Dominic who is ... pleading for us, not me, with Our Lord. [We] know that Our Blessed Mother's mantle, "after this our exile," will cover both you and your Innocent! ... Yes, my God, even though it breaks my heart, I accept the cross of complete separation, while in this "Vale of tears," from her who has been such a Mother to Thy little spouse!*

Innocent does not ask directly how Teresa is doing in her new convent, information that would no doubt have upset Bertrand and extended the time their letters would have been prohibited.

> *With diplomacy for the eyes of a censor, Innocent wrote concerning Swift's new sisterhood: I am sure you have chosen not only the Will of God, but loyalty to our dear Mother Loyola as well. For is not His will sweeter to her than all else and may our dear [deceased] Mother Loyola obtain for you the grace of Final Perseverance as well as Perseverance in your present vocation ... In Heaven I shall be able to prove how very tenderly you are loved by your little Sister–child, M. Innocent of Jesus, O.S.D.*[23]

When Innocent wrote again in June 1913, the May letter was still in her possession. "Were I to rewrite it, I would not change anything but the date; and I send it as it is, knowing that you will understand all." She could hear Teresa singing and wanted to sing with her "in the hope that soon I shall sing with you and her and all loved ones when we go Home, never more to be separated."[24]

Miss Tessie Swift Received at St. Clara Convent, Sinsinawa, August 28, 1913

On August 28, 1913 the St. Clara annals reported that the Sinsinawa Dominicans received Miss Tessie Swift, a first year postulant at age 51, along with seven other novices. Susie took the name Mary Imelda Therese. The change from "Teresa" to "Therese" may have indicated nothing more than an alternate French spelling, but it may have meant leaving her Albany Convent name behind. On August 28, 1914 she took her novitiate, a three–year temporary vow of obedience (black veil) with six novices. She would not live long enough to take the canonical novitiate (white veil) vow of obedience, chastity, and poverty "unto death," which is done after five years. She embraced the Dominican motto: "iuod Deus vult"—what God wills.[25]

On June 4, 1913 Miss Georgina Pell Curtis, editor of Swift's earlier "Road to Rome" testimony, had asked her to write an article by August 25th on her "present outlook—in a word, why you are satisfied you made no mistake." Interesting timing! Curtis was likely unaware of Therese's Albany troubles and her transition to a new sisterhood. She commended Therese's previous autobiographical article:

> *It would make you happy if I had time to tell you how many people have been influenced and led to the Church by your article in* Roads. *Many have written me to say so. The new book can include your impressions of what you have seen in others. Can't you bring in something about Havana and your work there, to knock away the prejudices of those who think everything Cuban is half pagan or worse?*[26]

If Swift had agreed to write the article Curtis requested, what would she have said about the turbulent years of yet another transition in her life? Certainly what she wrote would have passed the Catholic censors. She had followed Fr. Thuente's advice to make no fuss over her departure from Albany. She had only a six–week excursion into the devoted Catholic lay–world of the Russell–Byles household. After second thoughts Fr. McNicholas had steered her clear of a graduate course at Columbia University that would have exposed her to an "agnostic"

world similar to that of Vassar College where she had declared
agnosticism as her creed. Revisiting that experience might have
dimmed her commitment to religious vocation. But there is no
indication that the Albany misstep damaged her commitment to
Catholic theology, her loyalty to the church hierarchy, or her love
for Catholic sisterhood.

On June 18, 1913, Swift made a Retreat at St. Clara, and took
John McNicholas' "three requests" with her to focus her medita-
tion. Having learned submission to authorities, as John Carleton
or Bramwell Booth would have done, McNicholas urged her to
learn to:

1. never ... criticize superiors, equals or subordinates.
2. never speak of Albany and try not to think of it.
3. be loyal to Sinsinawa and never speak of trials to your
   life's end.
4. be sufficient in temptation, to recall that such a promise
   was made to God Himself [and]
   a. to my Dominican director, in whom I have full confi-
      dence and to whom I owe all things;
   b. because in a time of good spiritual health, it approved
      itself to my own conscience;
   c. at different times, recall as grounds [that]:
      1) the faith itself ... teaches us that lawful superiors,
         even secular, yet more religious, are God's dele-
         gates.
      2) from their position, their perspective is one impos-
         sible for those under them to require. This consid-
         eration also helps one to be just and considerate in
         speaking and thinking of subordinates. Recall Sr.
         Innocent, who never remarked without first 'sit-
         ting down and thinking how I would see it if I were
         a little girl.'
      3) with equals, consider differences of inheritance
         and education, which necessitate different degrees
         of responsibility—also that the critical words I use
         might mean far more to the person listening to
         them than to myself.
      4) and remember in all three cases that my [Salvation
         Army] years, with their attitude of "I am not as

other women," predispose me to spiritual *brateur* and criticism,

5) that my years as novice–mistress and director have made it a habit, and that I must, therefore, be the more stringent with myself than another need be.

Susie Swift—Sister Imelda Therese's prayer:

Lord, we know not what is good for us, nor what is bad. We cannot foretell the future, nor do we know when Thou comest to visit us, in what form Thou wilt come. And therefore we leave it all to Thee. Do Thou Thy good pleasure to us and in us. Let us ever look at Thee, and do Thou look upon us, and give us the grace of Thy bitter cross and Passion, and console us in Thy own way and at Thy own time. (Cardinal Newman in Meditations and Devotions*). The Holy man of Tours tells of a devout lady, who gained wonderful things from God by 'little things'—doing the tiniest and most insignificant acts of devotion, as one unworthy of great. For instance, she would kiss every step of a staircase she was ascending.*[27]

Susie Swift had learned her lesson of subservience. She respected Mother Samuel, as indicated in a poem she wrote for a 1915 Mother's Feast Day, the last stanza of which oozed with syrup:

Courage and Patience and sweet Content—These would we ask for you, Mother dear. Of all the treasures by Heaven sent, Courage and Patience and sweet Content. If the sworded Uriel smiling bent, And questioned our will for another year, Courage and Patience and sweet Content—These would we ask for you, Mother dear.[28]

In November 1914 an ex–Salvationist who, like Swift, had become a Catholic nun, wrote concerning Mrs. Stitt, who had mentioned Swift in letters. Mary Raphael (Teresa of Jesus) of Divine Providence, DCW, Lanhorne Convent, St. Columb, Cornwall, wrote that Stitt needed "prayers." She had been the Matron of the Dowager Duchess of Newcastle's Home for Penitents, and had worked with young girls at Lock Hospital. When she closed the Newcastle home on the death of the Duchess, she hoped that Catholic nuns would take up the work. But the Cardinal felt it was unsuitable for religious vocation.

Raphael then launched into news of ex–Salvationists who had become Catholic converts. Mr. Nicol's[29] conversion had seemed satisfactory at first, but she had heard "poor reports about him," and thought he was "not practicing his religion well" in Canada. Moseley had a "remarkable conversion" and was doing "good work" in the Catholic Reading Guild in London. Like Swift, Raphael still had Salvationist contacts. A London friend had sent a *War Cry* report of the deaths of General William Booth and Commissioner George Scott Railton. "The Army seems to be doing well in Germany, much better than when I was there about 20 years ago." It was hard for Salvationists who converted to break their ties to former comrades.[30]

Swift also heard from priests she had known. Bishop W. A. Jones, O.S.A. of Puerto Rico responded to a letter she had sent offering prayers on hearing of his parents' deaths. He noted the death of her friend Fr. Doyle and told her of Dominican sisters who were doing admirable work in Puerto Rican schools. He recalled her work in Cuba and the death of her father, and offered to serve her in any way he could.[31]

In March 1915, Fr Thomas Maria Gill, O.P. forwarded a letter from "dear little Sister Innocent." Innocent had found a way to circumvent the system. Sr. M. Thomas had written from Cuba that Innocent was in "great danger." Gill hoped that the report was mistaken. He was conducting missions in Minnesota and wished to pay a visit to the Mound, as Sinsinawa was called.[32]

Sr. Innocent's letter from Albany explained that she was in the care of the Infirmarian. Innocent said that her limbs were swollen and her heart was acting "queer." She said that she "would be happy to remain in purgatory, either earth purgatory or the real one, if He will grant the grace I ask of Him for those I love as well as for one I cannot love!" She must have been referring to Swift, her forbidden correspondent.[33]

Mrs. B. Ellen Burke, President of the *Sunday Companion* in New York, wrote to Mother Samuel to say that she had written letters to Swift after she went to Sinsinawa. She was pleased "because from the very first Swift seemed so much at home and so happy that I thought at last she had found the place where God wanted her to work. She is a dear good soul." Swift had written articles for the *Sunday Companion* in New York in 1897, the year she converted to Roman Catholicism.[34]

11

A Family Feud—a Matter of Money, 1910–1916

From 1910 to 1914 Susie Swift claimed that she had an on-going conflict with her sister Lil (Mrs. Brengle) over their father's will. Susie said that she had asked Lil for her half of their father's estate, although Susie had signed over her portion to Lil to pay his debts. Was Susie concerned that the dowry that he had agreed to pay to the church at his death had passed into the hands of the Albany Convent, and that she had not been notified of the transaction? Had she forgotten that she had signed over whatever remained of her portion of the estate at the time of his death in 1910 to pay his debts? Or had she become concerned about leaving a bequest to her adopted daughter Christobel after she experienced physical problems in 1910? This family feud lasted up until Susie's death in 1916.

In April 1915, a year before Swift's death, The Salvation Army's National Commander Evangeline Booth indicated in a letter that she was aware of her estrangement from her sister who had died on April 3. When she received news of Lil's death, Booth had asked if "news had been sent you." She had sent several telegrams, "but no reply had come from you." This may have been due to Susie's change of address. Booth had looked forward to seeing her at Lil's funeral. "I wonder if ever we shall meet again, and if so, when and where, and how it will be." Booth had seen her own family split by dissention when two of her brothers and her eldest sister had resigned from the Salvation Army. Her father's will included all of his children except Ballington, the first deserter. She saw the family split again in 1929 when she supported the removal of her eldest brother Bramwell as the Army's general. She assured Susie that problems between herself and Lil had not destroyed Lil's love for her:

> *No, I don't think she ever stopped loving you—I don't think she could, and I am sure you could not. These things cannot be explained down here. There is so much mystery in life—so much that when one's mind dwells upon its sorrows and misunderstandings, and ponders all its hidden meanings, one almost longs to get away from the night to the dawn of the everlasting Day.*

Booth was aware of Susie's closeness to her "adopted sister" Eileen Douglas, who was now living in the United States: "Dear little Eileen! I am trying to look after her. I think she is much stronger than she was, but she is frail enough. Her spirit is sweetness itself, and I love her more than ever." Eva had been "ill, but am better again"—a frequent phenomena for her. She inquired about Susie's well–being: "You don't give me any word of yourself—perhaps you will do, now that I have asked you." She wrote at the bottom: "Eileen and I often speak of you."[1]

George Brengle, Susie's nephew, answered her "note of sympathy" for his mother, but made no mention of the family problem over his grandfather's estate.[2] Eileen Douglas wrote about a vacation she was taking in Quebec and the welfare of mutual friends. She referred to "the money," but gave no details of her understanding of the part of the Swift estate that Susie felt was her legacy. She had wondered "what had become of you and Chris!" whom Susie had adopted when she and Eileen lived together as Salvation Army officers in London. Susie had told Eileen that Christobel had visited her at Sinsinawa, a visit that included a discussion of money Christobel needed to purchase a house now that she was married. Christobel had asked Eileen if she "thought it would do any good" to raise the money matter with Susie. Eileen told her "decidedly no," and explained that if Susie could lend her the money, she would get it herself. Eileen had not seen Christobel since. She had hoped that she would visit her and tell her all about Susie.[3]

On August 8 Christobel wrote to "Aunt Susie" about an investigation Chistobel had done on the estate problem.[4] Lil's death had left Swift without money of her own, since Lil's money passed to her husband and children. Susie had nothing to give to Christobel, who needed a loan. She had sent Christobel to a Poughkeepsie attorney to ask about the deed that she had signed to give Lil her half of their father's estate. Christobel located Ralph Butts, an attorney whose father had drawn up the deed, but Butts refused to advise her and told her that his father had died. He suggested that she ask Sam Brengle to provide information. Christobel visited "Uncle Sam," who explained that "when the deed was made out to Lil it was '*not* as a *loan*, but as a *gift*.'" Christobel asked Susie if Brengle was right: was it "a *gift* and not a *loan*?" She was concerned, "not only for myself, but for the position it places you in, when by right it should be yours." There is no record of Susie's answer.

Was Christobel agitating a situation that was transparent? Lil Brengle's family had inherited her estate. Christobel asked Susie: "Auntie you won't be hurt because I went to the Brengles [to] save you the bother of writing to the lawyer who would direct you to Uncle Sam?" Christobel said that she could get a loan from Uncle Sam, but he would want six percent interest. Since she and her husband Adolf were paying four percent interest for lots they were buying they would not want to pay six. She reasoned that the estate would be published in the *White Plains* paper, but she received only New York City papers. As for her adoptive mother, Christobel reasoned that "a loan would not be of any benefit at all to you, and as I said, I want you to have what Grandpa left you, if I can possibly do it." During Christobel's trip to Sinsinawa she and Susie must have discussed the money.[5] It is not clear why Susie needed money, having taken a vow of poverty, apart from helping her daughter and her husband.

On September 20 Susie gave Mother Samuel her version of the "state of affairs between my sister (Mrs. Brengle) and myself." She left out nothing that would "influence Samuel's decision on what to do next." Was the next step a legal one? She never indicated that she wanted to go in that direction. Susie wrote that her father, George H. Swift, intended that the sisters share equally in his estate, but in August, 1899, after she had taken the habit in Albany:

> *he made a final will in which he left all to my sister except the amount of dowry required at Albany, which he promised me verbally should be paid at his death ... My father died in November 1908 and this legacy was not to be payable until April 1910.*

Susie had attended her father's funeral and had signed a quit claim giving the estate to her sister Lil. She had promised not to litigate. About January 1909 Lil had written to Susie that their father was "thousands in debt." Mother Bertrand went to the Bishop of Albany to present Susie's request to give her dowry to her sister. The Bishop said:

> *If Sr. I.T. wishes to give her dowry to her sister, she must have good reason. In any case, she has earned it over and over again for the Congregation in Havana alone. Let her give it.*

So in November 1909 Susie signed over her dowry to her sister "by a deed of gift."

Susie told Mother Samuel that she "did not know then, nor till just before I left Albany, that [Lil] believed that $1,500 had been paid to Albany with my knowledge during my father's life."[6] This was the amount of her dowry. But the Albany convent denied that they had received the $1,500. But the presumption that George Swift had paid it influenced the Brengles and Susie Swift. Susie had thought concerning the deed of gift, that "if I ever need this money and she [Lil] can repay it, she will do so." Christobel had not found the amount of the total estate in her investigation, and apparently Brengle had not disclosed that figure to her when they met. If the deed of gift was less than $1,500, and Albany had received that amount for Susie's dowry from George Swift, then there was no issue.

When Susie left Albany in 1912, Lil gave her $200 to pay her board in Brooklyn and wrote her, according to Susie's letter to Mother Samuel:

I don't believe you will ever see the inside of another convent. Eileen [Douglas] says it is all a matter of money and you haven't enough. However, you can have the last cent of what papa left you to squander in trying to get into one, if you like.

Susie did not tell Mother Samuel that Lil indicated how much was left of Susie's inheritance at that time. Rather, Susie told Samuel that Lil had:

begged me to say no more than that she would give me what was necessary, although she was poor. She said: "You don't know them. It may be Albany right over again. I beg you—I entreat you as your sister, to let me keep that money, in case you are thrown on the world again. Still, if you insist, and Eileen says you will, you shall have it now."

With that advice, Lil gave Susie the $50 she brought with her to Sinsinawa and the $50 she asked for at the time of her reception. Susie said that she:

prayed a great deal about how and when to ask her for the full amount, and decided it was best, for her soul's sake, to wait right up to profession and let her see that it was not a question of money here.

Susie would not live to make her final profession (take final vows), but she told Samuel that:

two weeks ago I wrote her [Lil] and said that if she did not need it and would not use it, I did not think it right to keep it idle—that I wished to give it here. I wrote as fully and as urgently as possible—I enclose her reply.[7] I am indignant and hurt and ashamed of her.

But Susie acknowledged that "since the money is legally hers it seems best not to antagonize her unless one is sure of overcoming her."[8] Obviously, if Susie meant to give money to the Sinsinawa Convent, then she did not intend to give it to Christobel.

This is a difficult matter to sort out. There is the question of the missing $1,500 at Albany. There is Lil Brengle's willingness to give Susie money when she needed it. And Lil's side of the story is not in Susie's papers at Sinsinawa. Nor do we have Susie's letters to Lil about the matter. We only have Susie's letter to Samuel. But there had been a life–long chasm between the sisters. Their friends and family knew about the tension and took sides.

Mrs. B. Ellen Burke of the *Sunday Companion* wrote to Susie in October 1915: "Today I forgive your sister many things, and feel as if she needed our sympathy and our prayers more than anything else."[9] That this rift came to a head just as the sisters were dying within a year of each other is tragic. By "many things," Burke may have meant matters of faith as well as money. But Susie and Lil rarely spoke of faith differences. Yet many of their letters had a note of sarcasm in them. Elizabeth Brengle's estate went to her husband and their children's education. Christobel would have to fend for herself as she had for most of her life, about which we know little.

12

Vassar, Salvation Army, Dominicans
Assorted Sisterhood Notes, 1915–16

In September 1915 Swift was still receiving letters of sympathy concerning Lil's death from Salvation Army friends as the money episode ended.[1] From Roman Catholic friends she received updates on the Albany Convent that was in the throes of an "upheaval." Mother Bertrand had taken charge of a Dayton convent; Sr. Gregory was the superior at Philadelphia; Sr. Aimee was back in Albany and Mother Francis was in charge at Saratoga.[2]

Lura, an 1883 Vassar classmate, told Swift in January 1916 that Vassar was celebrating an anniversary and the class had gathered for the occasion. She gave resumes of about a dozen classmates. Minnie Sherwood was her "sweet, dignified self, a little intensified with the Bryn Mawr skepticism about everything." Mamie Cooley "is going through very deep waters, with a husband helpless mentally and physically, and a helpless father." Jessie Dewell was "efficient, thoughtful and gentle, and has kept the class together wonderfully by her quiet persistence." Sarah Iserdway was "elegant, sweet and dignified ... and beautifully dressed." And "Anna is Anna." Lura described the campus as adorned with October colors: "Surely, I have a goodly heritage."[3] The Dean, Miss McCaleb, for the sake of graduating students, made a plea for money to develop a fellowship fund of $600 out of which students could apply for loans for Vocational or Professional study. To the Committee for the Vassar Million Dollar Endowment Fund, Swift donated $15.[4]

Swift heard from Anna May Keenan in January 1916 that her closest friend, Sr. Innocent, had received the last sacraments, but had rallied and was "somewhat better." She asked Swift not to speak of it to the Albany community, but Innocent had "offered her life for your happiness, and surely her prayer has been granted!"[5] In November Dr. Stillman had said that nothing but a miracle could save Innocent's heart and kidneys. Sisters at Albany, to which she had returned in February from Cuba, had prayed to St. Vincent Ferrer and gradually her condition improved.[6]

On Maundy Thursday, Swift's teacher friend Florence Jeffrey wrote from the Brighton, Mass. convent of the Cenacle:

> How beautiful the Church's great days are, aren't they? High Mass began at 4:00 a.m., followed by the procession of the Priest and Religious to the repository with lighted candles singing the Pange, lingua, gloriosi, then returning for Vespers. The repository is beautiful. I have adoration at 3 p.m.

Jeffrey returned to the convent so fatigued that she collapsed and had to be nursed by the infirmarian, two refectorians, and a sister in charge of the retreatants' rooms. She recalled that Swift had tended to her at Saratoga with sodium phosphate and a mustard plaster. Jeffrey was translating a French book for the Cluacle in New York and was knitting heels for "the religieuses to wear in their stockings to preserve the real heel."[7]

13

Death of Susie Forrest Swift: Sister Imelda Theresa Swift, O.S.D., April 19, 1916

Sister Mary Imelda Therese Swift, O.S.D., died on April 19, 1916, at 8:00 p.m. of "acute dilatation and chronic valvular diseases of the heart," according to Dr. A. M. Loes of Dubuque.[1] It was Wednesday of Holy Week. Mother Samuel immediately notified Swift's family and friends by telegram and they responded to her death with memories of her life. Her Dominican friend, Mary Innocent of Jesus, wrote to the Very Rev. Thomas M. Gill on Good Friday:

> I have read a notice in the Catholic News that our dear Sister M. Imelda Teresa has left this "land of exile" and has gone, I sincerely hope and have reason to believe, to her Heavenly Home where in union with Father Leduc and Mother Loyola she will celebrate Easter. After having read what was a most painful surprise to me, I knelt down and with a peaceful and grateful, although bleeding heart, I gave her to God; and now I turn to you to ask you to pray for her who was a Mother to your child. Am I a coward to rejoice because our wonderful Sister is now beyond the judgment of men? Dear Sister! How often did she not say to me: "Little Sister, you must not be afraid to have me suffer!"[2]

Florence Jeffery wrote from the Brighton Convent to promise to have masses said. The Rev. Mother there asked the community to pray for Therese, a practice that Salvationists disdain, as when Lil Brengle had not acceded to Susie's request that she pray for Father Doyle after his death. Protestants believe in entry to heaven or hell without a purging in purgatory. Jeffery had received a "bright, cheerful letter" from Swift "after Laefare Sunday, seemingly full of health and spirits." She asked Mother Samuel to send "particulars" and possibly a photograph "of my dearest friend whom I have known for so many years." She noted that Swift had been taken during Father Thuente's retreat." She would inform Mrs. Byles, Fr. McSorley, C.S.P. and Fr. McNicholas, O.P.[3]

An obituary issued by the Sinsinawa's Saint Clara Convent gave an overview of Susie Swift's life in three sisterhoods, Vassar College, the Salvation Army, and two Dominican Convents:

> *Sister M. Imelda Theresa Swift died at Saint Clara Convent, April 19, 1916, in the 54th year of her age and the 2nd of her religious profession. The life of Sister Imelda Therese was a remarkable one, and has become a subject for a place in books and pamphlets in America and in England. A graduate of Vassar College, an ardent and distinguished officer in the Salvation Army in England and America, a convert to the Catholic Church, a writer for the* Catholic World *and other magazines, she finally entered the newly founded Community of Saint Catherine deRicci in Albany, New York. After about twelve years, finding it still impossible to make perpetual profession because of some delay in adjustment of the constitutions of that Community, she obtained dispensation to enter our congregation as a postulant chiefly through the influence and recommendation of the Reverend J. T. McNicholas, O.P., afterward Bishop of Duluth.[4] She made her novitiate with becoming humility and earnestness ... After profession she taught classes in Saint Clara College.[5]*

Mother Samuel wrote to the Santa Clara community and to Swift's friends and family who had asked for particulars of her death. Samuel sympathized with those "bowed down with great sorrow." Swift had been in good health to the best of Samuels' knowledge. She had taught classes in English and Spanish on Wednesday and was at supper at about 6 p.m., serving a table when the regular waiter was not there. At 7:30 the students began a spiritual retreat, a custom for the last three days of Holy Week. Swift had lined up a section of students to enter the chapel and urged a Protestant girl to get a head covering so that she would not miss the retreat. Before she went to the chapel she told a sister that she had a "queer sensation in my chest; am I pale or red?" The sister told her that her face was flushed. Swift said: "Would it not be strange if I were to die during Benediction?" She went to her chapel stall for Fr. Thuente's conference, but left before the Benediction. No one followed her since she seemed to be all right. She walked to her cell in the bay window of St. Aloysius' Dormitory and lay on her bed.

When Swift did not return for the Benediction, her friend Mary Ellen O'Hanlon noticed and hurried to the dormitory where she found Swift speechless and "almost breathing her last." She hurried to get help from sisters who were leaving the chapel. The infirmarian, a trained nurse, and others came immediately. Chaplain Fr. Kavanaugh arrived to give her "conditional absolution and anointing." Srs. Francesca and Kerin tried in vain to revive her. "Life departed." She was dead long before the doctor arrived. He gave the cause of death as valvular heart affection and said that this "nearly always brings sudden death." Swift had gone to confession about four hours before her death. Samuels wrote a warm personal tribute to Sr. Therese for her sisters at the Mound:

> When I think of her notable career in the world, a woman of fame on two continents, her gifted intellect and warm heart for the miserable, the thought of her dying in our humble dormitory makes me sad, but when I think that after searching for years for the Truth, and then finding it, and still not finding in the community she chose the ideal she sought, and her coming to us and saying frequently that she never expected to find again in her life as much happiness as she enjoyed here, I cannot but feel grateful to God. My one remorse is that we did not check her activity. She was tireless in her work among the pupils, and perfectly willing to assist any Sister in her duty, whether manual or intellectual. Her beautiful simplicity in continual happy association with our young Sisters of her own age in religion was touching ... [They] recognized in her a teacher of unusual parts and a woman of sterling character—a lady always. [Her students were] inconsolable, for they loved her as a teacher and a friend. [She helped] wherever it was needed—spiritual, intellectual or manual.

The sisters buried Swift on Good Friday. Since it was a high holy day, no Requiem Mass could be offered, but on Monday a Mass was "offered for her soul." After Low Sunday they observed a Requiem High Mass. Samuel wrote that "none of her immediate family is living." Had she forgotten visits by Samuel Brengle and Swift's daughter Christobel to the Mound? Swift's New York friends had wired their messages and given their reasons for being unable to attend the funeral."[6]

Since Susie F. Swift, Mary Imelda Therese, albeit 52, was a "young sister" when she entered the Sinsinawa convent, the Sinsinawa archivist, Sr. Benvenuta Bras, explained in 1986 that like other novices at the time she was not featured in the Convent annals. But years later Sr. Thomas Aquinas O'Neill held young "wide–eyed Sr. Mary Hunt spellbound as she recounted dramatically the saga of Sr. Imelda Therese." Sr. Thomas, who was present at the Mound when Swift was alive, mentioned that St. Clara College girls loved her even though "she talked above them and had trouble holding their attention."[7] The Sinsinawa archives hold Therese's World Literature lessons that vindicate this comment.

Swift had just written to an "ever dear Sister," possibly Innocent of Jesus, that she was teaching English Literature and Composition to novices of the Normal department at St. Clara College. As for health, she claimed that she "never missed a meal or a class or a Mass or an exercise."

Fr. E. O. Langlois, O.P. had responded from Ottawa in French on May 10, 1914, to Swift's request for a book by Fr. Hyacinth Cormier that indicates that she also taught Dominican history. Langlois had tried unsuccessfully to obtain information on "Father Cormier, instructor of novices." He advised her to write to Rome and ask about brochures by the Dominican Father General. Swift had apparently revealed her checkered past to Langlois who said that he was "unaware of all the paths you have tread," but prayed that as you were "looking for another *City of Peace,* and you have found it." *City of Peace* was a green–bound booklet published by the Catholic Truth Society of Ireland that contained sketches written by converts to Catholicism. One of these was by Susie Swift, "formerly one of the best known Salvation Army workers in England and this country."[8]

The *St. Clara annals* gave this terse report of Sr. Therese's death: "Miss Susie Swift had come to St. Clara ... late in life, educated, cultured, and of wide experience. We received her and she was a Professed Sister at the time of her death. During the time that she wore the Dominican habit in our community she was a model religious and a perfect teacher. She was respected everywhere. Her loss was deeply felt by students and Sisters.[9]

Sr. Benvenuta Bras' 1986 sketch of Swift drew on letters Mother Samuel had received from the Swift–Brengle family, her adopted Salvation Army sister Brigadier Eileen Douglas, from Roman Catholic friends in Albany, at Cuban schools, New York City journals, and from her 1883 Vassar classmates. All addressed Swift's "happiness" at Sinsinawa. They were also frank about her nature, with descriptions that matched what Swift had written about herself in her diary in the 1880s to1917, and about her troubled life at Albany prior to coming to Sinsinawa. Sr. Celestine of New York's Jesus–Mary Convent wrote on Easter 1915:

> *I knew that you would be happy among these Sisters, would find an outlet for your activities, and a sympathetic response to your efforts of zeal ... How glad I am that you are so well! How beautiful the prospect stretching out before you! The promise of long, useful, happy years.*[10]

At the time of her death Swift's family consisted of her brother–in–law, Salvation Army Colonel Samuel Logan Brengle, nephew George and niece Elizabeth Brengle, "adopted sister" Eileen Douglas, and adopted daughter Christobel. Her sister Elizabeth (Lil) had died in 1915. No family member attended her funeral mass, likely due to time and distance and, in some cases, health. Archivist Benvenuta cited a division in the family over a "misunderstanding" between Susie and Lil over "financial problems" that Susie had revealed in a letter to Mother Samuel.

Colonel Brengle wrote a gracious letter in response to Mother Samuel's obituary. He frankly explained his frustration over Susie's agitation over money. He was between revival engagements at Watertown and Syracuse, New York, and was "suffering from extreme exhaustion" following illness, the death of his wife Lil, and his hectic schedule as an evangelist. He heard of Sr. Therese's death after her burial, so was unable to attend the funeral or to communicate. When he had visited Sinsinawa he noticed that she was "entirely different from the [person] we have met previously." She was "in the best of health" and he was surprised to hear the news of her death. He wrote:

> I rejoice that her death was so peaceful and her last few years so happy, and employed in work amid surroundings and among friends and associates so wholly congenial to her. And I am comforted with the confidence that she, being "absent from the body," is 'present with the Lord' (II Cor. 5:8), and that some things which she did not know and misunderstood and misinterpreted to the disturbance of her peace ... she knows and understands there.

Then Brengle turned to the rift between his wife and Susie, "the only sister I ever had and I loved her with the love of a brother."

> Therefore it was a great pain and grief to me, and a source of astonishment above measure, when she abruptly and without a word of explanation to me, immediately following the funeral of Mrs. Brengle, broke off what I supposed were our wholly cordial and affectionate relations and as I learned later, began to write letters to our mutual friends, charging me with some things for which I was in no sense responsible, with others of which I had never dreamed, and with motives and intentions which were utterly foreign to me.

At the time of his wife's funeral Brengle was "coming up from the edge of the grave" after a second dangerous operation. He wrote that the previous year he was "overwhelmed by the death of my darling wife, and this action and attitude of Sister so pained and unnerved me that I felt I could not then write and answer the things she was saying to others about me." He explained the situation to Eileen Douglas, and hoped that she wrote to "Sister."

> I do not write this now that she is gone, to cast the least reflection upon her, but only that you may understand the relation that existed between us at the time of her death. I never ceased to have the most tender and brotherly feeling for her, and I rejoice to believe that the shadows have all passed away and that she now sees and understands this.

Brengle welcomed Samuel's invitation to visit Sinsinawa again. He had "a bright and pleasant memory" of his first visit. He signed off, "thanking you, and praying that God may in all ways richly bless and comfort you and make you a blessing to many, I am very sincerely yours, S. L. Brengle, Colonel.[11] Brengle's son George Swift Brengle, a Presbyterian minister and a Princeton University graduate, wrote a comforting letter. It is possible that he and his sister Elizabeth knew nothing of the money matter between their mother and Susie. Neither he nor Elizabeth knew their aunt well, apart from her writings. George wrote:

> *When I was in college I was greatly interested in the things that she had written for the Vassar Miscellany and since then I have read many of the religious articles which she wrote in connection with her editorial work in the Salvation Army. And her letters to Mother, better perhaps than anything else, made me feel that I knew her. As you say, she was a wonderfully gifted woman, and her powers of intellect as well as of body were always used in the interest of others. We knew that Auntie Susie was contented and happy at [Sinsinawa], but it was a joy to hear from you that she continually found peace and deep satisfaction."[12]*

Brigadier Eileen Douglas, whom Susie referred to as her "adopted sister" when they were Salvation Army journalists in London in the 1880s and 1890s, described Susie's complex personality as having a tendency to fear the worst. Douglas knew about the money matter between Susie and Lil, and had mixed loyalties. She had written a biography of Susie's sister Lil.[13] Of Susie's death she wrote:

> *I was terribly shocked at first, stunned, but later I have felt wonderfully comforted. Dear Susie had a strange complicated temperament. She had a marvelous capacity for suffering, she used to jump at conclusions and made herself sick with worry and then perhaps find out later her conclusions were quite wrong.[14]*

In May 1916, Susie's adopted daughter Christobel Janicke wrote to Mother Samuel from Brooklyn, the last address for which there is a record of her. She had visited Sinsinawa the previous summer to visit "Auntie," and thus was consoled by the fact that she "was the last one in the family to see her, and when I was with her she seemed very happy." Mrs. Byles, RSCJ, had told Christobel that Mother Samuel would be in New York for a couple of days and she asked if she could visit her. She did not say why, but it may have been to check on her mother's will.[15]

Swift's Catholic friends, Katherine Byles and Florence A. Jeffery, wrote to Mother Samuel to express a hope that someone would write Swift's biography. As for the circumstances of her death, Mrs. Byles could not understand why Dr. Mayo did not notice the heart problem when he had examined her earlier. She had "several such attacks," but none since her gall stone operation. Byles surmised that Swift's health problem had begun in the "torturing years" at Albany, prior to her rescue by the Sinsinawa Convent. She was grateful to Samuel for that!

Byles had thought of writing Therese's biography herself, and had boxes of letters and poems. If she did write with Sinsinawa's approval, she would focus on "intense interior experiences [that] were equaled only by those of some of the saints." Like St. Teresa, "no matter how holy she was, she was always clever and brilliant." Looking over her letters from Sinsinawa, Byles found that God had "inspired you to take her," so that she could "die in peace."

> She needed a little rest from suffering. All her mental torture was over, and she had these last few happy years in which to calm down... .
> Well, it is all over and she is safe with Our Lord at last.

Apparently Byles did not write her hagiography, but she did ask for Therese's papers and her ring, if she was not buried with it. And she enclosed $10 to have the Chaplain say mass "for the repose of her soul, or, if she is already in Heaven, for her sister."[16] Florence Jeffery proposed that a biography focus on Swift's brilliant intelligence and intriguing career. Her life story would inspire faith and trust in Christ. She thanked Samuel "for having made her so happy among you. Her every letter spoke of her great content at Sinsinawa."[17]

Jessie K. Dewell, one of Susie's 1883 Vassar classmates, wrote to Sr. M. Reginald to suggest that a biography trace Swift's 30–plus years of "service"—from her 1883 graduation from Vas-

sar to The Salvation Army (1884–97), and two Dominican sisterhoods (1898–1916). Dewell thanked Sr. Reginald for a $15 check
"in our friend's memory."[18] The check from a Catholic convent
to Vassar College, and notes from Salvation Army sisters, and
from Catholic lay and religious sisters, sealed the circle of Susie
Swift's sisterhoods.

In 1986 archivist Benvenuta Bras observed that a biography
of Sister Therese that Roman Catholic and Vassar College friends
had proposed in 1916 would not attract an audience in the
post–Vatican II era. Women Salvationists would almost certainly
agree, since the Army's single women recruits were also in de-
cline. All of Swift's sisterhoods had changed dramatically. None
of them would relish sectarian biographies of Susie Forrest Swift
that had been published in their magazines to celebrate her agnostic, Salvationist, or Roman Catholic conversions in the late 19th
and early 20th centuries. While such a biography may have been
appropriate in 1916, archivist Bras argued in 1986 that: "It is
doubtful whether the contemporary Catholic would be interested
in Sister Imelda Therese's career and conversion." The church:

> *is not the one which she knew. The intimate notes she left, and the*
> *books of piety among her possessions would be relics from another age*
> *for a young or even a not–so–young Catholic of today. The courage*
> *she manifested in leaving the Salvation Army for the Church and re-*
> *ligious life would almost surely not be evident to today's reader.*

But Bras thought it might be interesting for a biographer "to
trace her path of suffering," something she and her friends frequently mentioned. Mary Innocent of Jesus constantly referred
to it. Records at the Salvation Army archives and the Albany Dominican community archives at Elkins Park, Pa., and letters to
descendants of friends, might reveal "her interior anguish in a
way not obvious from her Sinsinawa years," for at Sinsinawa she
had "found happiness and peace."[19]

Bras found that Swift's personal papers from her brief time
at Sinsinawa "left little written testimony" of the peace that she
found there, or of her influence on that community. What was in
her papers was the troubled departures from The Salvation
Army and the Albany convent, and a family dispute over

money. While the stories that older sisters like Mary Ellen O'Hanlon, Professor of Biology at Rosary College, had told young nuns in the 1930s were "impressive" and "known to many at that time," by 1986 only the "oldest Sisters have ever heard of 'Brigadier General' Swift."[20]

By the 1960s and 1970s Roman Catholic and Salvation Army sisterhoods were failing to attract young women to their hospitals and homes for "unwed mothers," by then known as "single parents." Many parochial schools, rescue homes for poor women, orphanages, and day nurseries were closing. The work that Swift had done in her thirty–three years as a writer, teacher and social worker, had passed to secular professional women who did not don the Army's uniform or the Dominican habit. Soon elderly nuns and single women Salvationists filled convents and retirement homes to spend their last years. Neither organization was particularly interested in celebrating their passing with biographies of a lost era. In fact, there is no history of the Salvation Army women's social service department, and there are few histories of the social services of Catholic nuns in schools and hospitals.

Simple chronicles of a lost era may not interest modern Catholics or Salvationists, or women's movements for liberation and equality. Freedoms that single women like Susie Swift relinquished when they donned their uniform and habit and submitted to a male hierarchy are now too cherished to give up to subservience to male, or any other authority.

Yet there may be a story in why women like Susie Swift did what they did when and where they did it. Was it because few other options were open to women in the late 19th century? That may have seemed to be the case to women in the assertive days of the 1970s women's movement. Surely Swift's story of subjection to male authority, willingness to suffer burdensome and often unrewarding tasks, rejection by what may have been the only male who romanced her, may have limited her vision of secular possibilities in her era. And once committed to religious vocation she may have been unable to see herself back "in the world," away from religious sisters and a life of devotion.

This may explain Swift's attachment to educated, middle class sisterhoods. Yet she craved more. That craving might explain her movement from sisterhood to sisterhood—a migration that nearly always revealed both a push and a pull. That her migrations depended on male intervention into a sphere of sisterhoods may not be as surprising as we think. It may well have been the withdrawn love of a man that caused her to leave The Salvation Army. It was largely men who convinced her that Roman Catholic sacraments made that visible church the true faith.

Sr. Eva McCarty's 1952 history of the Sinsinawa Dominican Convent described Swift as having "remarkable humility," but a "naturally high–strung" temperament. Possibly these traits, kept in check by male advisors, allowed her to sustain a lonely life of penance, chastity, and hard work. McCarty wrote that Swift was "a valiant religious" and "a brilliant and inspiring teacher."[21] With this pithy analysis of her life her sisters at Vassar, the Salvation Army, and two Roman Catholic convents, would likely agree. She was a teacher, social worker, and writer of talent; she was a prickly personality; and she lived a deeply spiritual, even mystical life of the mind and spirit.

Conclusions

Following her 1897 Roman Catholic conversion, Brigadier Susie Swift—Sr. Mary Imelda Therese—continued to correspond with friends in the three sisterhoods in which she spent her professional life. She kept in touch with her Swift family, father George, mother, sister Lil, adopted–sister Eileen Douglas, and adopted–daughter Christobel.

She relished her Vassar College classmates to whom she owed her intellectual keenness and religious skepticism that led her to term herself "agnostic" during her undergraduate days. For three decades after graduation she never lost touch with them or with their middle–class values of proper breeding and lady–like behavior.

She also corresponded with middle–class Salvation Army sisters, Emma Booth, Eva Booth, Eileen Douglas, and at least one sister who had crossed over to a Catholic convent. She had met these sisters in London and New York during her twelve years as a Salvation Army officer. With them she edited journals, wrote hymns and poems, and prepared the outline for *In Darkest England and the Way Out* in 1890, the book that laid out the Army's social reform program, elements of which are still intact in the 21st century. She had, with working–class "slum sisters", gained first hand knowledge of London's poor. With other educated women she had supervised slum sisters who cleaned London garrets and cellars and established Salvation Army social services by insisting that souls detached from bodies are seldom won to God.[1]

As Sister Therese, Susie Swift spent her last two decades in Roman Catholic Dominican convents, under the supervision of Mothers Superior. She did much the same work that she had done in the Army in the presence of middle– and working–class sisters, both "lay" and "religious." As in her Army years, her spiritual directors were men in roles of authority who offered advice and sacraments of confession and absolution as well as harsh criticism to her often–troubled spirit. Had she risen in rank to Mother Superior, as one Salvation Army document thought she did, she still would have been inferior to males in the church. And had she risen in rank to Brigadier General, as one Roman Catholic document thought she had, she would still have been subject to male domination.

Mother Bertrand of the Albany Convent, when chastised by Fr. McNicholas, offered an apology that McNicholas suspected was written by a priest. Having a female supervisor and a male confessor was also the norm in the Army. In fact, married Salvation Army women, like Susie's sister Lil, were subservient both to a husband and a male hierarchy that regulated life in the church and the home. With Sam Brengle's permission, and that of Army commanders to whom he was subject, Lil spent her time raising two children and caring for her home and elderly father. But other married Army women followed Catherine Booth's lead and spent much of their time in the pulpit, with the acknowledged permission of their husbands, and raised children.[2]

A mystic on the order of Susie's patron, S. Teresa of Avila, Swift constantly questioned her devotion to the faith and the intensity of her devotion to her vocation. In Sir Isaiah Berlin's conceptual frame Swift was by nature a fox, always searching for absolute truth, but only occasionally expecting to find it. Men taught her at Vassar, acted as her superiors and confidants in the Salvation Army, and served as her Roman Catholic spiritual directors and career guides. Sisters offered solace or scolded her for her complex personality and her fluctuating intellectual–mystical faith that often stood in the way of simple trust and obedience that religious hierarchies demanded.

Although she spent her life in subjection to ecclesiastical rule, Swift's accomplishments, and those of her sisters who dedicated themselves to work in slums, schools, hospitals, and writing church journals, can only be adequately assessed with research into diaries and letters they left behind. Not many were as inclined to write so intimately of their lives as was Susie Swift. Perhaps Convent and Salvation Army archives have treasures that will yet yield a better idea of the sisters' lives and works. How much did their lives differ from sisters in the secular realm who also accepted spinsterhood as a requirement of

their professionalism in that era. But women who married the
church accepted a double subjection—one to their work and one
to the male hierarchy they served. They learned service and subservience, generally termed "submission," and only occasionally
challenged one or the other.

Endnotes for Susie F. Swift Biography

Notes to Introduction

1. O.P. after a name represents The Order of Preachers. Since 1920, O.S.D. (Order of Saint Dominic) was used interchangeably by men and women because the order's mission was to preach the Gospel.

2. "Sister Teresa M. Imelda, O.P. (Susie Swift), Dominican House of Retreats, 18th & Wood Streets, Philadelphia," *Herringshaw's American Blue Book of Biography: Men of 1913* (Chicago: American Blue Book): 1913

3. Historians Lillian Taiz, *Hallelujah Lads & Lasses: Remaking the Salvation Army in America, 1880–1930* (Chapel Hill: Univ. of North Carolina Press, 2001): 49–51, 193, & Diane Winston, *Red–Hot & Righteous: The Urban Religion of The Salvation Army* (Cambridge: Harvard Univ. Press, 1999): 65, 80, 86–7, mentioned Swift. Neither St. John Ervine nor Harold Begbie, William Booth's biographers, mentioned her. Salvation Army historians Sally Chesham, *Born to Battle: The Salvation Army in America* (New York: Salvation Army, 1965): 76, & William Clark, ed., *Dearest Lily* (London: Salvation Army 1985): vi, barely mention her.

Notes to Chapter 1

1. Clarence W. Hall, *Samuel Logan Brengle: Portrait of a Prophet* (New York: Salvation Army, 1933): 66–67

2. "The Conversion of Susan Swift (by herself), Later Sister Imelda Therese, Sinsinawa, Wisconsin, 1897," Salvation Army Archives, Alexandria, Virginia.

3. "Autobiographical Account by Brigadier Susie Swift," *War Cry* (March 1893): 4.

4. Abbreviation Fr. denotes a Catholic priest, referred to as "Father."

5. Sister Imelda Therese, "The Conversion of Susan Swift," 1897, 3, Salvation Army Archives, Alexandria

Notes to Chapter 2

1. "Autobiographical Account," March 1893, 5–6

2. The Salvation Army was Wesleyan: William Booth had been a Methodist New Connexion clergyman until 1861 when he and his wife, Catherine, became an itinerant evangelists. They founded a home mission in East London in 1865 that they named "salvation army" in 1978. See Norman H. Murdoch, *Origins of The Salvation Army* (Knoxville: Univ. of Tennessee Press, 1994), a study of the Army's early stages.

3. "Autobiographical Account, March 1893," 7–8

4. "Autobiographical Account, March 1893," 4.

5. "The Conversion of Susan Swift, 1897

6. Susie Swift, #510, *The Song Book of The Salvation Army* (London: Salvationist Pub., 1987): 322; Gordon Taylor, *Companion to the Song Book of The Salvation Army* (London: Salvation Army, 1989): 424–25.

7. Clarence W. Hall, *Samuel Logan Brengle* (New York: Salvation Army, 1933, 67.

8. Pamela J. Walker, *Pulling the Devil's Kingdom Down:* 32.

9. "Autobiographical Account," 9.

10. Clarence Hall, *Samuel Logan Brengle,* 70–1; 79ff for their marriage on May 29, 1887

11. Susie Swift and Eileen Douglas co–edited *All the World* until 1895 when Mildred Duff took over. Noel Hope, *Mildred Duff: A Surrendered Life* (London: Salvationist Pub., 1933): 70–2 & 85–9. The Booths gave Swift and Douglas, as well as Mildred Duff and Frances Forward the right to adopt children. Duff's child was an Armenian orphan, Helenko, c. 1896, whom she raised with Forward.

12. Gore Rd. was the Booth's home from 1866 till they moved to Clapham Commons. Catherine Bramwell–Booth, *Catherine Booth* (London: Hodder & Stoughton, 1970): 233, 288. See *Receiving House Girls Statements,* Book I., London, p. 203, and *War Cry* (22 Apr. 1887): Salvation Army Archives, London; "Gertrude King sent to situation," 6 Feb. 1888, Miss Swift, Penge; see H. 453, "In the Slums," and H. 210, "Eighteen Pence is Better than Nothing"

13. Adoption Agreement, Oct. 18, 1887, George & Mary Madeley, 29 Dark Lane Ardwick, Manchester, ("parents") & Susan Forrest Swift, 101 Queen Victoria St., City of London, "Spinster," (adopting parent)

14. Clarence Hall, 85, refers to the Swifts as "members of society's upper crust."

15. Susie Swift Diary, 1887–97, Salvation Army Archives, London, Dec. 11, 1887

Notes to Chapter 3

1. Andrew Mark Eason, *Women in God's Army* (Waterloo: Wilfrid Laurier Univ. Press, 2003) xii, on disciplining women officers to keep them submissive in the 1880s to 1930s. The Booths used similar tactics to discipline men.
2. Susie Swift Diary, Dec. 6, 1887–Jan. 1, 1888

Notes to Chapter 4

1. Susie Swift Diary, Aug. 10; Sept. 6, 1888
2. St. John Ervine, *God's Soldier: General William Booth*, vol. 2 (New York: Macmillan, 1935): 750–52, tells of Lucy Booth's 1892 engagement to John Lampard, who got cold feet at the thought of marrying "so excellent and noble a lady." General Booth had Colonel Lampard court–marshaled for breaking the engagement. A court of five officers, including John Carleton, got a specialist in mental disease to state that Lampard was "so far mentally deranged as not to be responsible for his action." Ervine says that Lampard may have gone to the U.S. "where his eccentricities, if he had any, would not be noticed, and there became an evangelist." Booth biographers do not mention the Herbert Booth–Susie Swift engagement.
3. Swift Diary, Sept. 17, 1888
4. Swift Diary, Sept. 6, 1888
5. "Autobiographical Account," 1893, p. 4

Notes to Chapter 5

1. *The War Cry*, London (Mar. 23, 1889): 8
2. Swift Diary, Jan. 29, 1890
3. R. David Rightmire, *Salvationist Samurai: Gunpei Yamamuro & the Rise of the Salvation Army in Japan* (Lanham, Md.: Scarecrow, 1997): 13–15
4. Ford C. Ottman, *Herbert Booth* (New York: Doubleday, Doran & Co., 1928): 88–91, describes Schoch's lineage, but does not say how she and Herbert met. Nor does he mention Swift.

Notes to Chapter 6

1. Susie F. Swift, "Sociology & Salvation," pts. 1 & 2, *All the World* 6 (Jan. 1890): 39–41, & (Mar. 1890): 110–13; "Glimpses of East End Life," *War Cry* (25 Dec. 1889): 17–18

2. I use the word "imperium" to describe the growing international scope of the Salvation Army that paralleled the growth of the British Empire in the 1880s & 1890s in style of leadership, and structure.

3. Frederick Whyte, *The Life of W. T. Stead* (London 1925): 213, on Booth's reluctance to promote a social program and how Smith changed his mind. See Frank Smith, "With the General" *War Cry* (13 Aug. 1887): 8.

4. Norman H. Murdoch, *Frank Smith: Salvationist–Socialist (1854–1940): Principal Ideologue of the Darkest England Scheme that Created Salvation Army Social Services* (Alexandria: Salvation Army, 2003): 24 pp.

5. Murdoch, *Origins of the Salvation Army*, 120ff; endnotes, 204ff.

6. Barbara A. Lundsten, "The Legacy of Walter Rauschencusch;" *International Bulletin of Missionary Research*, 28:2 (April 2004): 76–77, discusses a meeting Rauschenbusch, champion of the social gospel, meeting William Booth in 1891, and the influence Henry George on their social thinking.

7. Jeffrey Klaiber, S.J., "The Jesuits in Latin America;" *International Bulletin of Missionary Research*, 28:2 (April 2004): 64.

8. "Dear '83', Susie Swift's letter to the 1883 Vassar College Class reunion," at the Sinsinawa Archives

9. Susie Swift, "Sociology & Salvation," *All the World* (Jan. 1890): 39–41; (March 1890): 110–13

10. Bernard Watson, *Soldier Saint: George Scott Railton: William Booth's First Lieutenant* (London: Hodder & Stoughton, 1970): Chap. 17.

11. Murdoch, *Origins of the Salvation Army*, Chap. 6: A Christian Imperium's Growth & Stagnation," and Chap. 7: "Social Reform in Darkest England," membership "stagnation" and the Darkest England Scheme.

12. Swift Diary, Jan. 17, 1891

13. Lori Duin Kelly, *The Life and Works of Elizabeth Stuart Phelps: Victorian Feminist Writer* (Troy, NY: Whitston Publishing Co., 1983).

14. John S. Andrews, "Faber, Frederick William," *The New International Dictionary of the Christian Church*, ed. by J. D. Douglas (Grand Rapids: Zondervan, 1974): 367.

15. Swift Diary, Jan. 17, 1891

16. Swift Diary, Feb. 17, 1891

17. Ottman, chap. 5: gives Schoch's pedigree: her mother was the only daughter of Col. & Madame De Ravallet, a Huguenot with ties to

French royalty. Her maternal grandfather was a Colonel at the battle of Waterloo. (88–90)

18. "Susie Swift's Diary, 1887–1897

Notes to Chapter 7

1. Margaret Troutt, *The General Was a Lady: The Story of Evangeline Booth* (Nashville: A. J. Holman, 1980): 81ff.; "Ballington Booth," *National Cyclopaedia of American Biography* (New York, 1917): 14:54

2. "Major Swift," *War Cry*, US (July 1895): 80; "Auxiliary Department, US" (Dec. 1895)

3. If Swift wrote her diary in January 1893, 1894, 1895, they are not in the Sinsinawa Archives, nor are entries for 1899 to 1916.

4. Norman H. Murdoch, "The Salvation Army and the Church of England, 1882–83," *Historical Magazine of the Protestant Episcopal Church*, 55 (March 1986): 31–55.

5. Swift Diary, Jan. 4, 1896, Sinsinawa Archives.

6. In March 1896 General Booth appointed Emma Booth–Tucker and her husband as joint national commanders in the U.S. During their administration Swift became a Roman Catholic. Swift's mentor, Emma Booth-Tucker, died in a train accident on October 28, 1903 in Dean Lake, Missouri. Frederick Booth–Tucker, *The Consul: A Memoir of Emma Moss Booth–Tucker* (London: Salvationist Pub., 1927): 176ff and 316ff.

7. Sidney Williams, "Pudding and Policies: John A Carleton," in *The First Salvationist & Other Stories* (London: Salvationist Publishing, 1948): 177–189.

8. "Impetration," *Compact Edition of the Oxford English Dictionary*, 9th edn., vol. 1 (New York: Oxford University Press, 1971): 1386, cites Faber, *Growth in Holiness*, xv, 1972, 287, "no prayer has such a power of *impetration* as that which comes from a will conformed to the will of God." James Loomis, "From a Study Window," *The New World* (October 13, 1916) noted that Swift was reading Faber's *Growth in Holiness* and *Spiritual Conferences,* and had borrowed Catholic books from St. Joseph's Library, Mayfair, including a *Life of St. Teresa*. The Army's Literary Staff in London was writing short lives of the saints for the Army's *War Cry*.

9. Swift, "Letter to Bramwell Booth," Feb. 23, 1897, on her Catholic conversion, concerning Faber's influence. Salvation Army Archives & Research Center.

10. "Major Swift in US for Two Months," *War Cry*, New York (Apr. 4, 1896): 14.

11. Booth suspended the Army's use of sacraments in 1883, due to unwillingness to take sacraments from women. Walker, *Pulling the Devil's Kingdom Down* (Univ. of California Press, 2001): 118, found that the Army "instructed all officers to offer communion monthly," but was "challenged to explain why women were permitted to perform this sacred ritual." I have seen no evidence that women officers gave sacraments prior to 1883.

12. Swift, "Letter to Bramwell Booth," 6

13. Swift, "Letter to Bramwell Booth," 7

14. Swift did not mention Lil in references to family or Army friends.

15. Swift, "Letter to Bramwell Booth," 7

16. Swift, "Letter to Bramwell Booth," 9

Notes to Chapter 8

1. Reeve Lindbergh, "Born Again ... and Again," *New York Times Book Review* (Dec, 22, 2002): 24, reviewed Lauren F. Winner, *Girl Meets God: On the Path to a Spiritual Life* (Chapel Hill: Algonquin Books); on Winner's spiritual journey that began in Orthodox Judaism as a child of a Reform Jewish father and a lapsed Southern Baptist mother, and converted to Christianity. Lindbergh's analysis is that Winner's quest was not so remarkable for its theological purity as for her "search for religious truth, at whatever personal cost," combined with "honesty and flashes of wild humor ..."

2. C.S.P. after a name represents Congregation of Mission Priests of St. Paul of the Apostles, referred to as Paulists.

3. Swift, "The Conversion of Susan Swift," 9–10. Other accounts claim that Frs. Searle and Van Henssalaer were present. James J. Walsh, "20 Years of Converts," *The Missionary*, 39 (Dec. 1925): 357, exaggerated Swift's title as "second in rank to the members of the Booth family." "Brigadier" in British military ranks is below Lt. Colonel. Walsh invented Salvation Army "intrigues" to retain her. Nothing in the Army's attempt to dissuade her can be fairly termed an "intrigue".

4. Susan Swift, "The Conversion of Susan Swift" (1897): 3, Sinsinawa Archives

5. Mother of Lister Drummond of the Guild of Our Lady of Ransom for the conversion of England.

6. Susan Swift, "Letter to Bramwell Booth," Feb. 23, 1897

7. Sister M. Imelda Teresa, O.P. (Swift) letter to her 20th Vassar College reunion.

8. By "my own" denomination it is difficult to know what Swift meant. Did she mean the Episcopal Church she joined in 1883, that in The Salvation Army she received the sacraments in 1883? William Booth had administered sacraments as an ordained minister in the Methodist New Connexion, as the Christian Mission's superintendent and in the Salvation Army.

9. Swift, "The Conversion of Susan Swift" (1897): 5, correctly says that Booth did not prohibit Salvationists from taking sacraments. *The Sacraments: The Salvationist's Viewpoint* (London: Salvationist Pub., 1987): 1–4. John Coutts, *This We Believe* (London: Salvation Army, 1980): 126–31; and *The Salvationists* (Mowbrays, 1977) treat Army theology.

10. Fr. McDermot Letter, June 18, 1897; and hand–written sermons in the Swift File, Sinsinawa Archives, 1) *London Tablet*: "Defect of Intention"; 2) "Temptations against faith," May 16, 1897, *St. Anthony's Statue*, "Forty Hours," May 16, 1897.

Notes to Chapter 9

1. "Orders of Women, Monastery of our Lady of St. Catherine de Ricci, Diocese of Albany, *Catholic Directory, 1899*, p. 131

2. James Loomis, "From a Study Window," *The New World* (Oct. 13, 1916) for Swift's Catholic conversion and reasons she took the name Teresa.

3. John Delaney, "Teresa of Avila," *Dictionary of Saints* (Garden City: Doubleday, 1980): 542. The saint's father was Alonso Sanchez de Cepeda; his second wife, Teresa's mother, was Beatrice d'Avila y Ahumada, hence "Teresa d'Ahumada".

4. Swift diary, Sunday night, February 1898

5. S.J. refers to the Society of Jesus, or Jesuits.

6. "Salvationist a Nun," *New York Herald* (July 24, 1898); Sr. Benvenuta Bras, biographical sketch of Susie Swift, Sinsinawa Archives

7. "Salvation Army Worker to Become a Dominican Nun," *The World* (July 24, 1989) clipping at the Elkins Park, Pa. Dominican Archive, photos of "a Salvation Lassie," and "a Nun"

8. "Dear '83', 1

9. "Dear '83', 2

10. "Poke Bonnet to White Robe," (photos) clippings file, Sinsinawa Archives

11. "Dear '83', 3, Teresa had made friends with Señora Blanca Baralt, whom she called "probably the most learned woman in Cuba, a graduate of Packer, a Ph.D. from the University of Havana, and a disciple of Dr. Backus [Vassar professor] in English letters; "Our common training linked us in endeavor for Cuban girls."

12. "Dear '83', 3, Lena Bostwick, a Vassar friend, visited Susie in Philadelphia.

13. "Sister Imelda Theresa Swift, O.S.D.," *The Missionary,* June 1916

14. Brigadier Eileen Douglas, *Red Flowers of Martyrdom* (London: Salvation Army, 1907)

15. Sr. M.I.T., June 28, 1910, Drs. Griffin and Mayo diagnoses. Teresa wrote: "a lovely Sinsinawan infirmarian chaperoned me—two Dominicans are here—three sisters of Mercy from Pittsburgh came tonight." Possibly this was her introduction to the Sinsinawa sisters.

16. Sr. M. Celestine to "your dear Sister," no date.

Notes to Chapter 10

1. Fr. C. M. Thuente to "Dear Sister Imelda," Jan. 27, 1912

2. Fr. C. M. Thuente to "Dear Sr. Imelda," Feb. 5, 1912, in "M. Imelda Therese File Notes," Sinsinawa Archives

3. In April 1912, Josephine Delmonico Russell, widow of James Edward Russell, invited Teresa to attend the wedding of Isabelle Katherine Russell to William Esdaile Byles at St. Augustine Church, Brooklyn, Teresa's retreat in the fall of 1912. On May 28, 1912, Isabella Katherina Byles was presented to Pope Pius X, and was blessed by him, indicating the family's standing in the Catholic church.

4. Evangeline Booth to "Dearest Susie," Nov. 22, 1912

5. "Dominican Sisters of Media, Pa.," *New Catholic Encyclopedia,* 1967, 988: was Swift's Albany order of the Congregation of St. Catherine de' Ricci. After its move to Media, Pa. the order gained papal approbation in 1938. Founded in 1880 by Lucy Eaton Smith (Mother Maria de' Ricci), an American convert, with Francis McNeirney (1877–94), bishop of Albany as patron, it had conducted free parish schools in Glens Falls and Cohoes, New York for two years and then moved to Albany. As part of the Philadelphia Archdiocese, it had houses in New York, Cincinnati, Santa Fe, Trenton, Miami, Richmond, and Grand Rapids, and foundations in Cuba. Fidel Castro confis-

cated the order's three academies in Cuba in 1961. By 1963 the mother-house at Media and novitiate at Elkins Park, Pa. had 175 professed sisters responsible for 6 houses for closed retreats, 6 residences for women, a social center for Spanish–speaking people, and 6 catechetical centers.

6. Mother Bertrand, letter to Rev. John T. McNicholas, Dec. 15, 1912; and a Jan. 2, 1913, response to her first letter, Sinsinawa Archives.

7. John T. McNicholas' letters to Mother Samuel, from the *Holy Name Journal*, Holy Name Society, New York. See in the McNicholas–Bertrand–Samuel correspondence at the Sinsinawa Archives.

8. McNicholas to Samuel, late 1912 or early 1913. He had visited Sinsinawa and held a pleasant memory of it.

9. Mother Bertrand, to "Dear Child in Xto [Teresa], Jan. 10, 1913.

10. McNicholas letter to Samuel, Feb. 13, 1913.

11. McNicholas to Swift, the last of four letters he wrote on her behalf.

12. Samuel to The Council of our Congregation, Jan. 25, 1913, 140 W. 61st St., N.Y.

13. Sr. M. Imelda Teresa, O.S.D. to V. Rev. Mother Samuel, Feb. 1, 1913, from 119 Pacific St., Brooklyn

14. Sr. M. Imelda

15. Sr. M. Samuel to Sr. M. Imelda Teresa, Feb. 3, 1913, 1621 Park Row, N.W., Washington

16. Xto is shorthand for Christ.

17. Mother Bertrand to Sr. Imelda Teresa, Feb. 10, 1913

18. Lil Brengle to "Darling Susie," Feb. 26, 1913

19. Belle Katherine Russell to "My very dear one," Feb. 11, 1913

20. Florence [Jeffrey] to Sr. Teresa, Feb. 16, 1913, 492 Manhattan Ave., N.Y.C.

21. Belle Katherine Russell to "My own dearest one," Feb. 17, 1913

22. Mrs. Eduard Nienan to Mrs. W. E. Byles, Jan. 3, 1913

23. Sr. M. Innocent of Jesus to "Dearest Sister in Xto, May 4–16, 1913, from O'Donnell, 86, Cienfuegos, Cuba

24. Sr. M. Innocent of Jesus, O.S.D. to "Dearest Sister! July 6, 1913

25. Sr. Benvenuta Bras, pp. 6–7

26. Georgina Pall Curtis to Sr. Teresa, June 4, 1913, from *Beyond the Road to Rome*, 5000 N. Ashland Ave., Chicago.

27. Sr. Therese, "First Day of Retreat—June 18—made alone," St. Clara, Sinsinawa, 1913

28. Sr. Imelda Therese, read by her at Mothers Day Feast in 1915, Dominican Archives, Sinsinawa

29. Could this be A. M. Nicol, aid to William Booth, who left the Army? St. John Ervine, *God's Soldier: General William Booth*, ii, 650, 760, 779. Nicol was disturbed by Booth's rejection of his children and grandchildren who were not in the Army. He had served as the Army's Foreign Secretary in the mid–1880s. Murdoch, *Origins of the Salvation Army*, 120, 136–7, 140.

30. Mary Raphael, Divine Providence (Sr. Teresa of Jesus) to Sr. Imelda Teresa, Nov. 20, 1913 from Lanhorne Convent, Columb, Cornwall, England

31. W. A. Jones, O.S.A., Bishop, Puerto Rico, to Sr. Imelda Teresa, O.S.D., 18 Nov. 1914.

32. Fr. Thomas Maria Gill, O.P. to Sister Imelda, March 15, 1915, from Dayton, Minn.

33. Sr. Mary Innocent of Jesus, O.S.D. to "Reverend and very dear Father," March 5, 1915

34. Mrs. B. Ellen Burke to Rev. Mother M. Samuel, O.S.D., April 17, 1915 from New York City.

Notes to Chapter 11

1. Evangeline Booth, Commander, to "Susie" April 21, 1915.

2. George [Brengle] to "Auntie Susie," Feb. 1915, from 251 Beech St., Arlington, N.J.

3. Eileen Douglas to "dearest Susie," Aug. 15, 1915

4. Christobel to "Auntie Susie," Aug. 8, 1915

5. Christobel to "Auntie Susie"

6. Mother Bertrand to "Dear Child in Xto," June 19, 1912 concerns money the Albany convent claims that it did not receive in September 1904. Was this the $1,500 dowry Susie thought her father had sent to the convent? The convent bank balance, verified by Srs. Gregory, Teresa and Monica, equaled $668.49 in receipts that month. Bertrand wrote, "from what I have seen of your sister [Lil], she impresses me as being too noble at this late hour to want to make trouble on your father's account." He had died in 1908.

7. Mrs. Brengle's reply is not at the Sinsinawa Archives.

8. Sr. Benvenuta Bras, pp. 7–9.

9. Mrs. B. Ellen Burke, Pres., Sunday Companion Publishing Co., Oct. 7, 1915, to Sr. Imelda Theresa

Notes to Chapter 12

1. Letter from 43 Moresby Rd., Upper Clapton, London, Aug. 29, 1915, "My dear Friend," from a Salvationist whose "brother Arthur's eldest boy was killed on the beaches in France or Flanders in March," Sinsinawa Archives

2. Anna to "Sister Imelda," Sept. 10, 1915, Sinsinawa Archives

3. Lura to Teresa, Jan. 1, 1916, Sinsinawa Archives

4. Board of Directors Membership Committee to Susie F. Swift, Jessie K. Dewell, 232 Bradley St., New Haven, Conn., Committee for a Vassar Million Dollar Endowment Fund. Sinsinawa Archives

5. Anna, to "My dear Sister Imelda," Jan. 3, 1916, Sinsinawa Archives

6. Anna May Freeman, with Mrs. Alphonse Bechamp, to Mrs. W. E. Byles, Jan. 24, 1916, Sinsinawa Archives

7. Florence [Jeffrey] to Sr. Imelda," Apr. 20, 1916, Convent of the Cenacle, Brighton, Mass., Sinsinawa Archives

Notes to Chapter 13

1. Dr. A. M. Loes, Dubuque, Iowa, Apr. 20, 1916, to Rev. Mother Samuel, St. Clara College, Sinsinawa Mound, Sinsinawa Archives

2. Sr. Mary Innocent, O.S.D., to Very Rev. Thomas M. Gill, O.P., Good Friday, April 21, 1916; Fr. Thomas J. Marie Gill, O.P. to Mother Samuel, May 2, 1916, had Sr. Mary Innocent's letter enclosed, Sinsinawa Archives

3. Florence A. Jeffery to Mother Samuel, Good Friday, April 21st, Convent of the Cenacle; and to Samuel, April 26, 1916, Sinsinawa Archives

4. From 1909–17 Irish–born John T. McNicholas (1877–1950) was National Director of the Holy Name Society in New York, editor of the *Holy Name Journal,* pastor of St. Catherine of Siena Church, and prior of an adjoining convent, while he was corresponding with Susie Swift and Mothers Bertrand and Samuel. After eight years in New York he was assistant to the Master General of Dominicans in Rome, and Master of Theology and honorary provincial of Lithuania. He was Archbishop of Cincinnati from 1925–1950.

5. "Sister Mary Imelda Therese Swift," Obituaries 1:164–165, Sinsinawa Archives

6. Mother Samuel to "Dear Friends," April 24, 1916; "'Sister Samuel's' account of Therese's death," April 21, 1916, Sinsinawa Archives

7. Sr. Benvenuta Bras, "Biographical Sketch of Sister Theresa Imelda's Life," 1986, Sinsinawa Archives. Hereafter listed as Bras.

8. Quote from *The New World* (Oct. 13, 1916): 9; Sinsinawa Archives

9. *St. Clara Annals*, April 16, 1916, Sinsinawa Archives

10. Sister Celestine to Mother Samuel, Easter 1915, Sinsinawa Archives

11. Colonel Samuel Logan Brengle to Sr. [as she signed herself] Mary Samuel, O.S.D., April 26, 1916, Sinsinawa Archives

12. George Swift Brengle to Sr. Samuel, April 1916, for his sister and himself.

13. Eileen Douglas, *Elizabeth Swift Brengle* (London: Salvationist Pub., 1922): 117 pp. Other biographies of Elizabeth Brengle: Anon., *Elizabeth Swift Brengle: A Girl Collegiate*; "Elizabeth Swift Brengle," in Minnie Lindsay Carpenter, *Women of the Flag* (London: Salvationist Pub., 1945): 125–38, refers to Susie as *"a younger* sister"; William Clark, ed. *Dearest Lily: Correspondence* (London: Salvation Army, 1985): iv, notes that "after doing some literary work for the Army in London, Susie left the movement and joined a catholic order, eventually becoming its head [not true].

14. Eileen Douglas to Mother Samuel, Apr. 1916, Sinsinawa Archives

15. Christobel Janicke to Mother Samuel, May 3, 1916, Sinsinawa Archives

16. Mrs. Katherine Byles to Mother Samuel, Apr. 20, 22, & 27, 1916; James J. Walsh, M.D. to Mother Samuel, Apr. 20, 1916; Mrs. B. Ellen Burke to Mother Samuel, O.D., Apr. 21, 1916, had known "Sis. Imelda when she first entered the Church—a few weeks after her reception."

17. Florence Jeffrey to Mother Samuel, Mary E. McCall to Mother Samuel, April 1916, was present at Therese's "profession" ceremonies

18. Jessie K. Dewell to Sis. M. Reginald, May 1, 1916, Sinsinawa Archives

19. Bras, 13

20. Susie was a "brigadier" when she resigned from the Salvation Army, not the American army rank of brigadier general. This and Salvation Army accounts that made Swift a "Mother Superior" indicate the two groups' problems with each other's rank systems Bras, 10.

21. Sis. Eva McCarty, *The Sinsinawa Dominicans* (Dubuque: Hoermann Press, 1952): 282–83

Notes to Conclusion

1. Norman H. Murdoch, "Research Notes at the Dominican Archives, Sinsinawa, Wisc."

2. See Mark Eason for a study of Victorian women in the Army. They had the privilege of holding clerical status, but were expected to submit to the rule of their husbands as well as the Army.

Soldier of the Cross

Pioneer of Social Change

David Lamb

David Crichton Lamb, LL.D., C.M.G., F.R.E.S., O.F.
(1866–1951)

Salvation Army International Social Commissioner,
Governor of the Hadleigh Land Settlement and City Colony
Workshops, Director of the Emigration Department,
Director of the Assurance Society

Dedication

**Commissioner Dr. Harry W. Williams, O.B.E.,
F.R.C.S., O.F. (1913–)
Missionary Doctor—International
Administrator
and Admirer of David C. Lamb**

To Commissioner Dr. Harry W. Williams I owe the idea for a biography of Commissioner Lamb. Still living and working as an artist and writer on the Scottish border, Williams is an impressive Senior Commissioner of The Salvation Army at age 93. He has recently been honored by General John Larsson with the Order of the Founder, the honor that David Lamb received from General Eva Booth.

Acknowledgments—
David Crichton Lamb Research

First, I acknowledge that the source of the idea for this biography of David C. Lamb is the friend to whom I dedicate this work, Commissioner Dr. Harry W. Williams, who is now living in busy retirement near the Scottish border. In many ways Harry Williams is a replica of Commissioner Lamb. He is the senior international statesman of The Salvation Army, having served as a missionary doctor in India and Bolivia, as a territorial administrator in India and New Zealand, and at the Army's international headquarters in London. He was the Army's representative on the central committee of the World Council of Churches in Geneva. He is a man of broad vision, impressive talents, and enormous energy for humanitarian causes in which he believes. At the age of 93, he is a prolific artist, writer, and advisor. Harry Williams has read this work and made useful comments on its factual and interpretive content.

I am in the debt of Lt. Colonel Marlene Chase for her guidance as editor of Crest Books. She has been a delight to work with, the friend of any writer who is so fortunate to work through a project with the likes of her as editor and publisher.

To Salvation Army archivists in Alexandria, Virginia; London, England; Toronto, Canada; Sydney, Australia; and Wellington, New Zealand; I am indebted for your generous gift of time and patience in sending primary and secondary materials from your treasures. For an international figure like David C. Lamb I became an international sleuth, with your courtesies on the scene or by e–mail attachment.

To General John Larsson, Colonel Laurence Hay, and Commissioner Paul du Plessis, I am grateful for reading and correcting my facts and analysis in the epilogue. And for the patience of my wife, Professor Grace M. A. Murdoch, I am always at a loss for adequate words. As a fellow scholar and life partner she has made my work easier by permitting me to do "my thing" at the expense of being a better mate.

Introduction to David Crichton Lamb
(1866–1951)

The significance of David Crichton Lamb's life and work is in his durable dedication to social Christianity, the human face of Christian compassion. Although he was evangelically certain that saving a person's soul was the ultimate goal of his work in The Salvation Army, he was just as certain that the healing, peacemaking and feeding social ministries of Jesus of Nazareth were an equal part of the salvation plan. As the Army's founder, William Booth, discovered in his home mission in the East End of London from 1865 to 1878, the human condition could not be dissected into soul–body–mind compartments when it came to a Christian's compassion or a sinner's redemption.

This realization likely came to David Lamb gradually after The Salvation Army appointed him and his wife to social and administrative work in London. The couple served as officers (ministers) there from 1891 to the end of their lives—Minnie in 1939 and David in 1951. In 1888, when the Lambs arrived in London from Glasgow, Commissioner Frank Smith was beginning to organize the Army's social reform program. General William Booth had put Smith in charge of the Army's social wing that year as its first social commissioner. This early phase of the Army's formal development of a social program concluded in 1890 with the publication of *In Darkest England and the Way Out*. The general, his son Bramwell, the Army's Chief of Staff, Frank Smith, Susie F. Swift, and journalist W. T. Stead, were prime contributors to publication of the book.

After 1891, David Lamb and his wife Minnie were first and foremost "social" officers. By the time Lamb took his first strictly social wing appointment in England in December 1891, Minnie had already been working with rescued prostitutes—"fallen women" was the term in use at the time. The Lambs embodied the essence of Salvation Army work with the poor for 60

years. David's particular focus was in implementing the three–
tiered Darkest England plan. The idea was to move England's
urban unemployed in three steps from city slums, back to the
land in England for farm training, and then to Army land settlements in the British Empire's overseas colonies.

David Lamb's first social assignment was to assist the
Army's second social commissioner, Elijah Cadman, as his chief
secretary. They were running "city colony" workshops that provided temporary work, food and shelter for London's unemployed, the first step in the rehabilitation process. Next, Lamb
assisted the Salvation Army's Chief of Staff, Bramwell Booth,
with social planning and in seeking the support of government
agencies. Then in 1898 he became the resident governor of the
second step in the Darkest England program, a "farm colony" in
Essex County, southeast England, where he supervised the training of the urban unemployed in farming skills that they would
then use in the final step, an "overseas colony" in the British Empire.

In 1903 Lamb took charge of the third stage of the rehabilitation scheme, the "overseas colony," but he saw weaknesses in
the settlement scheme laid out by the writers of *In Darkest
England and the Way Out*. He proposed a broader approach.
The Booths, Smith, Swift, and Stead had envisioned land settlements, composed of small plots that a family would eventually
own, as the third stage of rehabilitation. But the plan was failing
in the United States, Canada, Australia, and South Africa.

Lamb reconfigured the plan and made it into a supervised
emigration program that moved the urban employed, mainly as
families, but gradually it included single men, widowed women,
young girls and boys. They were to go to Britain's vast colonial
empire—particularly to Canada, but also to Australia, New
Zealand, and Southern Africa. In the process The Salvation
Army would see that the émigrés were trained in domestic or
farming skills to make them acceptable to their new homeland's
employers. What they became after their initial employment
would be strictly up to them.

David Lamb's contribution to the restructuring of the Salvation Army's social program has been largely overlooked by historians[1], as has his 1929–32 involvement in efforts to alter the

Army's internal governance system, particularly its procedures for choosing its general, the leader of the Army's international Christian imperium.[2] And his post–World War II globetrotting missions for peace, after his retirement, have gone unmentioned in the Army's official and unofficial histories.

Lamb's 1929–32 contribution to a revolutionary change in Salvation Army polity came as an act of personal courage. He was the senior commissioner who put the resolution before the first High Council of the Army's international leaders in 1929, to remove Bramwell Booth as the Army's second general. Bramwell had succeeded his father as general in 1912 by a uniquely undemocratic method that William Booth had set up in a Foundation Deed Poll in 1878. Under that deed, generals would place their successors' name in a sealed envelope that the Army's solicitor would open after their deaths. When William died in August 1912, his son Bramwell's name was in the envelope, as everyone expected. Bramwell had served as his father's Chief of Staff for more than three decades.

But William Booth had adjusted the 1878 deed in a 1904 deed to accommodate the possibility that some future general might become so infirm as to be unable to efficiently conduct the office. The new deed called for the Army's international leaders to convene as a High Council to determine the fitness of the general, and if necessary, to remove him/her and elect a successor.

As Bramwell Booth became increasingly ill in 1929, Army leaders became concerned about his ability to continue as general. They also worried about whose name was in the envelope, and about the highly centralized, autocratic family imperium the Army had become. They were now operating in an age of a more corporate style of business operation, quite unlike the tycoon–led businesses of the late 19th century. For those reasons the High Council supported Commissioner Lamb's resolution that brought an end to the Booth dynasty and softened the general's autocratic rule. This included removing the general's personal ownership of all Army properties in the British Empire.

Following this 1929 settlement it was important to put the new system into law. So in 1931–32, Lamb was one of those who advised General Edward J. Higgins and a British House of Commons committee that prepared a Salvation Army Act to replace the Foundation Deed of 1878. The new act placed properties in a corporate trust, rather than a family one, and recognized that the Army was more than a British organization.

David Lamb's third significant contribution came after his retirement. In the late 1940s and early 1950s, Lamb's optimistic social vision and his post–World War II anxieties over international peace and economic recovery in Britain caused him to travel to North America, Australia, New Zealand, and Southern Africa as an ambassador of peace. He preached reconciliation between allies and with former enemies. He was concerned that a Cold War had begun to make enemies of allies who divided the world into Eastern and Western blocks. His social service work, particularly as the engineer of the Salvation Army's massive emigration program that sent as many as 250,000 of Britain's unemployed to former British colonies, had gained him a platform in the United Kingdom (UK), Canada, Australia, New Zealand, and southern Africa. The United States was also open to his Christian humanitarian message of hope and compassion.

The David Lamb story has nearly been lost in the 65 years since his death. There are no book–length or even chapter–long biographies of David or Minnie Lamb. Nor did the Lambs leave diaries or memoirs. In fact, the entire social wing of The Salvation Army has been largely neglected by historians, in spite of its prominence in the minds of the public. Yet, since World War II the Army has received more funds from governments and public giving than virtually any other philanthropic enterprise.

This biography aims to recapture the story of how Salvation Army social services caught the public eye through the work of two of its principal leaders in the early 20th century, David Crichton Lamb and his wife Minnie Clinton Lamb. The Lambs exemplified the spirit of Salvationists as compassionate Christians who put their concern for human betterment as well as spiritual redemption into programs and actions that met the need at ground level. This account also looks at the Army's organizational structure that needed reform that was painful to accomplish in a conciliatory spirit. David Lamb's awareness of business realities and his spiritual hopes marked his social and spiritual legacies.

1

Early Life, 1866–1888

D avid Crichton Lamb was born in Scotland on October 26, 1866, in the heartland of Angus, at the village of Friockheim, Forfar, in the parish of Kirkdon, not far from the haddock fishing port of Arbroath. Arbroath was the site of an abbey whose royal founder in 1178 was William I. It was also the site of the signing of Scotland's Declaration of Independence in 1320. When Scottish Nationalists stole the Stone of Destiny from Westminster Abbey in 1950, they placed it under Arbroath Abbey's high altar. The Stone was later returned to the Coronation Chair at Westminster.[1] Lamb was a proud Scotsman who carried his accent and Scottish heritage throughout his life.

Lamb's father and mother raised him in the Morrisonian Church,[2] founded by James Morrison at Kilmarnock in 1841. When Morrison and three other ministers were suspended from the United Secession Church they formed an Evangelical Union, which in 1896 merged with evangelical churches associated with Robert and James Haldane to form the Congregational Union. The Morrisonians' anabaptist theology[3] and the shorter catechism of Scotland's Free Church differed from the Wesleyan–Arminian dogma of William and Catherine Booth, but that would prove to be no problem for Lamb who rested his ecumenical doctrine on free will and a sense of divine destiny.

A basic element of a Salvationist biography is a conversion experience that yields a testimony to God's grace and personal faith in Jesus Christ. The more rowdy a Salvationist's past, the more exciting the testimony. Lamb's testimony was genuine, but hardly represented a U–turn from utter degradation. He had grown up in a Christian home. He attended Sunday School and a Free Church School. He participated in family worship, Bible study, reading the shorter catechism, and attending cottage prayer meetings.

At age 12 David's father apprenticed him to a chemist[4] in his hometown, and at 14 he joined a chemist's shop in Aberdeen. He continued to go to church, but over time became less faithful and more aware of the urbane world of science. He was exposed to medical students in a university city who "were always talking about evolution and rationalism." He "was beginning very seriously to doubt and to drift from Christianity." Still he believed in "sowing the seeds of a moral life and in not sinning." He continued to read his Bible "by fits and starts."

When he transferred to a branch shop in Boxton, near the Aberdeen #11 Salvation Army corps, he stayed with a friend who often attended Army meetings. The two also read books by Charles Bradlaugh,[5] a notorious atheist and political radical who, among other heresies, advocated birth control. From 1880–1886 the British Parliament excluded Bradlaugh for his heretical beliefs. Lamb had a life–long curiosity with new ideas, particularly scientific theories. No doubt Bradlaugh appealed to his curiosity, but there is no indication that he became a devotee of atheism or radical politics.

Instead, by 1882 David Lamb was attracted to a movement that William and Catherine Booth, Wesleyan evangelists, had founded in 1865 as a home mission in London's East End. In 1878 their Christian Mission became a "salvation army," modeled on a mid–19th century trend to form broad–based evangelical associations with a simple creed that virtually any Protestant could embrace. The Booths accepted evangelists and members from various evangelical backgrounds, as did American evangelist Dwight L. Moody at the time. The aim was to work for individual salvation from sin through basic biblical belief in God's grace and personal faith in atonement from sin provided by Jesus Christ's death on the cross.[6]

Conversion

On October 21, 1882, after work at the chemist shop, Lamb took a bus on a blustery night to the Woodside, Aberdeen Salvation Army corps that was staging a "singing battle." As he entered the hall around 9 p.m., they were singing the sentimental "Where is My Wandering Boy Tonight?" It was four days before Lamb's 16th birthday and he was away from home. At one point a Christian came who wanted to argue with him. Lamb had struggled over the divinity of Jesus and was always ready for a debate. He was bemused by the musical performers, but he spent the time entertaining his own thoughts.

When the service ended, Lieutenant Watson and Captain Rapkin came to talk with him. In a flash he saw the cross. The officers sang and prayed and talked, but he was "twisted" with argument and, in his own words, "lost in the thought of my own heart and God's goodness. At last I just cried out, 'Lord, break my proud, stubborn spirit.' I didn't feel I was a sinner in general; but I felt I'd been so obstinate. I'd hardly spoken for three–quarters of an hour before. I felt I'd wanted to set up a kingdom of my own, outside of God. That cry stilled the trouble in my heart, and the Lord filled my soul while they sang, 'My Happy Soul is Free.'" It was this experience that he later claimed as his personal testimony to faith in Christ. "When I went out everything seemed so new! ... I went home feeling completely changed."

In 1933, soon after The Salvation Army's turmoil over removing Bramwell Booth as general, the *War Cry* editor asked Commissioner Lamb to lead off a series of articles by international leaders on their conversion experiences. Lamb, contemplating his conversion from the distance of 52 years, gave this mature recollection.

> *"I cannot truthfully say that I felt overwhelmed with a sense of my extreme sinfulness." Citing a "rich young ruler's" response to Jesus' interrogation, Lamb wrote: "I had kept the commandments from my youth up. I did not smoke; I was a total abstainer." Nonetheless, on that dreary night in October 1882 "something overwhelming happened to me and very soon I found myself at the mercy–seat crying out in prayer, 'Lord, break my proud and stubborn spirit.' There and*

then it was that there came to me from the Cross of Christ a revelation of my spiritual need ... There at the mercy–seat free will manifested itself in choice! ... Since then, whichever way the finger of destiny has pointed I have realized that I had a will of my own which has enabled me, as God has directed, to make decisions for the good of those on whose behalf I labor."[7]

Call to be a Salvation Army Officer

In Aberdeen in 1883 David Lamb heard William Booth preach for the first time. Booth had held the title "general" of The Salvation Army since 1878.[8] When the Booths changed the name of their mission to "Salvation Army," they adopted military ranks and jargon, like many "muscular" Christian movements of the age. In the words of an Anglican hymn they were "Christian soldiers marching as to war."[9] In 1884, the second anniversary of Lamb's conversion, Colonel Alex Nicol came to Aberdeen for a night of prayer. Lamb felt God was calling him to "the work," a phrase Salvationists use for a career as an officer. He saw this as his "first spiritual difficulty." He was finishing his apprenticeship as a chemist, a profession he loved. Still, at age 17, he volunteered to become an officer in the Booths' soul–saving Army.

Lamb's early experience as an officer was a prelude to the way he would spend the rest of his life. He had "farewelled" from Aberdeen to go to the training home for men in London, but as he prepared to go, Colonel Henry Edmonds, the Army's commander in Scotland, ordered him to report to Major Deakin at the Aberdeen headquarters. There he would do office work and travel with Deakin on his tours of corps in the division.

Thus from the start Lamb was a "headquarters man." His officer personnel sheet yields no evidence that he ever ran a corps, a local self–supporting post that held nightly meetings to save souls, and visited soldiers (lay members) and collected funds to support the work during the day. Since he was from a middle–class family with an education and a profession, he was one of a select few officers who could take on management responsibility, particularly as a first appointment.[10] So in October 1884, at age 18, "Captain" Lamb was a scribe at the Aberdeen division "War Office." In August 1885 he took up the same work in Glasgow, where after two months he also became the cashier. In 1887, at age 21, he became "Secretary," to assist Glasgow's Divisional Commander, an office he held until 1889.

Army regulations required single officers, if they chose to wed, to marry another officer.[11] So on October 25, 1888, Staff Captain David Lamb married Captain Minnie Clinton who had been a corps officer since 1882. A new Scottish Marriage Amendment Act allowed a Salvation Army officer to perform the ceremony, in this case the Foreign Secretary from London. By now the Army had overseas territories to manage and a foreign office to keep track of its growing Christian empire. Prior to the new marriage law a state church clergyman had to officiate and sign the register. Lamb's four siblings were present; all were Salvationists. A crowd of 1,200 paid two pence each to witness the vows, a common practice to fill the Army's coffers. *The War Cry,* the Army's official paper, reported a diverse audience of the press, Presbyterians, Methodists, Congregationalists, Plymouth Brethren, and even "whiskey–drinkers." Following common practice, Salvationists had termed Lamb the "hallelujah druggist."[12]

As a single officer Minnie Clinton had been a feisty handful, often at odds with headquarters on matters of regulation. From the beginning, due to the influence of Catherine Booth, the Booths' mission had recognized the equality of women. By the 1880s women officers outnumbered the men. Born in Cornwall on March 3, 1864, to an Irish Roman Catholic father and a Cornish mother, Minnie had converted to the Army's brand of evangelical Christianity at Sunderland Corps where John Lawley, later a song evangelist[13] for William Booth, was the captain. Clinton, without spending a day at an Army training home, went to her first corps at Hetton–le–Hole (Houghton–la–Spring), Durham.

In February 1882, as a 17–year–old lieutenant at South Shields, at the mouth of the Tyne River in northeast England, Clinton took care of an officer who was physically incapacitated and ran the corps. In the 1880s that meant preaching every night and raising funds by selling *The War Cry* in public houses (taverns) and door–to–door to pay the mission hall rent and the officers' meager allowance. Visiting converts and performing janitorial duties extended long days into nights. On April 4,

1883, the Army transferred her to Eston Mines. The next month she moved to Dundee on the Firth of Tay, known for its jute industry and Mrs. Keiller's marmalade. Two months later she was in Patrick, near Glasgow, and two months after that the Army sent her to Perth, Scotland.[14]

On July 7, 1884, Clinton went as a newly promoted captain to Glasgow. But in August Army leaders decided that she should attend the training home as a cadet. The home would tutor her in the Army's Orders and Regulations, a book of discipline for its officer corps. After five corps appointments, now with a rank of captain, she was no doubt insulted by this all too apparent demotion to a mere "cadet." This would not be her last battle with the Army hierarchy.

Her "officer profile sheet" does not say where she was between August 1885, when David Lamb arrived in Glasgow, and March 1886, when the Army appointed her as captain at Wick, the leading town on Scotland's rugged North Sea coast, where the corps hall held 1,200 people. A "knee drill" prayer meeting at 7 a.m. on July 26, had 275 present when David Lamb visited the corps with the divisional commander. Lamb's estimate of Clinton was that she was "an out–and–out Salvationist, plain and blunt, but no one can be offended, she is so good and true."

In April 1886 Clinton was "resting," likely an indication that her health had broken, as was common due to the demanding work of a corps officer. In June the Army sent her to an Aberdeen corps to "rest." In March 1887 Clinton went to the Borough, near Southwark Cathedral in London. From there she had a week's "rest" in mid–August before she took an appointment at the large Marylebone corps in the central London district where William and Catherine Booth's daughter Eva had preceded Clinton from 1885 to March 1887.[15]

Marriage of David Lamb and Minnie Clinton

If David Lamb and Minnie Clinton had shown any romantic interests during the brief period when they were in Glasgow in 1886–87, Salvation Army leaders were not making it easy for them to cement their relationship when they sent Minnie to London. Just before their wedding Minnie was captain at another London corps at Battersea 1, on the south side of the Thames, from March 22 to October 25, 1888. She returned to Scotland to be married at Hamilton, on the Clydeside, east of Glasgow.[16]

Prior to her marriage Minnie had proven that she was a force that an army driven by orders and regulations would have to reckon with. To contain her independence had already proved to be impossible. So the Army put her on a longer leash that allowed her to do her work in her own way, including work outside her Army appointments. As it turned out, this was a wise choice. Many officer–wives wrestled with dual demands of family and a career that was tied to their husbands' appointments. While some spent little time on their ministerial careers as preachers, as Army regulation required, preferring the role of mother and housewife, others found their niche apart from their husbands' work, and at the same time raised children and cared for a home on the Army's small family "allowance." Minnie, like Catherine Booth, was one of the latter.[17]

In 1889, in an article in *The War Cry*, David Lamb, now 23 years old, revealed his philosophy of Christian work. "I believe the only way one can live to please God is to be busy all the time. There is no such thing as abeyance after one comes to a certain age." But he exposed a frustration with administrative chores. At one time, while he was visiting corps, "specialing [preaching] at week–ends," he experienced a "desire to go into the field [to work as a corps officer], and it unsettled me a bit. I felt it was such a blessed mellowing thing to keep in touch with the human, instead of being rolled up in cash and stuck away in books and letters! But I met that temptation and conquered it, and now business is spiritual work to me."[18]

Promotions: Staff Captain at International Headquarters (IHQ); Major and Chief Secretary in Southern Africa in 1889–1891

Before the Lambs left Glasgow in 1889, their first child, David Clinton Lamb, was born on August 25. In October, headquarters ordered Staff Captain Lamb to report to the Army's

Property and Finance Department at International Headquarters, 101 Queen Victoria Street, London. William and Bramwell Booth had become aware of his management and finance skills, talents that were in short supply among the Army's working class officers. The Booths quickly promoted the few educated men and women who had even limited business experience. The expanding Army in Britain and its outposts in North America, Europe (Ireland, France, the Netherlands, Switzerland, Sweden, Norway), South Asia (India, Sri Lanka), Southern Africa, and Australasia needed leaders of talent. The Lambs were members of a select few.

This was a busy time for acquisition of property, something William Booth had earlier sworn that he would not do. Property made movements less mobile, more settled. But in 1884 he set up a Salvation Army building association, and in 1886 a property league. By 1889, under Colonel Elijah Cadman's leadership, the Army was acquiring more buildings than ever before. Lamb's major contribution while he was assistant property secretary, was to oversee the transfer of the Charter of the Methodist and General Assurance Society, Ltd., established in 1867, to The Salvation Army in 1891. The transaction took place at the Lambs' residence at Kenmure Road, Hackney. The Booths consulted leading officers on whether to take over the insurance company charter; Lamb was likely one of these. He arranged for established insurance societies to take over the "working machinery" and "few remaining policies." The Army would transact annuity business at first, but in 1894 it would begin to issue life insurance policies. At the end of 1894 Commissioner John Carleton became the first managing director, with two full time and one part time agent. In 1904 the company became The Salvation Army Assurance Society, Ltd.[19]

In early 1891, as the Darkest England social plan was catching public attention, the Booths sent Major Lamb to South Africa to be Commissioner Thomas Estill's Chief Secretary. What was the purpose of this brief appointment? Did the Booths want to see if the third part of the Darkest England plan for an overseas land colony for Britain's unemployed workers could be developed in Southern Africa? Was it Lamb's mission to acquire property as he had been doing in Britain? Since there is no record of

Lamb's work in South Africa we can only guess at the purpose of his mission from his work before and after the assignment and from the situation in Southern Africa.

In 1883 General Booth had sent Francis and Rose Simmonds and a girl lieutenant, Alice Teager, to "take Africa for Jesus."[20] At the time Booth was focused on soul salvation. But by 1891, his mind had turned toward social, or as he termed it, "wholesale salvation." As early as 1884 the South African Salvation Army had begun social programs by opening Magdalena Home for Women in Port Elizabeth.[21] Rescue Homes for "fallen women" had begun in London in the 1860s, but they increased in 1885 as a result of W. T. Stead's "Maiden Tribute" crusade to raise the age at which a girl could become a prostitute. Stead was supported by the Booths and their women officers and cadets.[22]

In the late 1880s, Minnie Lamb had joined this rescue work, as did many women officers as "slum sisters." At the end of the Lambs' South Africa tour in late 1891, the Army invaded Rhodesia to preach to white South African miners who were migrating to this British South Africa Company (BSAC) colony. At the same time the Army in South Africa started a "Zulu Crusade," two years after it had begun work among natives at Weltevreden on Henry Cadle's farm.[23]

The Booths were obsessed with their Darkest England social program in 1891. It seems obvious that they saw a role for David Lamb. From 1891 to 1908 the general was looking for land for overseas colonies in the British Empire on which the Army could settle England's unemployed. Booth was particularly interested in Southern Africa, including Cecil Rhodes' new Rhodesian colony. He sought funds from several philanthropists to purchase land, and begged Rhodes' BSAC to give him a land grant, a promise the BSAC fulfilled in 1891 with a farm the Army named for William Pearson in Rhodesia's Mazoe Valley. But after Rhodesia's 1896–97 First Chimurenga (rising) of Shona and Ndebele warriors, the BSAC used Pearson as a center for a native corps, school, and clinic. In 1908 William Booth made a second arduous visit to Rhodesia to spy out the land for an ideal locale for a second settlement to be used for resettlement of white immigrants, but to no avail. After some encouragement, the BSAC board in London closed the door.

William Booth also lobbied the British and South African governments for financial aid and land grants. He emphasized the advantages to be gained by the British Empire in placing white settlers in Southern Africa. It would increase the reach of white Western Christian civilization and would cement colonial loyalty to the homeland. The advantage to The Salvation Army was that it would advance the cause of Christ, and, in terms of Booth's premillennial theology, it would speed the second coming of Christ as the leader of an international Christian imperium of peace. David Lamb would soon become the Booths' principal lieutenant in this millennial–imperial quest.[24]

Booth's dream was to move the urban unemployed in three steps from city workshops, to a farm colony training program in England, and then to an overseas land settlement where they would, in time, purchase their own farm on a small payment plan. The idea appealed to many in Britain and her colonies, including Booth's friends W. T. Stead and Cecil Rhodes. They shared a vision of an expanding Empire composed of "Little Englands" of white colonists. Booth's dream of a Christian Imperium, run by his Army, was in no way at odds with the prevailing British imperial vision in an imperial age. Americans endorsed this vision through their president Theodore Roosevelt, who also had imperialist views. Lamb's abilities in finance and property were just the ticket for handling land acquisition in Southern Africa. But his reports were for the Booths' eyes only, and thus there is no paper trail of his work during his Southern Africa tenure.

Booth's Darkest England message was not lost on politicians, business tycoons, and journalists with like–minded imperial designs. The general had many conversations with British and colonial leaders prior to 1908, the year the BSAC directors and British government extinguished his dream of setting up colonies on Army–owned land. Yet the core idea of placing Britain's unemployed in "little Englands" remained. The Booths and other empire builders still dreamt of moving England's excess population of "waste labor" to British overseas possessions that they saw as having enormous "wastelands."[25]

In fact, Africa's alleged "wastelands" were occupied by Africans whom white colonial governments were herding onto "native reserves" to make land available for white settlers and mining prospectors, just as the American government was herding Native Americans onto "reservations" in its Western states at the end of the 19th century to make room for white prospectors, ranchers and farmers. But someone would have to find a new approach to the overseas colony idea that did not necessarily include the gift or purchase of large amounts of land as "settlements" that would be divided into holdings for colonists.

That new idea occurred to David Lamb and social schemers in other organizations twelve years after Lamb's return to England, and after the Booths learned that the idea of land settlements under Salvation Army auspices was dead. The Army needed British or colonial government sponsorship for moving English families to land that was occupied by native populations, or was spoken for by companies like the BSAC. A few years after his South African tour Lamb turned the Booths' attention to Britain's largely white populated colonies of Canada, Australia and New Zealand. He would succeed in finding a common interest for all concerned in bringing Britain's trained unemployed workers to a "new world."

Within two years of the Lambs' return to London the Army in Southern Africa and elsewhere was continuing to expand social programs in the first two phases of the Darkest England scheme, the "city colony" and the "farm colony." The Army in Southern Africa set up a city colony "social reform brigade" in 1894 that included additional rescue homes for white women and, in 1896, it began a program of shelters for unemployed white men.

The Army opened three farm colonies in the United States in the 1890s for the urban unemployed of America's eastern cities. Ultimately they proved not to be viable programs for moving city folk "back to the land."[26] Within the British Empire the Army set up social farms in India, Australia, and New Zealand, and Southern Africa. In 1893 the Army in South Africa opened the Rondebosch Social Farm, then a Social Farm at Driefontein in 1898, and later a Prison Gate Home and Social Farm at Fairview.[27] But these farms were not for British colonists.

2

Major David C. Lamb and the Salvation Army Social Reform Staff at International Headquarters (IHQ), London, 1891–1898

In December 1891 Major David C. Lamb and his family returned to London where he took his first strictly social assignment as Chief Secretary to Commissioner Elijah Cadman, who had replaced Commissioner Frank Smith as the Army's Social Commissioner in January 1891. Smith had resigned the post. He had disagreed with the Booths over managing social funds. The funds came from a £100,000 campaign for public donations to establish the Darkest England program. Subsequent annual campaigns would try to raise £30,000 for ongoing expenses. Smith, as the ideologue who invented the program and set up its city workshops, pressed the Booths to place social income and expenses for Darkest England in the hands of accountants at his social headquarters on Upper Thames Street. The Booths insisted that the International Headquarters' accounting department at 101 Queen Victoria Street handle both Social and Spiritual Wing accounts. To Smith mixing the accounting departments responsible for the funds would endanger the integrity of the Army's two wings.[1]

Elijah Cadman was primarily an evangelist with no social experience. He needed Lamb's help in organizing and managing the social wing in line with the Booths' wishes. Ex–commissioner Smith soon won election to the new London County Council and found work as a political journalist, union organizer, and one of the founders of the Independent Labour Party with his friend Keir Hardie. In his last political campaign in 1929 he would win a seat in the House of Commons in his mid–70s, and serve in the first Labour government as Parliamentary Secretary to the Commissioner of Works, George Lansbury.

In 1892 Chief of Staff Bramwell Booth appointed Brigadier Lamb as his private secretary for social affairs. In August 1896 he promoted Lamb to Lt. Colonel.[2] As assistant to the Army's second in command, Lamb moved from daily oversight of social operations in Britain to helping the Booths plan international social programs. He advised on the management of urban workshops and social farms in Britain and on establishing overseas farm colonies. He also represented Salvation Army views to royal commissions studying remedies for Britain's social ills. On prison reform he proposed solutions to Home Secretary Herbert Gladstone; on unemployment he advised a panel chaired by future Liberal Prime Minister Sir Henry Campbell Bannerman. He also visited Europe to gain an appreciation for the Army's international character and the Darkest England social plan as it took root in Holland and Switzerland. Europe, as well as Australia, was providing innovative social ideas beyond the European and American ideas that Frank Smith had used to invent the Darkest England program.

Those ideas were quite simple. First, a "city colony," placed unemployed men in urban workshops that rehabilitated them physically and morally. Second, those who passed the test would move to a "farm colony" that early social planners termed moving the unemployed "back to the land" for training in agricultural skills, while continuing their moral rehabilitation. Some workers would remain in England, but most would move to the third step, "overseas colonies" in the Empire: in Canada; Southern Africa; Australia; and New Zealand.

Lamb discovered that the main problem in the system was the overseas settlements, most of which closed by 1910 or took up a different mission than that envisioned in Darkest England. When land settlements failed, Lamb and other social planners looked for emigration programs that had no land colony at the other end. Instead, English families would move to farm lands in

British colonies, or labor bureaus would find them city jobs. These emigrants would also populate the Army's corps in its overseas imperium.

After Frank Smith's resignation, no one had a background in social planning or his gift for publicity. Smith acquired his knowledge of social reform from Henry George's *Progress and Poverty* (1879) that proposed a single tax on land values. When the rich decided not to pay heavy taxes on land that was not producing a profit, they would sell it to divest themselves of a financial burden. Smith had traveled extensively in Europe to inspect German and Dutch land colonies and made contact with Fabians and other social reformers in Britain. During his term as Salvation Army commander in America (1884–1887) he was exposed to the ideas of Edward Bellamy's Nationalist social program.[3] Among his friends were George Lansbury, M.P. for an East London district, and American Quaker philanthropist Joseph Fels, who shared his single tax and land reform views. Lamb gradually sought the advice of socialists and social planners.

Lamb had Smith's taste for management, planning, and interaction with political leaders and philanthropists in fields of social reform and business administration. In October 1896 he became, for a little more than a year, director of The Salvation Army Trade Headquarters. This commercial venture sold Army merchandise: tea and teapots with the Booths' pictures on them; non–phosphorous safety matches from the Army's match factory; badges; uniforms and musical instruments.

But in 1898 Lamb moved permanently back to social service administration.

Governor at Hadleigh Farm Colony and General Secretary of City Colonies, 1898–1903

On January 12, 1898 David Lamb became the governor of the Salvation Army Land and Industrial Colony at Hadleigh, Essex. He also served as general secretary of the city colony's workshops, feeding and housing programs. In 1900 the Booths promoted him to colonel. He was largely on his own for five years, no longer working as someone else's assistant. Besides managing the first two stages of the Darkest England program, he increasingly became an activist in social program development in England.

The city colony, started in 1888 by Frank Smith, ran 28 industrial workshops by 1895 for unemployed men and women and provided food and shelter for the homeless. Workshops engaged in cutting: firewood; carpentry and joinery; cabinet making; sack making; mat making; carpet weaving; tambourine making; brush making; mattress making; painting; engineering; wheel–wrighting; saw mills; tin working; paper and rag sorting; tailoring; shoemaking; match making; and cardboard box making. It had a bakery; office clerks; and special training for cooks, night watchmen, gate–keepers, and scrubbers to work at Army buildings. Women worked in: book–binding; a knitting factory; laundry; white sewing; making texts for walls; and domestic work. The Army used these services and products in its own work and sold some products in its own stores.[4] The Army transported food from the Essex farms up the Thames to be sold or used in its homeless and workers shelters.

In March 1891 the Booths had put down a deposit on the Castle and Park Farms, 800 acres (later increased to five farms and 3,200 acres) in the Thames Estuary, about five miles from Southend, Essex, and three miles from the villages of Leigh, Rayleigh, and South Benfleet. The price was £12,000. From 1898 Lamb ran the Hadleigh social farm with a resident staff of Salvation Army social officers and employees. They trained men coming from city colony workshops in agricultural skills. Most of the men were single. Many transferred to the farm from London's East End slums. Most had learned basic work skills in the city where they had also gone through a program of character rehabilitation.

The Army, in light of its new social reform image and its dependence on public and government funds, did not press its evangelical message in social institutions. But neither did it hide its concern for spiritual change. While it attracted public support in the language of social conscience and a moral civic empire, its officers, who were trained as evangelists, did not resist the urge to bring men and women to a conversion experience that they deemed necessary to produce a U–turn in the lives of their clients.

Exhaustion from doing two men's jobs led to a breakdown in Lamb's health in 1901. He was not the only one among the Army's officers to suffer from the strain of increasing work loads.[5] His family lived in a home at Southend–on–Sea. By 1898

David and Minnie had five children: David Clinton, born on August 25, 1889; Catherine (Kate), born on December 12 1890; Marguerita (Meta), born on January 19, 1893; Patrick, born on February 28, 1895; and Janet, born on June 27, 1897. On July 20, 1899 their last child, Alexander (Alec), would be born. Catherine and Marguerita later became Salvation Army officers.

At Hadleigh the men learned farming and livestock raising techniques that would prepare them for overseas emigration to farms in the colonies. Initially the intent was that an overseas land settlement would be their destination. But Lamb later altered this third step to mean either employment on a farm or any suitable work that was available. He would use Labor Bureaus to explore overseas employment opportunities with the governments of Canada, Southern Africa, and Australia. When that change occurred after 1903, the Hadleigh's farms assumed broader training functions.

Countries outside the British Empire, like the United States, Holland and Switzerland, would not participate in the emigration phase of the Darkest England plan, but they did develop farm colonies for their own urban unemployed. The rather short–lived American colonies in Ohio, Colorado, and California, would initially transfer unemployed urban workers directly "back to the land," a program that had President Roosevelt's enthusiastic support.[6] But when colonization failed, the Army used farms for rehabilitation of alcoholics, discharged prisoners, unruly youths and orphans, and summer camp programs.

In addition to his work at Hadleigh and the city colony institutions, Lamb continued to plan social programs and present the Army's need for help in financing them to the British government and private philanthropists. At the same time, William Booth traveled extensively to gain financial aid from imperial and colonial governments and also led soul–saving missions. The city and farm colonies, as the first two–thirds of the Darkest England program, were essential to the tripartite plan. Lamb worked for their success until, in 1903, the Booths appointed him to set up a new approach to the third part of the plan—the idea to send England's urban unemployed to the British colonies to start life anew in a variety of occupations, but normally without small plots of land at the other end.

3

The Salvation Army Emigration Program, 1903–1938, in the Historical Context of 19th Century Social Reform Ideas

T he initial idea for the Overseas Colony—Darkest England's third step in social reclamation of England's unemployed—almost certainly came from outside The Salvation Army and largely from outside England. From 1887, when Frank Smith returned to England from the United States, to 1889, he was investigating ideas for land settlements that were available around Europe. From these ideas and those he brought back from America he put together the three–stage plan. He sold the idea to William Booth as they traveled together in Britain. Smith was Booth's private secretary and *War Cry* reporter. During this time Smith convinced Bramwell Booth to take the Army into the field of social reform. And Catherine Booth agreed.

The idea was to develop farm colonies as settlements in England and then in areas of the British Empire that had uninhabited "wastelands" that could be improved by the emigration of Britain's urban unemployed, whom they saw as "waste labor." Settlers would bond together in cooperative communities under the supervision of Salvation Army officers and employees. On a lease–to–purchase arrangement colonists would ultimately own their own farms and repay the Army for its initial investment.

But before the Army sent colonists overseas, it would set in motion a progressive plan for human reclamation. It would train colonists on private English farms or at its own farms in Essex. Only then would the Army move colonists to rural settlements overseas. There migrants would live as yeomen farmers in environments that nourished the soul and body. It was this program that was written up in 1890 for *In Darkest England and the Way Out*, a collaborative effort by a team of writers: Frank Smith, Susie F. Swift, W. T. Stead, and William and Bramwell Booth.

When General Booth appointed Colonel Lamb to develop the migration program in 1903, he and Bramwell were still thinking in terms of the original settlement idea and pushing it with the British government and Cecil Rhodes' British South Africa Company. Their passion for Salvation Army land settlements lasted to 1908, but it was becoming increasingly evident that they were not gaining support for the idea. Lamb soon began thinking of a better approach.

The outcome was Lamb's idea to broaden the program to include families as well as single men whom the Army had moved from city colony workshops and trained to farm at Hadleigh. Lamb would include women and young girls and boys in the emigration plan. When the Booths approved the plan, it would thrive until the onset of World War II. Bramwell Booth asked Lamb to direct the new Emigration Office at 122 Queen Victoria Street, across the street from the Army's headquarters.

Lamb's emigration program operated through labor bureaus in England, on the ships, and in the colonial areas. The bureau would locate work for men and boys on farms, but also search for jobs in urban areas, including domestic servant positions for women and girls.

In 1903 Lamb paid his first visit to the United States and Canada, to study three Army farm colonies in the U.S., and to investigate advantages of his new emigration plan with Canadian authorities. He would need to convince the dominions that it was in their interest to attract workers and to cooperate with the Army on the transportation and placement of the immigrants. For the rest of Lamb's life, immigrants and their descendants had his nearly exclusive attention. His travels and conversations with British and dominion[1] authorities would make him an expert on migration and would widen his moral vision to include a world at peace in the wake of two world wars.

The "back to the land" idea on which the Darkest England plan was built in the late 19th century was still alive. It took hold of the minds of many social reformers who revived an old idea and gave it new life during the turbulent decades of the 1870s and 1880s. Prof. Clark C. Spence traced land–based colonization history "at least as far back as the Greeks," who invited outsiders to help them hold onto their land against threats from invaders. Russia's Catherine II and England's George III embraced the idea in the late 18th and early 19th centuries. When Frank Smith organized the Darkest England plan in the late 1880s, he studied hundreds of farm colonies, sometimes termed land settlements, both religious and secular, established by individuals, societies and governments, to help the underclass improve their quality of life. There were colonies to reform criminals, drunkards, and beggars, and colonies to promote family cohesiveness. The 19th century "back to the land" movement developed on the European continent, in Ireland, in North America, and elsewhere.

As examples of 19th century farm colonies Spence cited several programs that Frank Smith and other 19th century social planners studied. The Frederiksoord colony of 1818, founded by a Dutch army general, was the first of several colonies organized by the Society of Boniface to assist veterans at the end of the Napoleonic wars. Urban, unemployed, married men, who suffered unemployment in a post–war economic depression, gained agricultural training on farms and then settled on small freeholds. In 1844 Emperor Louis Napoleon wrote *Extinction du Pauperisme* to propose state–subsidized farm settlements on vacant land for urban workers who had been displaced by technology or who failed in business ventures. Paris organized La Chamelle farm colony. Belgium had a farm near Wortel and founded one at Merxplas in 1825, mainly for beggars and tramps. Saxony, Holstein, and Switzerland developed work colonies. In the 1880s Pastor von Bodelschwingh, no doubt aware of these early 19th century land colonies, organized a settlement with philanthropic and government donations at Wilhelmsdorf to bring together German "wasteland and waste–labor,"[2] terms used by Salvation Army social planners.

In Britain in 1846–48, Feargus O'Connor's Chartist worker–based political movement proposed placing industrial workers on farmsteads and setting up for them. Displaced rural workers had been driven into what many saw as the evil environment of overpopulated cities. As a 13–year–old in 1842, William Booth heard O'Connor rally his forces on the streets of Nottingham. Booth's biographers speculate that this event turned young William's mind towards politics and the terrible living conditions of the poor.[3] But there is scant evidence of this in Booth's letters during his later career as an evangelist in the 1850s to 1870s when he devoted his energy to saving lost souls through preaching.

As late as 1886, in the wake of the socialist–led Trafalgar Square riots in London, Booth wrote an article on "Socialism" that showed how slowly his revivalist's mind was embracing a social creed. Booth claimed that nothing was "gained by destroying society's foundations in order to rectify its wrongs." Only God could radically mend society. He recalled how he had once admired O'Connor, but he now saw the Chartist ladder to bliss as a mirage. Only at the end of the decade, under the influence of Frank Smith, did Booth accept anything other than a spiritual solution to solving the chasm that had developed in industrial England between the rich and the poor.[4]

In the 19th century many social reformers embraced the "three acres and a cow" movement to reverse the trend of rural youth moving to cities and to revive rural living conditions. Inexpensive land in the British colonies was opening opportunities to settle British families overseas. Canada, South Africa, New Zealand, and Australia welcomed Britains who would help enlarge the dominions' economies and tie them to Britain's empire. Vast lands appeared to be "empty." That rural landscapes were in fact occupied by native people indicated that racism was another universal ingredient of the mindset of the times.

In the 1880s, General Sir Francis de Winton, Baroness Burdett Coutts, and Lady Gordon Cathcart, members of Britain's landed aristocracy, invested in land colonies in Saskatchewan, Canada.[5] Maurice de Hirsch set up a Jewish settlement in Saskatchewan. London's Mansion House Committee and the Jewish Colonization Association founded dozens of Jewish agricultural colonies after the 1881–82 anti–Semitic pogroms in Eastern Europe. Social reformers set up settlements in Palestine, Argentina, Canada, and the western United States.[6] The American government was providing free farms through its Homestead Act of 1862, and the Canadian government began offering free farms in 1873. Government aid gradually replaced private foundations in providing transportation by the end of the 19th century.

By the time David Lamb set up his Emigration Department in 1903, the Army's American branch, under the leadership of Commissioner Frederick de L. Booth–Tucker and his wife, William and Catherine Booth's second daughter, Consul Emma Booth–Tucker, had established farm colonies in Ohio, Colorado, and California.[7]

William Booth asked the British government to help the Army set up colonies in the British Empire. Prime Minister Arthur Balfour's Conservative government sent novelist Sir Rider Haggard to inspect the Army's U.S. colonies in 1903. Haggard's "white paper" report complimented the Salvationists' determination, but questioned the advisability of following their example to the letter. They had set up a Colorado colony for urban migrants on arid–alkaline soil with no source of water for irrigation. The 3–5 acre lots were too small and the untrained urban workers were unaccustomed to the hardships of farm life. While the Army's plans were faulty in estimating the acreage a family would need to turn a farm into a commercial success without irrigation, Haggard recommended that a better financed "back to the land" enterprise might work.

American social and political leaders, President Theodore Roosevelt and Ohio Governor Myron Herrick, were anxious to see the Army succeed.[8] But the Ohio colony, near Cleveland, named Fort Herrick for the governor, soon became a rehabilitation center for alcoholics and later a summer camp for children. The California colony became an orphanage. Thus none of them fit the Darkest England model of moving the urban unemployed "back to the land."

David C. Lamb's Emigration Proposal, 1903

Colonel David C. Lamb made his contribution to the emigration idea and promoted it as a new approach to the third phase of the Darkest England plan.[9] He would move entire families from Britain to British dominions, which after World War I would gradually become the British Commonwealth of sovereign nations. Immigrants would often move in stages: the father and older boys finding employment before sending for the mother and younger children. Lamb broadened the program to include those who could pay for their transport, but needed The Salvation Army's help in finding a ship on which to cross the Atlantic to Canada, or the Indian Ocean to Australia and New Zealand. The Army would find a place for the immigrants to live when they got there, and a means of finding employment in the new land.

Lamb assumed that overseas colonies would welcome families from Britain's overcrowded cities if the Army could show that they were willing to work and had good character. He was convinced that British and colonial authorities would embrace the cause of establishing "Little Englands" where land was plentiful and workers were lacking. It was their mutual interest. But all concerned needed someone they trusted who would mediate between them to connect British migrants to the new land and employer. The Salvation Army, like many religious and charitable societies, filled the "go–between" role. Lamb's talent for mediating between various parties in the program, including labor unions, proved to be the glue that held the system together on many occasions.

The Salvation Army migration plan showed how well its leaders embraced the mindset of the age and how wise they were in choosing the right person to direct the project. Early 19th century communal schemes had been more idealistic and less "business–like" and "scientific." At this point Lamb's administrative and financial skills made a difference. He thought in practical, not romantic terms. His enterprise would test how well members of the British working class could thrive if given a chance to prove themselves in the social/cultural setting of the new world. His proposal went beyond remaking, or transplanting, British families overseas. He wanted to reshape society as a whole, and he convinced the Booths to invent a plan that would be an example of what society could do to right itself socially, economically and spiritually. The migration plan, as a business–like enterprise, was less idealistic than the Owenite, Shaker or

Oneida utopian settlements of the 1830s and 1840s, but it fit the ideals of the times in which it had to work.

David Lamb, following the lead of Frank Smith, the Booths, and the Fabians, all early 20th century reformers, set out to gather financial support for the Army's social reform program from a diverse group of philanthropists, writers, politicians and educators. In the background was a deep anxiety in Britain over what the homeland had become. Social reformers saw degradation as particularly acute in urban tenements, massive unemployment, disintegrating families, and for evangelicals, the loss of religious sentiment, drunkenness, gambling, all set in the context of uncaring economic greed. Out of this frustration reformers contemplated an idyllic past that associated goodness with farm life and simpler times. Such an environment, they held, had produced sturdy moral values.

But country life was not, and likely never had been, as idyllic as early 20th century reformers believed it to have been. This came as a surprise to American sociologists when, at the turn of the century, "country life" studies pointed to weak, isolated rural schools and country churches without pastors, and a lack of medical and sanitation services in villages. But reformers saw that urban wealth was not the answer to rural poverty. They were anxious to tackle obstacles to urban unemployment in a practical manner and this included moving urban workers "back to the land."

The "waste labor" of Britain's cities would move to what reformers saw as "wastelands" of the country and overseas dominions by employing "waste capital" of governments to finance reform. In the process rural villages would consolidate schools and unify churches. Urban social planners would turn a trinity of waste into a trinity of wealth and efficiency; that was how the Salvation Army's American commander Frederick de Latour Booth–Tucker described it in his articles on farm colonies he had initiated in India and America.[10]

On David Lamb's June 1903 visit to the United States and Canada, he studied farm colonies and met academics, journalists and government officials, groups he would continue to meet with the rest of his life. He hoped to find support for his migration plan in Canada that would set the stage for the first shipment of British migrants in 1905.

William Booth had visited North America in 1898 and 1902 to encourage the "back to the land" settlement plan of his son–in–law, Frederick Booth–Tucker, who, when he was the Army's commander in India, had settled Indian Salvationist converts from outcast "criminal tribes" on land colonies near cities after they had been evicted from the land by their high caste Hindu employers. This occurred in 1884, six years before publication of the Darkest England plan. As missionary physician Harry Williams points out in his biography of Booth–Tucker, by the late 1890s Tucker was combining European and Indian experiences in developing farm colonies in the United States. He no doubt shared his ideas on colonization with David Lamb during his 1903 visit.[11]

In July 1903, a month after Lamb returned from his North America tour, the Salvation Army established an Emigration and Vagrancy Department at its London Headquarters. The Booths named Lamb its first Director. It was for this new work that Lamb gained recognition from the British and dominion governments along with other social agencies as a social reformer and practical, efficient administrator. It was this work that made him, next to the Booths, the Army's most visible international figure.

Emigration to Canada Begins in 1905

In April 1905, less than two years after Colonel David Lamb began to design his migration plan, he saw the first emigrant ship, the *S.S. Vancouver,* set out for Canada under a Salvation Army flag. On board were 1,047 emigrants, 600 of whom were wage–earners. Many paid their own way; to others the Army made loans, but none came from London's slums. The Army gave them a splendid sendoff on a train from Euston Station, London, where the Chalk Farm Band played and Salvationists presented Bibles to each emigrant. At Liverpool the Lord Mayor and Mrs. Bramwell Booth spoke, as did Commissioner Booth–Tucker and Sir Rider Haggard. Lamb knew that neither Canada nor other British possessions were inclined to accept what they saw as the riffraff from slums.[12]

In 1905, William Booth, now 76 and still an evangelist, wrote to the first migrants a message in a booklet that contained songs to be sung at Salvation Army meetings on the ship.

You are going over the sea, with its possible storms, to a country, with its unknown difficulties, in order to find conditions more favorable to your earthly welfare than those you at present enjoy ... On the other side of the sea of life there is a land of pure delight, where poverty, sickness and death never come, and I want every one of you to meet me on those eternal shores. The 'salvation ship' bound for that celestial country is ready to sail. Jesus Christ has bought you a free passage. If you have not started, enter your name forthwith, bid farewell to every evil way, hurry on board and sail with us not only to Canada, but to eternal glory.[13]

Discussing the 3,000 British emigrants the Army sent to Canada in 1905, General Booth mourned: "What a melancholy thing it is that old England has nothing better for such people than to show them the door! Still they are going under the British flag, and, after all, that is something. The whole thing has made a great impression on the country. We shall do better yet."[14] His combined British/Christian imperialism, of social and economic reform motives, would greatly increase the population of a British dominion and would tie it more closely to the British Empire and the Salvation Army's Christian imperium. David Lamb, a Salvationist, imperialist and social reformer was a champion of all these realms.

The Salvation Army's Canadian *War Cry* in May 2005 quoted British statesman Earl Grey's address at the Toronto Club on "the immigration question." Grey observed:

In every crowded city of the United Kingdom there are a large number of men who, because they have arrived at what is termed the dangerous age—between 40 and 50—find it most difficult to obtain employment. The present problem is how to get these worthy folk, with their rich assets of children, upon the land. The colonies of The Salvation Army in the United States, which Mr. Rider Haggard is now reporting on to the imperial government, also teach the same lesson. I am certain it will be a good thing for Canada, and for the Empire, if we can concentrate the disinterested enthusiasm which at

present animates the Salvation Army, by using it for the purpose of
settling on your unoccupied lands worthy and respected families, se-
lected from the poor of the cities in the United Kingdom."[15]

Canada: Emigration from 1905 to 1912

The influx of British citizens into Canada under Salvation
Army auspices, with the cooperation of Canadian and British
government migration authorities, continued for more than
three decades after the arrival of the first ship in 1905. By 1938
more then 200,000 migrants would book passage to Canada with
the Army. Many of these would then travel to the Canadian
prairies by train to work on farms. The Army also sent migrants
to work on farms in Australia and New Zealand, and women to
do domestic work in cities.

In the first phase of the migration, from 1905 to 1910, the
Army sent 50,000 men, women and children to Canada. Of that
number only 10,000 needed financial aid for their transportation.
Canada, according to Sir Rider Haggard, became "the mecca of
the Salvation Army emigration policy," the exemplar of its capacity for cost–cutting managerial efficiency and moral purpose.
Canadian authorities returned less than one percent of the
Army's migrants to England as undesirables.[16] David Lamb was
the architect and administrator of the plan during this period.

Canada insisted on quality immigrants, as did all British dominions. Canada's population grew from 5,371,315 in 1901 to
10,376,786 in 1921, thanks to the generous number of immigrants. There were 189,000 immigrants in 1906 alone, the year after The Salvation Army's first boatload arrived. The Canadian
government invested large sums to entice immigrants through
pamphlets, Department of Interior advertising, and by giving
land to railroads to build main and trunk lines to open up western land. The railroads would then sell land adjacent to the
right–of–way to farmers, and railway junctions would develop
into business centers for shipping out wheat and cattle and
bringing in farm equipment and other goods. In four years after
the settlers put down a small payment for government land they
would own their quarter section (160 acres) outright and, hope-
fully, become efficient farmers.

Private and charitable organizations received Canadian government grants for finding prospective settlers in Britain. Prof. R. G. Moyles points out that The Salvation Army was not alone in this empire– building enterprise. Besides the Army, charities involved in emigration included: the Church Emigration Society; the East End Emigration Society; the Quebec and St. John Colonization Society; Dr. Barnardo's; the Women's National Immigration Society; the Ottawa Valley Immigration Aid Society; and the Western Canadian Immigration Association. Each worked on a similar plan and coordinated their programs with the British and Canadian government migration departments. They set up emigration headquarters to recruit settlers, arranged ocean passage on steamships and land transportation by rail, assisted government agents to acquire land for settlers, and set up labor bureaus to find jobs for them in cities.

Canadian government grants to The Salvation Army included a bonus of 12 shillings for each immigrant over twelve years old and 6 shillings for immigrants under twelve. There were also grants for giving lectures to attract emigrants in Britain, advertising in *The War Cry*, and taking care of the migrants on the ships and after their arrival in Canada. Moyles writes that the Army received $8,124.90 in bonuses between 1906 and 1907, and additional grants of approximately $25,000 between 1906 and 1908. By his analysis, that "the Canadian government got excellent value for its money was a fact no one could deny."

When immigrants arrived at a Canadian port the machinery of the Salvation Army Immigration Bureau went into action under its first Canadian director, Brigadier Thomas Howell, and his staff. Processing included assistance in: 1) setting up immigrants with their prospective employers; 2) collecting information on the general fitness of prospective emigrants and sending the report to the Canadian port; 3) at the point of boarding the ship the Army's agents helped emigrants pass through the official medical, customs and immigration process; 4) upon arrival in Canada the agents examined the emigrants' papers, exchanged money, cashed letters of credit, gave them the name of their employer and a card of introduction, issued them a railway ticket to the station closest to their new job, checked their baggage, answered questions, gave details on food needed for the trip, and got them on the train headed for the next port of departure; 5) the officers who accompanied the migrants on the ship to Canada took them to a central point (Montreal, Toronto, Winnipeg) where the final distribution took place. The Army even arranged for a Commissariat Car to be attached to the train where emigrants could purchase provisions. And the Army kept in touch with émigrés in order to continue to advise and help them by sending corps officers to visit and by other means.[17]

The Salvation Army in Canada did all it could to attach the immigrants to the Army's spiritual wing—the local corps. Every immigrant received a card that introduced them to the nearest Army corps. The Army expected corps officers to communicate with newcomers as soon as possible and invite them to attend Army meetings. The officers would report their meetings with immigrants to the Migration Bureau in Toronto. Often the Bureau asked the officer to meet the immigrant at the railway station. This strategy established a permanent connection between the Canadian Salvation Army and those the British Salvation Army's Emigration Bureau in London had sponsored.

Moyles estimates that of the Army–sponsored immigrants, about 75 percent went to farms in Ontario or the West. But only a few could afford to buy land on arrival. Therefore, most were farm laborers during their early years in the dominion. The other 25 percent, those who did not want farm work, settled in eastern cities, many of them in the town of Cobalt as part of a "New Ontario" development.

A third group, with whose welfare The Salvation Army was particularly concerned, were women "domestics," some young and single, others widowed and older. Wealthy families in Toronto and Montreal were pleased to have them in their homes. The Army was determined to ensure their fair treatment and saw to it that they received a second class fare of $42.50 from Liverpool to Montreal and a rail fare of $6.65 from Montreal to Toronto. The employer paid two–thirds of the passage money and a $2.50 registration fee. The women paid one–third of the passage before sailing and re–paid two–thirds in monthly installments out of their wages. Their wages were not to be less than $10 a month and they had to agree to work at least 12 months.

By 1914 The Salvation Army had brought over 100,000 immigrants to Canada. The Toronto *Globe* reported that less than 100 of these were unemployed and few had been returned to Britain as "undesirable" Before they found housing, many stopped at the Army's "newcomer hotels" and rest homes in Toronto, Montreal, Winnipeg and Vancouver, or at the government lodging house in Toronto run by the Army. Moyles estimates that "perhaps 10 percent of the more than two million who came to Canada" before World War I came under The Salvation Army's auspices. But his analysis found that the Army's "Christian concern, scrupulous dealings, friendly manner and continued contact" set it apart.[18]

Canadian Settlement Colonies Fail and Trouble with Labor Unions in 1906

On his trips to Canada David Lamb inspected two early land "settlements" that the Army ran as joint ventures with organizations that owned large tracts of land in the West. He was satisfied that the Tisdale colony, established in Saskatchewan in 1906, and Coombs colony, organized in British Columbia in 1910, were working out well. Moyles describes these colonies as "bloc settlements" a "common feature of western settlement." They were not "planned ventures," but were the outcome of requests made to The Salvation Army to settle immigrants on land tracts that belonged to other colonization ventures. Outside of the nearby town of Tisdale, the Army settled men from its Hadleigh farm colony and experienced Canadian farmers from Ontario. Eighteen families had settled on 740 acres by 1907. The Independent Order of Foresters provided land at $2 and $3 an acre, a house, food for six months, oxen, a cow and farm implements. They gave each settler a loan of $500 to be repaid in installments through the Union Trust Company at 6 percent interest on the land's value, plus 6 percent on the unpaid portion of the loan's principal. Moyles mentions that the Army did not include this last part of the payment in its ads. Mr. A. Ready advised the settlers on farming and the Army's Adjutant Hanna would be their spiritual counselor. The plan called for 20,000 acres to be made available as the colony developed.[19]

David Lamb returned to Canada in 1908 to see how things were going with the immigrants and how Canadians were responding to the new citizens. He arrived in time to meet union officials who had created a tempest over the displacement of Canadian workers by British immigrants during a period of economic depression. With thousands of migrants arriving in Canada any downturn in the economy and rise in the rate of unemployment were bound to catch the eye of union leaders and members.

By the time Lamb left on the *Empress of Ireland* on October 2nd he realized that "emigration must be controlled," and that he would need to reassure governments and trades unions that the Army's filtering process would send only the best British stock to the dominion. While he continued to believe the "prospects for the future are bright" for migration programs, the Canadian situation convinced him that he had to "bend his energies to even more careful selection and specialization."[20]

A British *Young Soldier* (paper for Salvationists under 14 years of age) article in 1909 reported a conversation with Colonel Lamb concerning his 1908 visit to Canada, including a stop at Tisdale colony on the Canadian Northern Railway, 450 miles northwest of Winnipeg, and 90 miles east of Prince Albert, Saskatchewan. Lamb described the English settlers, including about 100 boys and girls, mostly under 15. The majority were boys. He called them "state children." They included "orphans;" "deserted;" or "children taken from dangerous surroundings." Some may have come from Minnie Lamb's Millfield children's home in Essex. As for families, Lamb noted that generally the father came first, "taking perhaps two of the elder ones." When he was established the mother followed with the girls and younger children. Two of the families were as large as 12 and 13 members. Lamb said that "few of the settlers" at Tisdale were Salvationists, and various denominations conducted meetings in the school room. The Army held a Sunday School and the officer assigned to the Colony paid his own rent for his own land out of his farm proceeds.

Lamb described "C" as a Tisdale settler who had "fled from the polluting influences of an English Midland city's streets, to give his family a chance of growing up in the fear of God, and under the healthiest possible conditions, moral and physical. He and his wife had nine children. They were "a bit untidy," but when he began to sympathize with them the mother broke in to tell him that neither she nor her husband regretted their move to the Canadian West. In England their garden backed onto a football field, and the filthy language there and in the streets had "caused them to flee with their family" to this refuge. At Tisdale they drank "fine, rich milk," as if it were water. Their untidy clothes were due to the fact that their best were being washed in anticipation of Lamb's visit.[21]

The Salvation Army signed a similar contract for a much smaller tract of land in 1910 with the Nanaimo and Esquimault Railway for a land colony on Vancouver Island, British Columbia. The Army brought in twelve English families, mainly Salvationists. The first settler received 22 acres, five of them cleared, and a frame house. Ensign Crego, an experienced farmer, was the Army's project director. At this colony, named Coombs for the Army's Canadian leader, the Army, rather than a bank, held the mortgages. The Army built a school and Army hall and employed teachers.

Prof. Moyles concludes that neither Tisdale nor Coombs was a success. Poor supervision at Tisdale, and the fact that the Army did not fully inform settlers of their obligations, led most settlers to leave the colony to seek free homesteads. Only the Gregory family, who were Salvationists, held out at the Coombs colony. In their case, Moyles reported that their "front five acres turned out to be a gravel heap and the back five a swamp."[22] These failures, much like the Army's three U.S. colonies, turned David Lamb against expanding this type of venture in Canada and caused him to focus on working with individual migrants whose settlement and employment the Army could manage. So they returned to Lamb's plan to settle families and single men or women for whom the Emigration Office Labor Bureaus in Britain and Canada could find work and a home.

The Immigration Act of 1910

W. D. Scott, the Canadian superintendent of immigration, returned from London to explain Canada's new Immigration Act that called for immigrants to have $25 on arrival in the dominion. As a result of his meeting with British emigration agencies Scott intended to modify the act. If an immigrant found a job and proved to immigration officials that he and his family were not likely to become public charges, then he would "be allowed to bring out the members of his family without their producing additional funds." The purpose of the act was to keep "undesirable persons" out of Canada. The measure defined "undesirables" as: "imbeciles, feeble–minded persons, and persons who have been insane within [the] previous five years." It also excluded persons with a "loathsome disease" or who were "dumb, blind, or otherwise physically defective," and "persons convicted of certain crime." It excluded "immoral women" and those who lived off their earnings, and "professional vagrants." Those assisted by charitable organizations, like The Salvation Army, had to have, in writing, the support of the superintendent of immigration or the assistant superintendent.

Scott commended The Salvation Army for complying with the act. He considered the Army's success as being the result of its appointment of a selection board that was composed of people whose knowledge of the emigrants was "sound and extensive." The Army also placed Canadians on this board, since they knew the kind of persons Canada wanted. Scott compared the number of rejected immigrants from Britain with those coming from the United States. There had been 104,996 immigrants who arrived at ocean ports in 1909. Those who crossed the U.S. border into Canada had numbered 103,798. But Canada had rejected 8,997 of those from the United States. Only 1,515 from England and the continent had been turned away.

Superintendent Scott also commended the Army for paying "a great deal of attention to its immigrants after they have landed." The Army had found them employment, cared for the sick until they were well, and attended to their "moral and spiritual interests." Canada needed more immigrants who met the criteria of "the Britisher of the true type." For accomplishing this the Army could proudly point to "the carefulness of its administration and the soundness of its methods. It could claim "a foremost place among British emigration agencies."[23] This was a fine tribute to David Lamb and his British and Canadian social officers.

According to the 1910 edition of the *Salvation Army Year Book*, the Army's emigration program had benefited the Army in Canada. By then about 44,000 migrants had passed through the Army's hands. Rather than give the number of immigrants who had become Salvationists as a result of the Army's aid, the *Year Book* pointed to the public's support to its 1909 annual fundraising "Self–Denial Effort." The $40,343 campaign indicated that the Canadian public liked what the Army's migration and other social departments were doing.[24] But there were more tangible results for the Army than dollars. The impression made by its effort on behalf of the unemployed in resettling them in a land that wanted them had increased the number of Salvation Army soldiers (lay persons) and officers (ministers). And for this there was a multiplying effect that would increase its ranks over the years as the immigrant's children and more distant descendants continued their membership in the Army.

Hadleigh and Boxted Colonies in England

In 1912 David Lamb turned over the management of the Hadleigh Land and Industrial Colony to Colonel W. L. Simpson when General Bramwell Booth made him the Salvation Army's International Social Commissioner. It was the Army's highest rank next to the general. By 1914, the Hadleigh colony that Lamb had developed on 3,000 acres of marshland had been drained and was under cultivation. The colony was providing work for "destitute but able–bodied men," and was giving farm training that prepared them to earn a living on the land in England or abroad.

As the *Salvation Army Year Book* put it, the colony took in "pauper, reckless, hopeless, unfortunate men," and like an efficient machine it sent them back to the world as "capable, industrious, honest citizens." More than 7,000 men had gone to Hadleigh. The Army had placed 4,444 of them in jobs. It expelled 1,595 for various causes. Of the rest, 457 had emigrated to Canada, 261 had been sent back to the Army's city colony or to

Poor Law unions[25], and 183 had left the colony due to illness or death. In 1912 the Colony had 190 residents.

Hadleigh, which was meant to be self–supporting, nearly paid its expenses by selling its farm produce. The Army estimated that it was saving British taxpayers the cost of keeping the men in workhouses, jails, and asylums. The men came to Hadleigh from the Army's city colony institutions, from boards of guardians, and on personal application.

Most of Hadleigh's men worked in the Market Garden that had 125 acres of fruit trees. The farm department featured a dairy and stock–raising, and was proud of its pedigreed prize–winning herd of Middle White Yorkshire pigs. Hadleigh sold produce at nearby Southend market and produced nearly two million bricks annually at a mechanized Brickfield with greenhouses containing 193,000 square feet of glass. Colonists ate in a common dining hall and had recreation rooms, a sports field, and a library in the Home. To Salvationists, the "most important" function of the staff of officers and employees was their "spiritual efforts" to change the men's "character and moral regeneration." The two–fold work aimed at "helping the poor and the Empire." In the long run, the Hadleigh colony adapted to new demands for its services, as had the North American farm settlements. It gradually turned more in the direction of training youth than rehabilitating older men.

While at Hadleigh, David and Minnie Lamb kept in touch with the English world beyond the Army's farms through public service in Southend, Essex county. Voters elected them to boards of guardians for the poor in their home county. Minnie was also working with the courts as a justice of the peace and a probation officer. On top of that, she ran a children's home.

Another venture during David Lamb's time as general supervisor of The Salvation Army's city and farm colonies in England was a failure. The Army purchased 400 acres at Boxted, Essex as a small holdings settlement. The intention was to move families onto 67 holdings of four and a half to seven acres.[26] The "settlement by credit" idea, or "Raiffeisen system of cooperative lending," had been used in Germany, England, Holland, Sweden, and India. It placed small farms in the hands of city workers who had gathered enough capital to begin such an investment.[27] Boxted was the only Army effort at using this means to move urban families back to the land in England, and it was short–lived, and unsuccessful, as were true of similar efforts in the United States and Canada.[28] City workers were not sufficiently qualified for farm work, and the land often needed to be analyzed before the new landowner took title to it.

Since Salvation Army polity was a monarchical hierarchy operating under the rule of the Booth family, it is difficult to determine what, if any, credit was due to underlings in its achievements or what fault they deserved for its occasional failures. Almost always, General William Booth from 1878 to his death in 1912, and Bramwell Booth from 1912 to 1929, received credit for achievements. All publications went out under the general's name and by his authority. Thus the historian assigns credit to others, including David Lamb, only by reading between the lines or by reading outside sources. Official Salvation Army histories seldom attach Lamb's name, or that of his wife Minnie, to accomplishments in areas for which they were responsible.

4

The Character of Salvation Army Social Officers & their Leader, Commissioner David C. Lamb: The Army's Bifurcated Two–Wing Mission

Assessing the impact of the Army's emigration program in Canada, R. G. Moyles claims that: "There is no doubt that The Salvation Army in Canada has reaped great results from this program as it became the fourth largest religious denomination in that country."[1] If he is correct, the social wing, through the work of David Lamb and his colleagues in the migration departments in England and Canada, found a way to tie the Army's social program to its founders' revivalist evangelical mission to save the poor urban masses for Christianity. And to the delight of the British government it also assisted the British society and economy by sending so–called "waste labor" to allegedly "wastelands" of the empire. The Army's early 20th century migration program may be the most remarkable evidence that its social services have had a major impact on its evangelical side, at least in Canada, and likely in most of the more than 100 countries in which the Army sustains a dual ministry of spiritual and social salvation. More research on the social side of Salvation Army history may uncover proof that social services are at the heart of the Army's work.

Moyles' assessment counters the notion, held by some, that social reform programs have detracted from the Army founders' initial purpose to save lost souls, with only passing attention to their physical needs. Some Salvationist contended, from the beginning of the Darkest England social program in the late 1880s, that God had called the Army to one mission, to "rescue the perishing" in religious meetings led by its evangelists (corps officers).

David Lamb's genius was to ask the spiritual side (corps) officers to care for the new immigrants and, if they chose, to welcome them into the church (corps). On subsequent visits to Canada, Australia, New Zealand, and Southern Africa, he met with many who had been met at the train, taken to their new employers or farms, and introduced to the community and the church of their choice. In many cases that church was The Salvation Army.

There can be little doubt that the Booths' decision to divide the Army into two wings, social and spiritual, in the late 1880s, split the movement in much the same way that medieval monasteries divided priestly monks who prayed and offered sacraments, from their lay brothers who worked to feed them and offer hospitality to the poor. The Army's spiritual wing officers have seen their main work as preaching, although most of them have done a fair share of social work, especially in small towns where the Army has few separate social institutions.

This view of the supremacy of evangelical work over social work has often alienated social–wing officers and employees from spiritual–side officers. To work in social institutions to mend physical, mental and moral ailments has been seen as a second class chore. In some cases the alienation has worked in the opposite direction when social institutions have received funding from community and government sources not open to the corps.

It must be noted that all Army officers, including the Lambs, began as evangelists. Only in the late 1880s did the Army open separate training centers for men and women it expected to assign to social institutions. Since those separate training schools closed, the Army has again trained all officers as evangelists, including those it planned to assign to social services.[2]

As late as 1955, 65 years after William Booth published *In Darkest England and the Way Out*, Colonel Robert Sandall, in the third volume of the Army's official history, raised the veil on the battle for the Army's soul; it was seen as a campaign between its spiritual and social wings. Sandall claimed that "The Salvation Army did not begin as, nor has it at any time, anywhere, become, a social reform organization."[3]

That anyone, particularly a Salvationist, would make this assertion is difficult to comprehend. General Booth made the Army "a social reform organization" with his Darkest England proclamation in 1890, as Sandall surely knew. Yet more than six decades later, he included this line to the contrary in his Army–sanctioned history. By that time the Army's dual character was undeniable. In fact, in the public mind in the post–World War II era, the Army was best known as a charitable institution. Due to its own publicity and appeal for funds, few people in many countries knew that the Army was a Protestant evangelical church with a clergy, lay members, and a Wesleyan–Protestant creed. Even though Sandall's statement was obviously untrue, it indicates that the Army's bifurcated organization, whose missions were only superficially connected, had made the Booths' and the Lambs' case for unity difficult to support.[4] In far too few instances the Army had successfully married its social and spiritual ministries.

That Moyles saw a nexus of the two wings in Lamb's plan for Salvation Army–sponsored migration and hospital programs in Canada is an impressive testimonial to the potential for the interdependence between the two wings. This is all the more significant in that a large number, possibly a majority of those who have worked in the Army's social services as employees are not Salvationists, nor are they necessarily advocates for its evangelical creed.[5]

Recent examples of the problems of bifurcation have awakened the public to this division. Peter Seinfels pointed out in his March 2004 *New York Times* column entitled "Beliefs," the American government has found ways, "in accord with the Constitution's guarantees of freedom of religion and church/state separation," to accommodate or even finance religious organizations that provide "health care, social work, emergency food and shelter, higher education and charities of all kinds." In fact, this has been true from the beginning of the Darkest England program in virtually every country where the Army has run hospitals, rescue homes for women and men, schools, city workshops, food and shelter centers, and migration programs. This is obviously true in Canada, Australia, New Zealand, South Africa, and other outposts of the British Empire. But for their part, the religious charities, like The Salvation Army, have had to agree not to hire only members of their own faith, nor to limit services to their own members, nor to proselytize. And from the beginning William Booth was willing to make these concessions.

Seinfels noted that most religious charities in the United States had incorporated their social services as units that were separate from their "worshiping or preaching communities."[6] This was the plea that Frank Smith made in 1890, but the Booths rejected the idea of separate accounting departments. Unlike the U.S. organization Catholic Charities, which the Roman Catholic Church separated from parish churches, the American Salvation Army did not incorporate its two wings separately. Instead, the American Army was slow to accept separation and government regulation.[7] When Booth sought public funds in the early 1890s he assured the public that the money they gave to social programs would not be used to proselytize. Soon the words "character building" replaced "soul saving" in Army fundraising literature.

The Salvation Army's dual mission has occasionally confused the general public. Consider two unrelated situations in early 2004. Joan Kroc, widow of the McDonalds Restaurant chain founder, gave the Army $1.5 billion, likely the largest gift it ever received anywhere. When the U.S. National Commander W. Todd Bassett announced that the Army would use the gift for its spiritual mission as well as social programs, a *New York Times* reader took exception to this use of the windfall bequest and wrote: "While one can argue that food for the soul is necessary, food for the body is more so." Another wrote: "this is the end of my donations to The Salvation Army. Having worked for many years for and with the hungry and homeless, I know that what they need is food, housing, shelter and social services. Once they receive these, the body, mind and spirit will react holistically." A Quaker wrote: "As a 40–plus–year contributor to The Salvation Army, I am appalled by the reversion to 'spread the Gospel' ...

Change comes by good work, not by preaching. The harm done all over the world by missionaries is only assuaged by their contributions to education and relief of misery." This critic said he would "re–evaluate my commitment to this great organization that seemed only to want to relieve suffering."[8] There can be little doubt that the public is confused by the Army's dual mission and about which part of that mission receives their philanthropic support.

A second problem of bifurcation has come from the Army's relationship with non–Salvationist, non–evangelical employees. While not all social wing employees were secular, many were. On February 2, 2004, the *New York Times* announced that: "The Salvation Army of Greater New York, long known for its network of thrift shops and shelters, has begun an effort to reassert its evangelical roots." The Army in New York City had announced that its "core mission is not just social services but also spreading the Gospel." The director of the National Association of Social Workers' New York chapter saw ominous implications in the announcement. "First, social workers are likely to find that they cannot continue to work in their administrative and supervisory roles, since the profession's code of ethics prohibits discrimination in employment on the basis of religion and sexual orientation." And "since services are provided under contract on behalf of the city, it will be our government, by extension, that will be engaging in religious practices if this relationship is allowed to continue."[9] The Army and Roman Catholic Church in New York had earlier taken a stand against the hiring of homosexuals to work in their community centers with children.

Some Salvationists and members of the public saw problems in the late 19th to early 20th centuries when Frank Smith, Elijah Cadman, and David Lamb were putting the social wing together. Prof. Roger J. Green of Gordon College claims that William Booth's "theology of redemption" had become far more inclusive after 1889 than it was before the Army developed the Darkest England social scheme." In other words, as Smith planned the Army's social reform program, Booth's salvation theology had become more "inclusive." Greater religious tolerance had followed the development of social services. Booth was returning to a more ecumenical philosophy that he had embraced in the early days of his East London home mission when he appointed evangelists who adhered to various non–Wesleyan evangelical creeds. But social programs made the Army visible to a broad spectrum of the population and social services aided its spread as a global mission to the poor. In the late 1880s the Army chose not to labor in a narrow cultural trough, and invited people into its buildings for social services who were not of its religious persuasion.

Green asserts that: "Booth and his Army would be perceived from that time onward as a man and a movement engaged in social redemption on a much larger scale and with a fuller vision of such redemption than had been present thus far in either the Christian Mission or The Salvation Army."[10] While the Booths and the Lambs agreed that the Army's ultimate goal was a person's spiritual salvation, they saw a new means to that end in what Booth termed "wholesale salvation" through the Army's social programs.

At the same time, many in the Army continued to argue that the preaching of soul salvation by its spiritual–side officers was more important than social redemption supplied by social–wing officers and employees. The Army had a caste system. When Catherine Booth, the "Army Mother," commissioned rescue work officers who cared for "fallen women" in the Army's urban rescue homes in 1888, just before cancer forced her to retire from public life, she advised them not to wish that they had been called to do "more spiritual work." They could be just as spiritual while sewing on buttons as they could in dealing with wayward girls about their souls.

The War Cry called for the recruitment of slum sisters, social–wing officers who were godly but "did not possess great powers of leadership." "Great powers of leadership" signaled that some officers had the ability to save souls rather than to sew buttons. Major James Cooke, the slum work commander in London, was perturbed when a spiritual–side commander wrote on an application form of an officer candidate: "A nice little lass, she has offered herself for the slums [social work], but is really fit for the field [spiritual work]." Cooke fumed: "I suppose they think if a girl is good and sympathetic, and loves the people, and is willing to scrub their floors, these qualifications are all that are needed [for social work]."[11]

As for the character of David and Minnie Lamb and their fellow Salvation Army officers, a late 19th and early 20th century Fabian socialist reformer, Beatrice Webb, may have penned the best description of their virtues. Mrs. Webb claimed that Salvation Army officers as a whole, social and spiritual, were, by her Fabian classification, a "Samurai caste." They practiced equality between men and women. For them "home life and married life are combined with a complete dedication of the individual to spiritual service ... More cultivated than most persons of their social status, they were better at conversation than an elementary school teacher or trade union official." They exuded "a power of command."

But Mrs. Webb had particular affection for the Army's social officers, and her description of them fit the Lambs and Frank Smith, whom Mrs. Webb knew as a fellow Fabian in the 1890s. The Lambs were not known as outstanding "platform" officers who could move audiences with emotional rhetoric. Rather they were behind the scenes social planners, movers and shapers of large social agendas. Webb argued that "officers on the spiritual side have more the characteristics of the artist or public performer—more emotion and less intelligence."[12] Social officers were, for the most part, men and women of intelligence and character like David and Minnie Lamb, who organized and led the Army's social programs from the late 1880s into the mid–20th century.

In spite of their success in capturing public attention and support, within The Salvation Army social officers remained a class apart. Seldom did they rise to the Army's highest rank (commissioner) or the top positions of general and chief of staff. In fact, no general has come directly from the social wing. Seldom have its national, territorial, or even divisional commanders come from "the social." On occasion spiritual side officers who have had a physical or emotional breakdown have been assigned to "the social," another suggestion that its work was seen as less important, less demanding, less "Army." And within the Army social officers and employees frequently spoke of demeaning assumptions about their work for "wholesale salvation." Yet many on the social side have been the Army's most educated personnel, largely because their professional fields required degrees and certificates as physicians, nurses, medical technicians, hospital administrators, social workers, teachers, accountants, and pharmacists like David Lamb.

Nor has The Salvation Army published as much history of officers in its social wing as of its evangelical work officers. In proposing a biography of David Lamb, Commissioner Harry Williams, a missionary physician who was one of the rare social officers who broke through to high command positions, abhorred the Army's neglect of Lamb, quite possibly its most distinguished officer during his lifetime. While the Army Literary Department commissioned biographies of many early spiritual side officers as "Notables," only a few of its social officers were so honored.[13] While an academic historian, Prof. E. H. McKinley, has published a history of the Men's Social Services in the United States, no one has published a history of the Women's Social Services whose personnel were nearly all unmarried women working in hospitals, homes for unwed mothers, and children's' homes. Yet recent academicians have shown an interest in the Army's social side and particularly in women officers who were engaged to rescue "fallen" sisters.[14]

The Lambs themselves wrote no memoirs of their social services, and revealed little of their family life, apart from their letters home due to frequent absences from their children while on Army business. The family experienced a great personal tragedy on May 1, 1909. Their eldest son, David Clinton Lamb, died of heart failure at nineteen years of age. At the time of his death he was an Assistant Master at Lindisfarne College and was attending classes at the Technical School of Art. The Lambs were living at "Clinton," Ailsa Rd., Westcliff. They published a memoir for which David and Minnie wrote prefatory notes. The passing of a child before his parents is a violation of the natural sequence of life and thus an apparent eclipse of providential timing. The author of the biography, *Dave*, appears to have been Minnie Lamb's friend Major Winifred Leal.[15] Another son died on the front lines during World War I.

5

David C. Lamb's Leadership as International Social Commissioner: The Growth of Salvation Army Social Services, 1912–29

On October 30, 1912, soon after William Booth's death, his chosen successor as the Army's second general, William Bramwell Booth, promoted David Lamb to "commissioner," the Army's highest rank, equivalent to bishop in Episcopal churches. In his new appointment Commissioner Lamb would work directly under the General and Chief of Staff as the Army's international secretary for social affairs and assistant to the chief of staff for the oversight of the Men's and Women's Social Work in the United Kingdom. "Commissioner" is not a military rank, but was adopted by the Booths from its use in the diplomatic corps. A diplomat of that title was the ranking representative of the English monarch's government in the British Empire. In The Salvation Army a person of that rank acts as the general's personal representative. In addition to being international secretary for social affairs, Lamb would continue to be responsible for emigration affairs, and have oversight of the Army's work in the British dominions, India, and "some other areas." Surely few, if any, Salvation Army officers other than the general and chief of staff has ever had such a breadth of responsibility.

In late 1912 Lamb visited China, with side trips to Siberia and North America. China had been on The Salvation Army's expansion list since 1887, with numerous visits by Army leaders to scope out the land. Lamb visited Tientsin to inquire into Ou Yang's "Eastern Salvation Army," which he apparently was able to locate. But a follow–up visit in 1913 by Colonel Joseph Hammond revealed that Yang's "army" had disbanded and the £10,000 of Salvation Army funds that he had allegedly spent on its creation had been lost.[1] In 1913 Lamb visited Australia and New Zealand, and in 1919 he visited North America again, this time with General Bramwell Booth. Put simply, as a commissioner, Lamb was given responsibility for all social service programs in the Army's growing international Christian imperium.

Between 1912 and 1929 many governments and social service agencies gained an appreciation for Lamb's keen sense of how to administer huge programs for the benefit of the poor. As he presented his ideas in public forums and private consultations, his stature rose as an expert in fields of social planning and efficient management.

He also maintained a spiritual keenness when it came to affairs of the heart. He never lost his belief in an individual's need for salvation from sin by God's mercy. Yet his audiences were more often secular than sectarian and his appeals were more often to a universal compassion rather than a patriotic allegiance to any nation or church.

David C. Lamb's Ideas on the Salvation Army's Relations with Governments

In 1902 Lamb began to set down his ideas in print, often after he had given them as public speeches or radio addresses. Occasionally Salvation Army publications printed his essays, but more often he published them personally or in secular journals. Since he left no autobiography, these essays and widely circulated family letters are the best sources for his thinking in the years he served as the Army's Emigration director and International Social Secretary prior to his "promotion to glory" in 1951. He wrote about the reform of drunkards, emigration, the Empire, world peace after the 20th century's two world wars, conditions in countries he visited, and Salvation Army social work and internal organization.

An early essay to Army colleagues expressed his concerns about the Army's working with governments and the constraints that placed on its spiritual ministry and independence. While Lamb and the Booths welcomed endorsements and financial assistance from government officials for the Army's work, Lamb wrote in an article for the Army's *Officer* journal to warn officers to avoid the dangers of too close ties between the Army and governments in whose countries they served. Lamb addressed the Army's need to gain financial support from governments for its social programs without endangering its two–fold mission. While stressing the need for cooperation between British and Colonial governments and the Army, he warned that cooperation must be done with caution. Governments, he knew from his own experience, had "a wonderful capacity for regulating the village pump." He bluntly told Salvationists: "Never trust a State official to do a generous thing."

Lamb reminded officers that their work was not the same as that of government officials. His succinct advice was that Salvationists were not "heralds proclaiming the advance of the victorious army of human progress; rather are we ministering agents of the divine Solicitude working in the debris of the sin–stricken field, seeking 'midst the word's travail' to rescue those in whom there may yet be left a spark of spiritual vitality; to quicken in them fresh hope and is treated by us under Government authority with a deep sea barrier to prevent him or her coming within the temptation zone of the fatal besetment." Army officers must not see themselves as "social servants of the State; [because] the State can buy better service than any Salvation Army officer or ex–Salvation Army officer can render it." Officers must not think too highly of themselves.[2] At the same time he did not demean the working–class background from which officers generally came. Many would rise above their class origins to be recognized by their communities as having a native genius for doing good.

David C. Lamb on Emigration

In 1915, as a measure of Lamb's growing reputation in the emigration field, *The Herald of Stars,* published his "Lecture on

Susie Forrest Swift in her Salvation Army officer's uniform. She was an officer in the Army from 1885 until 1896.
Source: The Salvation Army Archives, National Headquarters

The Swift family in 1898. Pictured clockwise from top are Susie Forrest Swift; Susie's niece, Elizabeth Brengle; a family friend holding Elizabeth; Susie's brother-in-law, Samuel Logan Brengle; Susie's father, George Swift; Susie's nephew, George Swift Brengle; Susie's mother, Pamela Forrest Swift; and Susie's sister, Elizabeth Swift Brengle (Lil).
Source: Sinsinawa Dominican Archives

George H. Swift, father of
Susie Forrest Swift.
*Source: The Salvation Army
Archives, National
Headquarters*

Pamela Forrest Swift,
Susie's mother.
*Source: Sinsinawa Dominican
Archives*

This article describes Susie Forrest Swift's decision to leave the ranks of The Salvation Army and join a Catholic convent. (*The World*, July 24, 1898, London).
Source: The Sinsinawa Dominican Archives

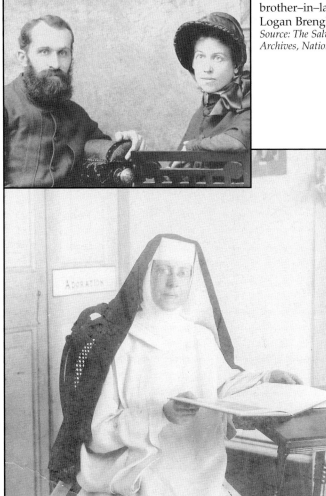

Susie Swift seated with her brother–in–law, Samuel Logan Brengle.
Source: The Salvation Army Archives, National Headquarters

Susie Forrest Swift dressed in the habit of a Dominican nun. She became a nun in 1897, after leaving the Army. Taking the name Sister Imelda Teresa, she remained a devout Catholic until her death in 1916.
Source: The Sinsinawa Dominican Archives

David Crichton Lamb early in his Salvation Army officer career, when he held the titles of Brigadier and Lt. Colonel on the staff of the Army's International Headquarters in London.
Source: The Salvation Army Archives, International Heritage Centre

Commissioner and Mrs. Lamb on board a ship docked in Sydney in February 1926. The trip to Australia was made in the interests of Lamb's Salvation Army migration and settlement scheme.
Source: The Salvation Army Archives, Australia Southern Territory

This publicity photo of Commissioner Lamb was published in *The War Cry* during his 1926 visit to Australia.
Source: The Salvation Army Archives, Australia Southern Territory

Commissioner Lamb talks with a young Salvationist in New York City in 1925. Visiting New York fell under Lamb's responsibilities as International Social Secretary.
Source: The Salvation Army Archives, National Headquarters

The five nominees chosen for the post of General by the
second High Council in 1934. Pictured from left to right
are Commissioner Samuel Hurren from the International
Training College; U.S. Commander Evangeline Cory
Booth; Chief of the Staff Henry M. Mapp; Catherine
Bramwell–Booth from the Women's Social Services
Department; and Commissioner David Lamb.
Source: The Salvation Army Archives, National Headquarters

David Lamb pictured in his
Aberdeen University robe
and Doctor of Laws sash.
The school granted him an
honorary degree in 1934.
*Source: The Salvation Army Archives,
Canada and Bermuda Territory*

Minnie Lamb in her
Salvation Army officer's
uniform.
*Source: The Salvation Army
Archives, Canada and Bermuda
Territory*

Commissioner and Mrs. Lamb being received by Queen
Mary at a garden party at Buckingham Palace in 1934.
Source: The Salvation Army Archives, International Heritage Centre

A program from a memorial service given in honor of Commissioner Lamb. Salvation Army Chief of the Staff Commissioner John J. Allen presided at the service after Lamb's death in 1951.
Source: The Salvation Army Archives, International Heritage Centre

Lamb during his 1941–42 tour of Canada and the United States. As part of the 12,000–mile tour, he used a gas mask to demonstrate what life was like in London during the war.
Source: The Salvation Army Archives, National Headquarters

Emigration." That journal also carried an article by George Lansbury, a member of the London county council and later member of Parliament and leader of the Independent Labour Party. Lansbury was a close friend to Lamb, Frank Smith, and the Booths.

Lamb began his lecture by introducing The Salvation Army with a snippet of early history in East London, the riots of the 1880s, and its 32–year growth into a 58–nation body. In 1915 there were 9,415 corps and outposts and 1,142 social institutions for men, women and children, plus 572 day schools. There were 15,988 officers and cadets. Officers received a salary that would not "attract people to make a livelihood out of it," and furnished quarters. Young men received 5 shillings a week (he failed to mention that women received less pay for equal work). Maximum salary was 18 to 20 shillings a week. The 5,601 employees received an "ordinary rate of wage." He did not give the number of soldiers (lay members) apart from 55,688 the Army termed "local officers" (lay leaders). He noted that there were 23,315 senior bandsmen in some good and "some rather indifferent bands." Salvationists picked up from their Methodist ancestors this fascination for statistical records.

The Army's spiritual wing gained much of its financial support from selling, often in pubs, 81 Army periodicals that published 1,029,804 copies per issue. Every week a "tea league" sold "tons" of "Triumph" tea from the Quaker Tea Company to support missionaries. Profits from the Insurance Society that Lamb had set up in 1901 went to the Army's "ordinary work." Lamb did not mention other sources of income: offerings of its soldiers and officers; an annual Self–Denial appeal; government grants; and income from its social centers and migration programs.

Then Lamb turned to statistics from his social department, which had 2,860 officers and cadets, about 20 percent of the officer corps. In 1915 these officers and the social wing's employees ran 25,755 shelters and hotels, 259 homes for inebriates, 2,133 children's homes, 3,457 rescue homes for "fallen women," and 590 maternity homes. The total capacity of the "industrial institutions" was 6,527.

Lamb then turned to his emigration work, beginning with the Hadleigh Land and Industrial Colony, where he claimed that the Army served "six to eight hundred men, women, and

children, who were the byproducts of our modern civilization."
The men had "got into trouble and gone astray." The idea for
Hadleigh was that "by work and a good influence they can be
helped to regain their place in society." Some emigrated to
change their conditions. William Booth had said that there were
"two classes of outcasts:" 1) "the man who became an outcast
through the force of circumstance, in which case a change of condition is of no use, and you must then bring some external influence to bear upon him;" and 2) "victims of circumstances,
[who] if their circumstances where changed, then they would
become useful members."

It was up to the Army's social officers and employees to determine which men were essentially good, but needed a change
of circumstances. Lamb had begun his work at the social headquarters with only an office boy. In 1915 he had a staff of 19 men
and women, who had sent out 10,000 men, women, and children
to the Empire, mostly to Canada in 1914. Chancellor of the Exchequer Lloyd George had told Parliament that as many as a
million British workers received disgracefully low wages. Lamb
proposed that Britain take that million or so with their children
and "submit them to wholesale emigration." The result would
be better conditions for those who are left. But this required a
centralized management, including insurance that guarantees
against unemployment, sickness, and loss of luggage. The Army
issued this insurance for 10 shillings. If the man did not find
work, the Army brought him home and refunded his 10
shillings. The Army had made a profit of £200 on emigrant insurance in 1924. As a Scotsman Lamb claimed that someone told
him that the "Scotch" preferred to keep their 10 shillings and accept the Army's guarantee.

Lamb then described the process that the Army's social and
corps officers followed in getting emigrants from their British
homes to their destinations in the dominions of the Empire. At
each step, from British train stations and ports to on–board labor
bureaus to disembarkation and the final rail passage in the dominions, The Salvation Army protected its émigrés. Lamb discussed the "excess of women over men" in Britain—including
"40,000 widows" with 138,000 dependent children receiving
"outdoor relief of 2 shillings 6 pence and a loaf, and 1 shilling

and a loaf for each child. Lamb had discussed the problem with Poor Law guardians and found that they regarded the widows as "most dreadful people," who "wanted to desert their children." Lamb had sent 300 widows with about 300 children to the dominions in 1914. He had suggested that the widow would take one child, while the Army took care of the other children. Once settled with a job and place to live she would ask the Army to send the other children.[3]

David C. Lamb on the Reform of Drunkards

As David Lamb and William and Bramwell Booth saw it, much of the problem behind unemployment and other social ills such as broken marriages and families was the consumption of alcohol. As an evangelical church The Salvation Army asked every officer and soldier to pledge not to drink any alcoholic beverage—total abstinence. This demand came from William Booth's wife Catherine, whose father was at one time a Wesleyan lay minister, but who became a binge drinker who frequently abandoned his family to indulge his habit. Catherine convinced William that a glass of port, apparently a favorite drink of Methodist ministers, had no medicinal value. Furthermore, she could not marry a man who was not a total abstainer. For himself, Lamb declared that he had never imbibed or smoked. But in his social ministry he had seen the devilish effects of alcohol.

In 1917 Lamb wrote an essay on "The Reform of Drunkards," for the *Herald of the Star,* which he introduced with a hope: "The best that we can hope for from the tremendous trouble in which the world is seething is that, with the return to peace, the nations will have awakened to a truer conception of life and life's responsibility." This was the hope of a father who had lost his second son in World War I. As a result of that war he saw "signs of quickening to a larger sanity." In particular he saw forces causing "the Russian to give up his vodka, the Frenchman his absinthe," while Canada and Australia were moving towards becoming "dry" countries. England's temperance reform to achieve greater national efficiency by shortening the hours of sale and other restrictions, had led to a decrease in drunkenness and crime.

Lamb argued that "every inebriate is either a potential criminal, a burden upon public funds, a danger to himself and others, or a cause of distress, scandal, or nuisance to his family and to those with whom he associates." And by his precept and example he was "reproducing his like to the detriment of national welfare in years to come." For this conclusion he cited an unnamed "eminent authority." But Lamb was certain that a man or woman "who has fallen to the lowest depths through the drink curse, may be lifted out of his wretchedness" to become "a responsible citizen" and better yet, he could be "rehabilitated in his own esteem."

To achieve this rehabilitation and soul cleansing Lamb recommended the treatment program at Hadleigh Colony. Hadleigh was not merely "a sort of glorified inebriates' home." It was "a commune of prodigals," where under a "benevolent autocracy," sinners "worked out their salvation while they tilled the fields, and tended the herds and flocks." He described Hadleigh as an "agricultural community" of 550 colonists housed in 12 buildings and 20 cottages for married couples. He estimated that two–thirds of the colonists "owed their ruin directly or indirectly to their indulgence in strong drink. During the war Hadleigh had welcomed several hundred Belgian refugees and even provided them with a Roman Catholic chapel.

Hadleigh had three "cardinal aims:" 1) "to eradicate from these poor fellows the fatal craving for stimulants;" 2) "to instill willpower and energy into their invertebrate make–up;" 3) "to transform them into beings capable of fulfilling the functions of honest citizenship—in fine, to make new men of this vagrant legion of society's rejected." As Lamb put it:

> To one fossicking for treasure on the scrap–heap of civilization, the ravages of the drink traffic appear in all their appalling significance. Misery, naked and unashamed and noisome, meets him at every turn—the starving wastrel, the fallen and degraded woman, and the ragged and famished children—almost all, except the children, apparently beyond the hope of reclamation.

When a colonist entered the colony, quite likely he had once been "in a good position." But "shame had driven him from his native place." He "ceased to count as a human entity." He once had "a secret spark of optimism that can only be extinguished with life itself—the Wilkins Micawber feeling that something better will turn up; but God alone knows when." When he could no longer find money for a lodging house, he put up at "the 'spike,' as the casual ward of the workhouse is known to the fraternity." There he is given a small cell and a half ton of granite rocks. He receives a pound of bread three times a day and as much water as he can drink. "If he is sent to jail, he discovers that prison is heaven compared with the casual ward" of the workhouse. Then "Providence intervenes" and he is picked up by The Salvation Army. He is grateful to God for a square meal, clean clothing, and a comfortable bed. "And there his regeneration begins if he has any moral stamina left."

The Army achieved its "cardinal aims" by what might be termed "tough love." Lamb, ever the disciple of William Booth, notes that the founder "was not given to namby–pamby methods." For a minimum amount of labor the person received "the regulation allowance of food, which is generous." Failure to do the allotted work led to an inquiry. If laxity continued rations were curtailed. There was monetary reward for work done beyond the established minimum. And it was possible to move up if performance warranted it. A man could go from the lowest grade to the highest grade and even become a superintendent.

Through this regimen Lamb claimed that "the vast majority" were "permanently cured of their disease." By "disease"[4] he may have meant sin, or he could have meant drunkenness. For Lamb there was no particular difference between the root cause and the behavior. Men who wanted to avoid going back to their old environment might choose life in overseas dominions. But this was only done for men who had "proved their worthiness." Religion played a role in this change. Lamb quoted William Booth as saying: "once the man was right in himself he would seek a new environment." In that new place, Lamb argued, "the ex–tramp may work his way back to decent livelihood, freed from his evil propensities." He allowed that the "hallowing influence of a good woman is inestimable," as he sheds his "armour of callousness."[5]

This in a nutshell was David Lamb's social creed with its desire to see Christian regeneration, humanitarian hope, and military strictness.

David Lamb's Migration Program Plans
for the Post World War I Era, 1917–1918

By the time The Salvation Army published its 1917 and 1918 *Year Books*, David Lamb was looking forward to the end of the "Great War," which was still more than a year away. Still, Lamb was anticipating his migration program's post–war problems before American forces arrived in Europe to join the warriors from the dominions of the British Empire. The 1917 and 1918 *Year Book* essays on migration were likely written by, and certainly approved by Commissioner Lamb, although as usual no credit was given for authorship. First, the author made the claim that the Army's program was "the largest emigration organization in the Empire," although its functions were "greatly curtailed" during the war. In the interim it was "adjusting its machinery" to take advantage of opportunities in the post–war reconstruction process.

General Bramwell Booth, in an interview with *Lloyd's Weekly News*, stated that: "Very probably the new aspirations of our soldiers will find their fullest expression in a big migration to the Overseas Dominions." He surmised that the soldiers' expanded outlook on the world and their "newly acquired physical needs," would make a sedentary life distasteful. These needs would require The Salvation Army to find work for them overseas and to be prepared to transport them to wherever the Army could find places in the Empire. Their wives and children would be sent out as soon as the men were settled. All of this should be a "war charge," paid by the state.

To charge the expense to the British government was a normal expectation at the end of the war. How could European governments spend so much money on shedding blood and not be willing to spend at least that amount on the social needs—the health and welfare—of their people. Thus the post–war era spread socialist thinking across Europe, and led the electorate to vote into office the first Labour government in Britain in 1929.

The Salvation Army had for years worked with dominion governments receiving immigrants. Now Canada, Australia, and New Zealand were preparing to settle soldiers of the Empire and were looking to the Army for assistance. In July 1917, Earl

Grey, former Governor General for Canada, addressed a conference of the British and Dominion Parliaments at the House of Commons with this testimonial:

> *My experience leads me to believe that you would be acting wisely in your own interests by making much use of the organization of the Salvation Army. I have seen a great deal of their work in Canada, at home here, and in Australia, and wherever I have examined their work I have found it to be quite first–rate. They have machinery ... here and overseas, and they have 4,000 commissioned officers overseas, and thousands of helpers under them. They have placed 90,000 people in the dominions in the last twelve years, and they have only 1 percent failure.*

How did Earl Grey know so much about the Army? He was chairman of the empire land settlement committee of the Royal Colonial Institute, of which Commissioner Lamb was a member.

The 1917 *Year Book* article claimed that The Salvation Army had successfully placed widows and orphans overseas in 1916 through its "widows' counselors' scheme" for war widows and others. The Army accepted responsibility for the welfare of each widow for four years. It was also settling orphaned and neglected children in "younger nations under the British flag." These children came from the 150,000 British children who depended on Poor Law guardians and 100,000 in the care of charities, who were "spoiling physically, mentally, and morally in an atmosphere of vice and squalor." This was a "wanton waste of the Empire's most valuable raw material ... when the everlasting cry of the dominions is for more people!" The Army had placed "hundreds of them" in its children's homes in Canada and Australia, where the "bairns" (surely a Scottish author) had "kindly and sympathetic training" until they located proper foster parents. The children were periodically visited and reports made. The cost of obtaining overseas connections was £10.

For certain classes of emigrants "assisted passages" were available: wives and children of settlers who had established themselves; widows and single women who were willing to do domestic work; young agricultural workers; boys in "blind–alley" occupations; and children in unwholesome surroundings. The Salvation Army claimed that its emigration department

had pioneered the "personally conducted party system." It had
agents and representatives and correspondents in "all parts of
the world."[6]

A 1918 *Year Book* article followed up on "After the War Migration" plans for "beneficent reconstruction." The author gave
total credit to the general for his visionary planning. British
Colonial Secretary Walter Long had appointed a committee and
named David Lamb as a member. Other members represented
the dominions and their provinces or states, and members of the
British government, to be chaired by Lord Tennyson. The committee report echoed "The Salvation Army's system of Migration" and followed William Booth's recommendation of a central
emigration authority. In Canada, the Army's Resident Secretary
for Immigration, Colonel Jacobs, would work on a plan from his
Montreal headquarters. Lt. Colonel Charles Taylor had visited
South Africa in 1917 to locate areas suitable for British settlers,
and Major Tudge, Western Canada's migration supervisor, had
visited Australia and New Zealand on a similar mission. They
sent their reports to Commissioner Lamb. The Army's military
huts in France were circulating literature to determine settlers'
needs and the customs of several dominions. They were also registering the names and qualifications of men wishing to go overseas after the war ended.[7]

Minnie Lamb's Personal Social Philosophy and Work

Despite David Lamb's warning against The Salvation Army
becoming too enmeshed in government affiliation, he and his wife
were extremely active in local government affairs in their home
county of Essex and their home town of Southend. During this
busy period in her husband's life from 1903 on, and despite having
five children to raise, Minnie Lamb, J.P.[8], was involved in personal
and governmental as well as Salvation Army social activities. She
had done social work since they moved to London in 1888, and
then on the Army's farm colony at Hadleigh, Essex after 1898.

In 1907 she had opened a privately funded day nursery for
working mothers at 369 Leigh Road, near their home at Southend.
The newspaper announcement of the new home pointed out that
"Col. and Mrs. Lamb have no official [Salvation Army] respon-

sibilities in the neighborhood." But they kept a personal social service calendar, separate from their Army assignments, until 1939, the year Minnie Lamb died.

By 1911 Minnie Lamb's home, known as "Lamb's House," had become a place of refuge and counsel for persons in need. She also began to work with the "Rochford Hundred" in Poor Law administration. In this government program she served for 24 years as an elected Poor Law guardian, a position to which David was also elected. During this period she was also a probation officer for Southend, and she served as a Salvation Army representative in the local court of petty sessions. She was one of the first women justices of the peace, serving at the police court at Rochford, Southend, and she was a member of the board of governors of Lock Hospital in London.

Minnie Lamb opened Millfield Children's Home in Southend, near their home. As the president of a committee of eight local women, she raised £1,000 to find more suitable premises for her children's home. The fundraising brochure promised that the home would ultimately be taken over by Mrs. [Florence] Bramwell Booth of The Salvation Army. But for now donations were to be sent to Mrs. Lamb at 6 Ramuz Drive, Westcliff, Southend.[9] In 1912 she appeared in a photo with Millfield children that the Salvation Army was sending to Canada under the auspices of David Lamb's emigration program.

Generally speaking, a Salvation Army officer's wife who held her husband's rank, was assigned a lesser office and a smaller allowance until the 1960s. But Mrs. Commissioner Lamb found her own work and gained her own reputation, as had other Army women who bucked the tide of bureaucratic regulation and gender discrimination.[10] Like William Booth's wife Catherine, Minnie Lamb began her mainly "outside" work while bearing six children between 1889 and 1899. Of the six, two became Salvation Army officers, Catherine and Marguerite. David died of heart failure at age nineteen. Janet and Alexander (Alec), who died in World War I, found other work. Minnie Lamb also assisted in her husband's work and joined him on a world tour in 1925 that ended on Empire Day 1926.[11] The tour took them to the United States, Canada, New Zealand, Australia, and South Africa to reconnoiter the Army's international social programs.

A New Outlook for Unwanted Children
and Widows with Families in the 1920s:
The Empire Settlement Act of 1922

In March 1923 David Lamb wrote an essay on "A New Outlook for Unwanted Children and Widows with Families." He saw the Empire Settlement Act of 1922 as more than a significant change in Britain's relations with its overseas dominions. Its provisions would also "prove to be of vital importance to tens of thousands of fatherless youngsters." Those who were "unwanted" in Britain's crowded districts would find opportunities "in other parts of our vast British Empire." The hopelessness of widows was "perhaps the most tragic and pathetic feature our existing social system has met with in the British Isles."

First, the 1922 act empowered the secretary of state to pay 50 percent of the cost of any scheme that he approved. This, as Lamb saw it, would lift the heavy cost of resettling widows and their children. Second, Lamb saw this new source of funding as covering the gap that had existed in that local boards of guardians did not have the means or power to maintain children overseas, and there was a considerable financial commitment needed. Voluntary organizations that had been offering this service could now look to the overseas settlement department of the Colonial office for grants to maintain and transport children and widows with families.

Lamb commended the Canadian government for inspections and after–care of widows and children, and wished that Poor Law children in England "were as well looked after as the youngsters sent overseas, where they have such great opportunities. The preferred method in most cases in Canada was adoption. For that reason the Army advocated early transplantation, at about 7 years of age. From 10 to 14 was more of a problem for adoptions, "although not prohibitive." For boys 14 to 18 the Army had a special program that offered an intensive course at Hadleigh in rough carpentry, shoe–making, personal laundry, digging, planting, milking, and horse–harnessing. Boys would be placed with "selected farmers," and the Army's officers would stand *in loco parentis* until they reached 18.

In the previous two years (1921–22) the Army had sent 412 widows and 692 children overseas. Lamb had found that "the bigger the family, the more easy is the transplanting, since such families had two, three or four workers. For the success of the program he praised his social officers overseas and the "judicious use of cable and telephone systems that assured widows of a warm welcome in the receiving country. The Army was ready to serve any family, not just Poor Law cases, at its Emigration and Colonization Department, Migration House, 3 Upper Thames St., London, EC 4.

Lamb gave two examples of how Poor Law guardians saw their role in emigration. Remember that David and Minnie Lamb were elected members of boards of Poor Law guardians in Southend, Essex. The first case he discussed was of a widow with nine children who were inmates of a Midlands workhouse when the local guardians requested the Army's aid. The Army's plan was to take the family overseas in stages—first, the mother with an infant and two girls of working age. The guardians realized that even if there was no hope of transporting the entire family, they would be ahead financially in caring for the rest of the family. The next year two more children went to join their mother, and the following year the rest of the family. This, Lamb held, was the right way to do it.

As for doing it the wrong way, Lamb gave an example of a widow with nine children who was in desperate straits in 1922. Her husband had been killed in a quarrel with a neighbor. After twelve months in prison the neighbor moved back to the neighborhood, a few doors from where the widow and her family lived. This caused tension for the whole family. The widow's daughter told one of the man's children: "We are hungry in our house, and if it had not been for your father we should have had plenty to eat." And one of her sons threatened one day, when he was older, "to get it on him." The widow pleaded with the Army to get her overseas "right away," "anywhere." She was receiving 35 shillings a week in outdoor relief. Lamb thought the Guardians would cooperate to help such a distressed family, particularly since it could be done at a great savings to the taxpayers. They declined, even when the Army offered to pay half of the costs. Later they agreed to take care of three children, ages

5, 7, and 9, if the Army would agree to send them to their mother in a year. The Army agreed to the deal.

Lamb concluded the article with a description of the migration work in New Zealand and Australia. In New Zealand the Army had a "fine farm school with up–to–date equipment" for receiving and maintaining children. Australia also had "ample provision" for the "care and oversight of all children sent out under our auspices." All of the children were linked to a Sunday School and church, and agreements with foster parents or employers called for the child's spiritual life to be cared for. The Army's inspectors looked for spiritual as well as material progress on their visits. The Army aimed to place the children in "such surroundings that they will truly feel that 'goodness and mercy had followed them'—and deepen in the hearts the desire that they may 'dwell in the House of the Lord for ever.'"

Commissioner Lamb's statement in 1923 was critical to an understanding of the government investigations of child placement and care several decades later when the children, who had become adults, recalled the trauma of their transplantation. Many of them accused voluntary associations of lacking oversight and record keeping of adoption records and of the children's natural parents, their place of birth, siblings—in other words, their roots.[12]

The 1923 *Salvation Army Year Book* article on migration would underline Lamb's emphasis on families and on Australia and New Zealand. That *Year Book* stated that the migration department at 8 Upper Thames Street was under new leadership. Commissioner Lamb had moved from day to day management of the department to oversight of all of the Army's international social services. Commissioner Henry Bullard was the new secretary for immigration under Lamb's supervision. Otherwise the goal remained the same: "to relieve the Mother Country of her surplus population" and "develop the natural resources of the King's Overseas Dominions." As William Booth had put it: "transfer from a land of poverty to a land of plenty." In the Army's canon: "Of all the schemes yet propounded for the immediate and permanent relief of distress arising from unemployment, *emigration still holds the field.*"

The *Year Book* claimed that the Empire Settlement Act of 1922 was "as important as Magna Carta." Since Lamb was a member of the committee that drew up the act, it is possible he was writing the annual report and touting his achievement.

Australia would, according to Viscount Northcliffe's statement in *The Times*, "become the most promising home for those British men of brawn who wish to seek a career overseas," as world trade improved. Already, working men there were "better off in almost every respect than any I have encountered in any other part of the world." He predicted that by 1925 Australia would be accepting 100,000 immigrants a year.

Lamb had written in the *Telegraph* in March 1922, that: "All are now agreed that within certain reasonable restrictions, inter–imperial migration on a large scale will be good both for the homeland and the Empire, in order—1) To relieve the present surplus population and unemployment; 2) To populate and develop the dominions; 3) To solidify and strengthen the whole British Empire." He held that emigration is "badly needed on both sides ... for the necessary re–distribution of the population [due to] our present war–depressed conditions."[13]

In 1924 the *Year Book* reflected Lamb's frustration with the scope of the Army's international work. There were terrible economic conditions in Europe and the near East, and in "poor, persecuted, downtrodden Armenia," but there was little the Army could do outside the British Empire. In 1923 General Bramwell Booth had agreed with the secretary of state for the dominions to provide "the greatest assistance" in carrying out the Empire Settlement Act of 1922. The Army would work with five "special classes:" 1) single young women; 2) widows with families; 3) youths between 14 and 18 years of age; 4) orphans and "unwanted" children; and 5) men, women, and children of the poorer classes.

Since 1916, the Army had transported 1,769 widows and 1,019 fatherless children. When plans for a recent sailing had gone amuck, Lamb was "humiliated" by the late arrival of 20 widows with their families on Christmas Eve in Melbourne. But the report from Australia encouraged him that overseas officers had remedied the situation. Within two weeks some of the widows were earning £2 a week with board and lodging that included keeping of one child. Another widow's children had found work, and a war widow who had been in Melbourne three months had an income of £9 a week at three jobs.[14]

David C. Lamb on Juvenile Migration
and Settlement, 1924

In July 1924 Lamb wrote an essay on juvenile migration for the *Edinburgh Review*. The article is important in light of the post–World War II epidemic of outrage by children and youths who were transported in the 1920s to British colonies. The Salvation Army was one of several volunteer organizations called to testify before a committee of the House of Commons on charges brought by the complainants who could not locate their natural parents or records of their emigration. So what was it that The Salvation Army was doing in the 1920s and how did they assess their methods at the time?

Lamb began his 1924 essay with a response to a May 1924 report to the Overseas Settlement Committee's president from a delegation appointed to inquire into the conditions affecting British settlers in Australia, in particular "boy settlers." Lamb noted that the Army's migration work in Australia was not nearly as extensive as that in Canada. He was disappointed that the delegation had not heard of the Army training farms in Essex, or "hundreds of centers and thousands of workers in Australia cooperating and ready to cooperate further in this work." He complained of government ignorance of the Army's work and added that "no government official in this country has yet been able to see The Salvation Army except as one of the many philanthropic societies whose 'sphere of activity in this country at any rate lies chiefly amongst classes which are not the most likely to prove successful overseas.'" He quoted the report of Mr. Lunn, chairman of the Overseas Settlement Committee, on the work of volunteer migration societies. From April 1, 1923 to March 31, 1924, The Salvation Army had transferred "more migrants than all the other voluntary societies put together." The total numbers were 2,529 for The Salvation Army, and 2,216 for all other societies. Had they forgotten Earl Grey's comments in 1912 in response to a charge that the Salvation Army was "purely and simply a commercial undertaking?"

Lamb claimed that at this point the Army had taken 150,000 men, women, and children from the British Isles with only a 1 percent failure rate. And that this was a far better way to curb population growth than was used in the past: "infanticide; famine; and pestilence." The present problem was "the absorbing power of the receiving country, and not the social or economic pressure of the emigrating country ..." Migration plans must transfer "city–born young people to farms and villages overseas," as difficult as it was to reverse the country to city flow. Success depends on working for the good of the individual, the emigrating country, and the receiving country.

As for the "boy problem," Lamb held that it was "constantly changing." After World War I returning soldiers filled boys' places in the work force. Now, with increased trade, boys were again moving into industrial jobs. Boys and their families were more interested in their capacity to earn money than they were in extending their schooling.

Lamb saw the "dole" as a demoralizing system, a "cancer" on the breast of the nation that must be surgically removed. He did not see public welfare as a proper replacement for unemployment. And the "fuller life and earlier independence" that boys and their families craved could be best supplied in the dominions. Lamb believed migration was the easiest solution because the boys want to go, and they were wanted overseas.

For this reason Lamb would turn the Army's farms in Essex over to the preparation of boys for migration, and cease its work with "derelicts." Representatives of the board of agriculture and the treasury had visited Hadleigh and immediately recognized it "as an ideal place for the short course of intensive training." Soon after that visit the secretary of state for the colonies signed an agreement with General Bramwell Booth.

Hadleigh had all of the facilities needed for an eight to twelve week training course. Besides farming experiences the boys attended hygiene classes, lectures on thrift, character building, health care, kindness to animals and courtesy. Practical work included: cooking, laundry, shoe repair, rough carpentry, feeding, harnessing and driving horses, market gardening, milking and dairy work, care of livestock, trench digging, and draining. There were lessons in simple surveying and engineering, measuring rainfall, reservoir and cesspool construction, care and repair of implements, and seasonal work of plowing, sowing, pruning, and harvesting.

In all, Canadians and Australians preferred "a British immigrant to those of other nationalities." There was no need for training centers in the colonies since "every boy can be placed with a selected farmer immediately on his landing overseas." For those who want "a more scientific study of their calling," there were winter courses at government–run agricultural colleges overseas. The Army's job was to find "suitable homes in selected districts."

The Salvation Army's agreement with the British government was that a dominion government immigration authority "approved the boys before training commences and has undertaken to accept them on completion of a satisfactory course of training, provided The Salvation Army may provisionally accept boys for training without such prior approval, on the understanding that no charge will fall on the overseas settlement department in respect of such boys if they are not accepted for overseas after training."

But before the Army accepted a boy for training at Hadleigh, he was seen by an officer who inquired into his "antecedents." The boy needed a doctor's certificate and had to give assurance that if he was accepted, after training he would go to an overseas dominion. For Australia the boys had to be 16 years of age, 5' 4" tall, and weigh 8–9 stone. Boys with eyeglasses were not accepted. Canada had no rule concerning height and weight, but was careful in making a selection.

In the previous 18 months, The Salvation Army had sent 1,000 boys with an average age of 16 years, 2 months. Half were from large cities and half from small towns and villages. Seventy percent said that they belonged to the Church of England; 25 percent were Presbyterian and Nonconformist; 5 percent were Salvationists, Roman Catholics, and Hebrews, etc. The boys would be under the guardianship of Salvation Army officers in the dominions until they were 18, or 21 in some cases. The care given was not "coddling," but "guidance," and "the helping hand of a friend when they are in difficulties or suffering from home sickness." "After–care" included receiving, placing, replacing, supervising, and if necessary, repatriating the settler.

In case of illness, there were no Poor Law infirmaries in the dominions, and public hospitals required payment from the patient or on his behalf. After long negotiations the British government agreed to pay 50 percent of certain after–care expenses, but the Army would pay for repatriation. The British government would not pay for funerals, marriage expenses, and "home plenishments." They did agree to "reasonable charges" for health care.

As for finding "suitable positions," this required a "commonsense method" in dealing with many contingencies. "Misfits" had to be "adjusted." The general principle was: sickness, discouragement, accidents, even death would be treated by the Army with "the same attention" that the Army would give "to a Salvation Army officer on foreign service." "The boy is cared for; everything possible is done to save the life; the headquarters is kept advised by cable; the boy's friends communicated with, and if the worst happens, the Army undertakes all the necessary arrangements."

The Salvation Army had opened four new centers in Canada, each staffed by a married couple who devoted their time exclusively to after–care. Lamb had visited Canada to examine the situations of 300 boys sent out before June 1923. All but five were working on farms. One of the five was "quite a failure." Two were too sick to remain in Canada. The other two were homesick and "made themselves a nuisance." Lamb had received "numerous interesting letters" attesting to the success of the "boys immigration" program. A government inquiry had found that the only limitation was financial. One province had 1,000 applications for 75 boys; another had 500 requests for 100 boys; while in Britain there were 500 applications a month for training and re-settlement in the dominions.

David Lamb estimated the total cost for each boy at £48. It included: selection; outfit; training; transportation; and after–care. This depended somewhat on the district from which the boy came and where he was placed overseas. After payments from each boy and from the government The Salvation Army paid £10 per boy on average. Lamb noticed that the first hundred boys paid £7, but that the amount fell over time until "the last 100 averaged less than £3 per boy." At the time of his writing, Lamb reported that "none of the Overseas Dominions have so far been induced to contribute anything towards the cost of the training."

Under General Booth's "self–help" and "help–others" principles, each boy contributed to the cost of transportation, and when he was settled he repaid a flat rate in Australia. But transportation to the West Coast of Canada made a flat rate impossible in the dominion. So Canada was divided into four sections, with a fixed amount for each zone. A two–year limit was set for completing the payment. If the Oversea Settlement Department made loans to boys, the Army acted as the collection agency. If the percentage of repayments fell below 70 percent, the secretary of state would evaluate the plan. Lamb found that loan repayments by women, at 90 percent, exceeded those by other settlers.

Lamb asked: "What are our statesmen and politicians going to do about this matter?" He found quotations indicating some awareness by Labour, Liberal, and Conservative leaders that they were aware of the unemployment and population surplus problems. In "the past three years more than a million workers have been unable to obtain employment." And the "re–distribution of the population of the Empire is not primarily a political, economic, or even an imperial issue, but a human business operation."

In support of this idea, Bramwell Booth had written to the *Times* to call attention to the unsatisfactory results of the Empire Settlement Act of 1910. In asking for "British business methods" he proposed that "a commission of business men looked at the administration of the act," particularly "the inadequacy of its financial provisions." As for British boys, "Idleness is the most demoralizing influence that can enter into the human life. If not rescued they soon begin to injure the communities which support them, for it is the idle dog which worries the sheep."

In summary, Lamb restated his two–decade long plea. Population in the British Isles was growing faster than its ability to provide employment. And there were "unpopulated parts of the Empire" that "will have to look elsewhere for the population they need" if Britain does not support them with immigrants. Sir Henry Fairfax–Lucy had suggested that an organization such as The Salvation Army be given a block grant out of the unexpended money voted by Parliament.

This led to the Empire Settlement Act of May 1922. The measure proposed spending £3 million per annum for 15 years "for the better distribution of the people of the Empire." But the results were disappointing. Of the four and a half million pounds available between May 1922 and the end of March 1924, only £452,000 was spent to assist 55,000 people resettling. Lamb compared this to the 250,000 who emigrated each year in the pre–war period.[15]

6

David & Minnie Lamb's Eight–Month Tour of North America, Australia, New Zealand, and South Africa in 1925–1926

I n their only overseas tour together, David Lamb, as the international social secretary, and Minnie Lamb, J.P., spent eight months in the United States and Canada in 1925–26. They left London on September 12, 1925 and boarded a ship at Southampton for New York. They spent a day in New York and Brooklyn, separate cities at the time. The focus was to visit Salvation Army social institutions in Eastern and Western Canada, the United States, New Zealand, Australia, South Africa and Southern Rhodesia. They traveled more than 52,000 miles and seldom stayed in the same place four nights. At one point they spent ten nights on trains, while occupying their days with meetings, interviews, and inquiries. They returned to England on Empire Day, May 24, 1926.

At the end, in a lecture to Fellows and friends of the Royal Colonial Institute and in published recollections of the tour, Lamb gave this judgment of the British Empire: "I have seen nothing better, and with all its faults, I love it still." He was not optimistic about the current situation, but for the future there was hope if the Empire developed "a strenuous, continuous, and elastic migration policy on the lines agreed definitely between ourselves and the dominions, or forfeit what we have so hardly won."[1] David and Minnie offered their impressions of the dominions and the United States in writing.

New York and the United States

The United States was an awkward colony in The Salvation Army's Christian imperium as a former British colony. Its difficult relations with the Army's London headquarters had always been tenuous. Americans preferred a federal association rather than centralized rule from outside. This had led to Thomas E. Moore's schism in 1884. William Booth sent Frank Smith to heal the split as commander in North America. In 1896 the Booths' second son, Ballington, who had replaced Smith, "left the work" and founded the Volunteers of America. The Booth–Tuckers took over. By the mid–1920s Evangeline Booth, as the Army's U.S. commander, was having difficulty with what she saw as over-reaching control by her brother Bramwell. David Lamb's only notes on America concerned his visits to New York City and Washington.

Their first crowded day after docking in New York was a Sunday. They began with prayers and a counseling session with "officers and girls" of the Booth Memorial Home and Hospital on 15th Street. Residents of what had been rescue homes had gradually changed as the clients had moved from "fallen women" to "unwed mothers." Before the Army closed the maternity hospitals in the 1970s, the phrase had become "single parents;" women bore their pregnancies openly and needed no period of seclusion. Leaders of the women's social department: Colonel Mrs. Bovill; Lt. Colonel Clara Van Der Schouw; and Commandant Ella Bergner accompanied the Lambs.

The next stop was the Brooklyn men's social service center, part of what had been called the "city colony" in the Darkest England plan. The chapel was full of men. Commissioner Lamb, according to *The War Cry*, represented the men's problem "in an enlightening way, pointing out the sin that had brought them to grief in the majority of cases and the great eternal remedy that was free for the poorest and all–powerful for even the weakest of men." Mrs. Lamb told the men to "go out into the world to fill your place in it as men. The world needs you and the work you can do. And with God's help, each one of you, even the worst ... can make the world better for [your] having passed through it.'"

The Lamb's next stop was the Brooklyn #1 Corps for a Sunday morning holiness meeting, which had already begun. Commissioner Lamb took charge and for more than an hour the crowd "sat at the feet of these Army leaders." He spoke of his boyhood and conversion and reminisced after hearing them sing, "We'll roll the old chariot along, and we won't drag on behind," a song Scottish Salvationists had sung in Aberdeen after he gave his first testimony.

Mrs. Lamb recalled her father's piety and influence on her early life and asked the Brooklyn soldiers to be true to "the highest and best to which the hearts of men have ever aspired, but you don't want people to salute your uniform only—you want them to salute you—because they believe in you." She told them that they had come to the meeting "to partake of the Bread of Life, which was the truest sacrament" and led them in singing, "Holy, Holy, Holy!"

The next stop, before they went to the Bowery, was for prayer with officers of the Brooklyn Nursery and Children's Hospital (Superintendent Lt. Colonel Mrs. Hamon). At the Bowery Memorial Hotel that evening, jammed with "denizens of New York's notorious waste," according to a reporter, the Holy Spirit wooed them "from the maelstrom of sin and vice and debauchery and encouraged them to grasp the lifeline of salvation held out to them." Major Wood led the "preliminaries" and Colonel Mrs. Bovill prayed before the men gave the visitors a royal welcome.

The War Cry reported: Mrs. Lamb "hit these men right where they stood." She walked into the congregation and stood on a chair and "uncompromisingly exposed the sin that had brought the men before her to the unspeakable condition in which they now found themselves, and then held out unqualified mercy and salvation to the uttermost for all who would come." She "denounced the liquor" that had ruined most of the men and praised God "for the soberness and prosperity which now is so conspicuous in the places where the demon rum wrought such havoc of poverty and drunkenness and misery before he was outlawed and started on the run to banishment from the land." Commander Evangeline Booth had been a staunch supporter of the 18th Amendment that in 1920 prohibited the manufacture and sale of alcoholic beverages. It was a political stand taken by the Army on the side of the Republican–backed constitutional change.

Mrs. Lamb also let it be known that she had opposed the recent war—"the shame of it and uselessness of it—and before she finished tears filled the eyes of the hardest of the men who listened to her impassioned plea for peace, universal peace, through the acceptance of the Christ who came to bring peace and good will to men." She spoke of her son who died in the war, whose grave was marked by a white cross in a French field. She asked, "Why can't men invent means of saving life and blessing instead of scheming ever and inventing machines for destruction?"

Commissioner Lamb invited the men to receive Christ. "There are men here before me this evening who would give anything, even their right hand, if they could blot out some memories; if by some process they could forget some ... despicable sin, and start life again with a clean heart." They want "absolution and freedom from all sin." "God forgets, as well as forgives, and through the Christ of Calvary the past may be forgotten and left behind as we start along the new, bright path of righteousness to the City of Eternal Life." The reporter sensed "hearts burn behind shabby, ragged coats," and "men stripped of all sham and unrealness in the light of eternity." Lamb invited men to come and pray, and the "penitent form was soon lined with heartbroken wanderers from the path of right, and freedom came as shouts of victory ascended to the eager ears of the angels in Heaven.'" Lamb was an evangelist as well as humanitarian.

On their way to the Bowery Hotel the Lambs traveled through congested east side streets. Mrs. Lamb noticed men and women filled the streets to gain a breath of air on a hot summer day, but there was a "total absence of any disorder, especially any evidence of drunkenness and drinking." She was "untiring in her praise of the prohibition regime, which had so successfully brought about such a pleasing and beneficial contrast to the days when this section of New York was a festering sore of debauchery, misery and poverty because of the open saloon."

Other than New York and Washington, Lamb listed American cities they visited without comment. They made brief stops at Star Lake, Montrose, Washington, Baltimore, Pittsburgh, Detroit (where his sister lived), Chicago, St. Paul, Minneapolis, Seattle, Portland, Sacramento, Salt Lake City, Los Angeles, Lytton Springs (site of one of the Army's farm colonies in the 1890s), San Francisco "and other places." There is no reference to seeing Evangeline Booth or other members of the American Army leadership.[2]

Toronto and Canada

David Lamb was well–acquainted with Canada, the gem of his Migration work. The Canadian *War Cry* described the Army's Social Work under the caption, "The Salvation Army in Outline," in its Christmas 1925 edition. Special departments provided "shelter for the homeless and employment for the workless, for reclaiming the criminal and fallen, for assisting suitable people to other lands, finding them employment there, and exercising a wise after–care over them." But, it added, "the means used to alleviate temporal misery have a spiritual end in view; a change of heart, by the grace of God, being regarded by Salvationists as the only foundation of true and permanent upliftment."[3]

Lt. Colonel Tudge of Montreal, Immigration officer for Canada, accompanied the Lambs from New York to Eastern Canada to begin a second phase of their world tour. They visited St. John, Moncton, Halifax, Quebec, Montreal, Ottawa, Hamilton, Dundas, St. Catherine's, London, Woodstock, and Windsor before they arrived in Toronto, site of the Canadian Salvation Army headquarters.

In Toronto a Canadian *War Cry* reporter trailed the outspoken Minnie Lamb to collect her views on Canada. He found her at Woodside Lodge, one of Toronto's immigrant lodging houses, where she was doing what she'd done all her life—"mothering" young women the Army had brought to Canada and placed in situations. At the Langstaff Jail Farm she was impressed by the "absence of officialdom." "The method of dealing with law–breakers in this jail is evidence of the enlightenment which is possessing the minds of our governments in regards to the wisest treatment of 'short term' men and women." Kinder terms, "inmates" and "delinquents," had replaced "prisoner." Exposure to nature helped. She approved of a "grading system" that separated men and boys. It suited her idea of how to deal with first offenders.

She was pleased with Canada's progress in dealing with "the drink evil." Instead of main street corners occupied by public houses there were banks. This was "significant!" In England she had often gone into pubs to threaten that she would call the police if mothers did not take their children home. "So I have felt I have been in a wonderland since being here. Does Canada know that she stands out among the nations of the world because she had had the courage to boldly deal with this evil which saps the life–blood from the nations!" On Yonge Street she was not pleased to see cinemas, which she blamed "for half the crime that takes place." They put the "idea of crime into the imaginative minds of our youth."

These were sentiments of a woman who had been a justice of the peace since 1920. After conducting a trial in England she would go into the jail to "have a word with the poor convicted people and thus at once link them up with the Army's helping hand." "So often we see a lack of compassion on the bench with childish offenders." She felt strongly about everything, but was especially proud of Salvationists who worked in prisons and police courts, as she had done as a probation officer.[4]

In his history of The Salvation Army in Canada, R. G. Moyles gives a detailed look at social services with an eye for praise and criticism. In 1916 a "Widow's Scheme" brought war widows to Canada. G. A. Aylesworth indicated that "the Army had not maintained contact with them," and the government refused to award $100,000 requested by the Army. In 1926, just after the Lambs were leaving Canada, the English boys' program, which had received $45,837 in government aid in 1923–24, ran into trouble. For each boy the Army had received $80 from the Canadian Department of the Interior. But the Army expected each boy to repay the Army from £12 to £20 from his wages. The government saw this docking of wages as illegal. An investigator's report suggested that the Army's grant be reduced from $25,000 to $5,000 per year. The Interior Department had concluded that "the Army's immigration work is not as altruistic as is generally believed and that its present business methods should be completely overhauled."

Moyles concludes that despite its support from some politicians and the Montreal *Daily Star*, "The Army never recovered from the unfavorable publicity." But beyond this flap, Moyles found "criticisms of [the Army's] handling of new settlers were very few and praise of its humanitarian treatment frequent." Its later immigration work focused on: 1) assisting war brides after World War II; 2) providing translators for immigrants; and 3) running reception centers for immigrants. Overall Moyles accepted estimates that the Salvation Army brought 250,000 immigrants to Canada.[5]

Minnie C. Lamb, J.P.: Impressions of their North American Tour

Minnie C. Lamb gave six "impressions" of her tour, starting with the "effect of drink restrictions, because it is the most wonderful thing I saw." Restrictions that benefited the working classes included: prohibition in the United States; state control of intoxicating drinks; and limiting drinking hours in public houses. She was impressed by provisions for "water–drinking" in North America, whereas "Adam's wine" had to be requested on "other continents." Second, she liked the "hospitality of the people" and a "simplicity" that did not lack "excitement and romance." Americans were "energetic, confident, determined, ambitious, and hard–working." She corrected a guide in the capitol building in Washington on a point of British Naval history, and had a strange physical reaction to "the intensity which seemed to mark everything" and "made my wrists ache."

Third, on prisons and the treatment of offenders, a particular interest as a justice of the peace, she held that "Britain has little to learn from overseas." But she would make fuller use of probation for offenders at home," and give the Salvation Army facilities to visit prisoners and hold meetings; and make sure that "every offender has a fighting chance when he leaves prison." She was impressed by U.S. and Canadian farm prisons. Young inmates were "on their honour," and there were few walls and fences. She was not pleased with the lack of decorum in American court rooms. But as a J.P and Salvation Army officer, judges invited her to "sit on the bench" in every city. She did not like mixing young offenders and "old hands," and inadequate accommodation in some districts. Invariably she spoke with prisoners, wardens, doctors, nurses, and governors.

Fourth, on Salvation Army social activities, she found the equipment was splendid, particularly for hospitals and children's homes, especially in "growing communities in the British Empire where we have a freedom, unhampered by privilege and prejudice, and stand on our merits." She was pleased by the prison visitation and prisoners' aid system in the United States. Fifth, children of the Empire of European working class background were "happier, freer, better fed, and perhaps more alert than those at home." Was it due to longer periods of sunshine or "more easy general conditions of life for the parents?" When she compared children in the poorest parts overseas with the poorest districts of Britain the contrast appeared to be even greater. Sixth, on women, she objected to her husband's reference to Britain's numerical excess of women over men as "tragic," but she had noticed that overseas "women enjoyed themselves in their wide freedom ... and their quick response to their new environment."[6] Arnold J. Toynbee was correct in advising: "the first thing any student of human affairs should do is travel." For Minnie Lamb North America, Australia, and Southern Africa were a "distant mirror" that reflected on conditions in her homeland.

David C. Lamb's Impressions of the Tour

David referred to Minnie and himself as "Apostles of Empire," and so they were. They took the tour at Bramwell Booth's request, but Lamb spoke on "my own responsibility of those things that I have seen and heard." He informed the fellows of the Royal Colonial Institute that to date the Army had sent 160,000 emigrants overseas, of whom less than 15 percent were Salvationists. He saw two "evils" that would respond to a single cure for Britain. First, "we are slow to take up and develop our great inheritance overseas," and second, "we are overcrowded at home." In the dominions there was under–population and under–production; at home there was over–population and under–production. This was an economic problem, but Lamb asked the Royal Colonial Institute to see it as a moral problem as well. British young people had no "land sense." This must be rekindled by agricultural training to prepare them for emigration to the British colonies.

On the economic side, in the Empire Settlement Act of 1922 the British government had committed itself to spending £3 million in one financial year on new emigration. Since the World War I Armistice in November 1919, public "relief for able–bodied men and women" had cost the government at least £500 million because of the dole. For six years Britain had registered a steady one million unemployed. While it should have spent £10 million on Empire resettlement by 1926 under the 1922 Act, it had spent less than £2 million. Population was growing by 1,000 a day. A conservative estimate for the amount of emigration that would need to occur to stabilize the population was 250,000 a year. But in the last four years Britain had sent 432,899, less than half of what was called for. In 1925 only 85,398 emigrants went to the dominions.

Lamb called these economic figures demoralizing. To put £500 million into the dole (welfare costs), "a negative and demoralizing enterprise," and at the same time put a pittance into a "moralizing enterprise" of emigration that would energize the Empire, "is morally wrong" and "economically wrong." Lamb's favorite mantra at this time was: "What is morally wrong cannot be economically sound." As he saw it, it was Britain's duty to "keep our people in, and for, our Empire, and to keep our Empire for them."

The American 1924 National Origins Act had dammed the flow of Europeans and others to the United States. In pre–war years the flow had been a million European immigrants a year to America. From 1853 to 1888, 6 million of the 8.7 million emigrants from the United Kingdom had gone to the States. Lamb estimated that the number of descendants of those English, Scotch, Irish, and Welsh migrants in 1926 numbered about 30 million U.S. citizens. Between 1847 and 1850 multitudes of Irish who could have gone to British Colonies went to the United

States to develop American resources, and "to nourish revenge-ful thoughts on the cruel elder sister who drove them into the wilderness." If America reopened its doors again, Lamb judged that there would be another exodus from Europe, including Britain. He asked: "Is a politic act the worse for being a generous one?" In his judgment what was good for Britain was good for the dominions.

He argued that the British still nourished "the spirit of indi-vidual enterprise." He gave individual examples of enterprising immigrants that he met on the tour. He argued that the £3 million the government had committed itself to spend on emigration was "a fraction of the unproductive coal subsidy," and "a fraction of what has been spent in relief." The Empire Settlement Act had provided for a system of "half shares with the dominions." Un-like doles that "do not produce dividends," a "generous scheme of migration and settlement, free of false sentiment," would ben-efit individuals, help Britain, and improve the dominions.

Lamb found that Canada supported "an aggressive and ac-tive immigration policy." But he was aware of negative voices. There was a belief that "every fresh immigrant is a competitor for an existing job." But he saw this as a treatable malady. The "old bogey" of absorption of immigrants by the United States had passed. A plan to put 3,000 British families on abandoned or semi–developed farms had been met in three years. But the British increase in Canada was much less than the non–British increase.

Before their trip to Toronto the Lambs had visited cities in the East (already mentioned). Before they left Canada they would visit the West where most of the Army's British emigrants lived. The Lambs stopped at Winnipeg, Brandon, Regina, Saskatoon, Edmonton, Calgary, Vancouver, and Victoria, British Columbia. Then they moved on to cities in the western part of the United States, before they embarked for New Zealand via Honolulu and Suva on December 31, 1925.

After crossing the international date line they arrived in New Zealand on January 1, 1926. They found that New Zealand was "keenly interested" in The Salvation Army's social programs. Lamb met with the Prime Minister and Governor–General, but was particularly delighted with his welcome by Chambers of

Commerce, Rotary Clubs, and agricultural societies. They convinced him that "New Zealand is ready to receive an increased number of emigrants from home." Throughout the trip the press reported his message. He was always available for an interview. They visited Aukland, Hamilton, Putaruru, Rotorua, Napier, Masterton, Wellington, Christchurch, Dunedin, Timaru, Omaru, Palmerston (North), Wanganui, Eltham, Cambridge, and New Plymouth, and left for Australia on February 2, 1926.

In Australia, where Labour governments dominated in most states, the Lambs found a "general willingness" to listen to their message. The Australians were, due to an international solidarity of labor, concerned about high unemployment. This was the main threat to his immigration message. But Lamb found that a migration idea that General Bramwell Booth had floated in the *Times* in 1925, a "small permanent Empire Settlement Commission," had taken hold among business leaders. The Lambs began their tour in Sydney, New South Wales, on Friday, January 5th, then went to Brisbane, Purga, Toowoomba, Melbourne, Adelaide, Mount Barker, Kalgoorlie, Perth, Peel, and Freemantle. They left Freemantle for South Africa on March 6th.

In Australia, Prime Minister Bruce was forming a Migration and Development Commission outside of politics, but the £34 million that Australia had agreed with the British government to spend in the next few years was "quite inadequate" for the "opportunities of the day." Lamb insisted that governments would have to "get over the economic stumbling block ... beyond immediate concrete returns and budget for the distant, but not less certain, harvest." "Harvest" meant "land and training" of urban populations for migration to empty lands. He drew the comparison to preparation for war in 1914, when "thousands of men, at enormous cost, were made ready speedily enough." And he asked the question many in Europe were asking: "For the purposes of peace, shall we do less than we did ... for war?" Emigrants must not go to the dominions untrained, and their families must be cared for at home until the men are settled. "Let their wives have the dole to enable them to carry on."

The Lambs arrived at Durban, South Africa, on March 21 and visited Salvation Army social centers at Cator Manor, Pietermaritzburg, Nel's Rust, Johannesburg, Benoni, and Mafeking. It had been 35 years since William Booth sent Lamb there as the Army's chief secretary. In Southern Rhodesia, where several of Lamb's siblings had emigrated from Scotland, they went to Bulawayo, Salisbury, the Mazoe Valley, Victoria Falls, and to Livingstone, Northern Rhodesia. They then returned to South Africa and Kimberley, Bloemfontein, Port Elizabeth, Rhondebosch, and Cape Town, from which they left for home on May 7th.

In South Africa and in the two Rhodesias, not surprisingly, the "colour question" made immigration an issue of "life and death to the people." Lamb was quoting E. R. Grobler, Administrator in Bloemfontein, who was saying that Southern Africa needed white people. Lamb noticed that native races were increasing and were "moving southwards from the interior, learning Western methods, adopting Western manners." Native and "coloured" [mixed race] populations outnumbered whites about six to one and a half. In this light, Lamb found that "old racial antagonisms of Dutch and British" were receding; they were uniting in their antagonism for black Africans. But with native and colored populations providing the "rough and unskilled labor," migration of workers from other countries was "a matter of extreme difficulty."

David Lamb's New Recommendations for the Migration Program

David Lamb recommended five steps to rejuvenate the migration program. First, "drastically amend the Empire Settlement Act of 1922." It had not worked as planned by the committee on which he had served. Second, "amend the Unemployment Insurance Act so that the government can pay the dole to the wife and family of a man who is in training for farm work overseas." Third, "develop a ten years' program of intensive emigration." Fourth, "provide a big–scale system of training for potential emigrants, especially lads and young men." And fifth, "create a commission to carry out the last two of these proposals." Lamb and Bramwell Booth had suggested that this be a commission of businessmen.

The group settlement scheme in Western Australia had impressed Lamb. Similar to the American 1862 Homestead Act and a similar program in Canada, the Australian plan provided for a free grant of 160 acres to each settler. Office and survey fees would amount to £13, plus the Agricultural Bank's help with improvements, stock, and implements. Each group of 10 or 20 families would work under an experienced foreman. The cooperative effort would lead to speedy settlement of rich forest land where dairying would be the main industry. On each 160 acre holding, 25 would be developed, of which 20 would be for pastures, and 5 for gardens and a cottage. There would be work on fencing, roads, and water supply. At the end of 24 to 36 months of sustenance allowance of 10 shillings for a day's work, settlers would take over their own land. Rules would govern equipment, labor, bank advances, etc. Medical care and educational facilities would be provided. By February 1926, 135 groups of nearly 10,000 people had already been established. The cost was £2,390,349.

Lamb was impressed by the cooperative group plan. By "group" he did not mean families with a common religious or ethical basis, such as farm settlements of the 1840s, but rather families gathered from all parts of Britain, "without too much regard to anything but their adaptability and general suitability for life overseas, and settled in a group, and, if possible, one or two families with local experience interspersed."

In concluding a speech to the colonial forum, Lamb quoted the Prince of Wales, Chancellor of the Exchequer Winston Churchill, and W. A. Appleton, secretary of the General Federation of Trades Unions, who had all stated similar views. When Churchill was Colonial Secretary in 1922, he told a Royal Colonial Institute deputation: "'Inter–Imperial migration was the main path along which the Imperial government should endeavor to advance in regard to the consolidation of the British Empire ... A year would show practically nothing; ten years would begin to show some results; in 50 years great and lasting changes in the groupings of the population of the world might be set on foot, and in a century a revolution might be effected in the balanced of population."

The Prince of Wales, with whom Lamb had met at St. James Palace on his return to London, had said: "This great subject [migration] provides a problem as wide and intricate and as vital as any of the multitude which face us today; but to any one who has traveled, it cannot fail to appeal and to interest. Most of you are travelers, and I hope you share my interest, and if so, you ought to share my optimism, because it is that that wins through in the long run. We have a very long way to go indeed in the matter of Empire settlement, but we have made a start since the armistice seven years ago."

W. A. Appleton had surveyed the migration problem in 1921 and came to a morbid conclusion: "Either you transfer the people who want food, or you increase the variety and the quality and salability of the goods your people manufacture, and also your capacity as world–carriers of merchandise, or you starve and deteriorate until your effectiveness is less than that of the cheaper yellow and brown men, and then you go out."

Lamb summarized his reading of the *Story of the Empire* series of books, and Saxon Mills' *The Future of Our Empire*. He concluded by quoting John Stuart Mill: "There need be no hesitation in affirming that colonization in the present state of the world is the very best affair of business in which an old and wealthy country like ours can possibly engage." Lamb, asked Britain to "speed up" and stretch to bigger things, realizing that if the overflow is of our best, it will give those who are left at home a better chance to grow and develop." But "the flow of Empire migration must ever be determined by the absorbing power of the Overseas Dominions and never by the social or economic pressure at home." The Empire had "vast tracts of land capable of close settlement" that waited for "willing hands to make the wilderness blossom as the rose." He called for a "super–economic" point of view. The economic leg was "too much in evidence of recent years." It "developed at the expense of ... the humanitarian. Let the two [legs] take equal and regular strides and carry the British Empire steadily on."[7]

Commissioner Lamb's Report to General Bramwell Booth: Some Excerpts

David Lamb concluded his tour book with a "Report to General Booth." For Lamb and Booth redistribution of the British population in the Empire was not "an economic, political, or even an Imperial matter." It was "a human business proposition." They agreed that "a state–controlled movement is predestined to failure," and wanted businessmen to take over the program. They agreed that no British. government was likely to "openly advocate emigration," and that in the dominions it was becoming a partisan political matter. Thus a "new effort" must be made on "independent lines." Migration had to be made easy for those who go, but not "easy for them to return until they have made good." "Moral stiffening" had become necessary "after a long period of enforced idleness."

As for where new migrants should go, Lamb observed that "life is easy in Australia—probably easier than in any other part of the Empire," at least in attaining the "bare necessities of life, food, clothing, and housing." And on the plains of Western Canada he had admired the "vigor, the sparkle, and the spirit of battle against the elements [that] foreshadow the growth of a strong, virile and dominant people—as a strong big brother to be relied upon should need arise."

Lamb reviewed several practical ideas for Booth. First, he wanted to find "farm openings for part–trained married men between ages 30 and 40, with families that could be "absorbed under existing Government Schemes." Their families would need support during their training. Second, "the widow and the fatherless" had done well in Canada and new legislation would make things easier for "widows with sufficient vision to see the opportunities for their children overseas." But they would need their pensions to be transferred overseas.

Lamb pointed to "outcroppings" of emigration—as second and third generations of emigrants who had done well in Western Canada came to meet him and Mrs. Lamb at "reunion gatherings." At Woodstock, Ontario, the center of a large agricultural district, 80 percent of those at a Town Hall meeting were emigrants brought to Canada by The Salvation Army. At Halifax, Moncton, Toronto, Winnipeg, Regina, Calgary, and Vancouver, there were reunions, as there were in New Zealand, Australia and South Africa. Lamb concluded that "many thousands who have gone to the 'New Lands' have established for themselves a reputation for character and ability which is gratifying to all concerned."

The Lambs found "a strong call for women" in the dominions to participate in "management" of homes. Canadian authorities had set regulations that were keeping The Salvation Army from sending "unwanted children of school age and under." Foster parents were refusing to adopt children they had not seen. Lamb saw "racial stock safeguards" as being at the center of the refusals. He claimed that New Zealand and Australia had overcome the problem, but the Army had not many children there because "special organization for such work does not so far exist."

South Africa presented the "most complicated and difficult problem which has ever confronted statesmen." The British and Dutch had mended fences, but their antagonism to what they termed "native and Asiatic perils" persisted. Lamb saw it as a duty to develop "native and coloured races spiritually, socially, intellectually, and economically," to "standards of life and conduct which have made ... races and nations truly great." A "shrewd observer" had argued that "South Africa may accept the solution of degeneracy and perpetuate a Eurafrica civilization: a course utterly inconceivable, involving as it would do, the dishonoring of racial ideals tenaciously held by both of the great European races of the Union." Not until 1994 did that old course yield to a new day with majority rule and one vote per person.

While in South Africa Lamb visited Nel's Rust, an estate left to benefit South Africa by Joseph Baynes, an acquaintance of William Booth who had visited him there in 1908. The Baynes' trust revenues would beautify and develop Nel's Rust, expand existing industries, and assist scientific agricultural research, agricultural schools, lay out a public park, and establish and equip two industrial institutes, one for poor children of both sexes of European descent, and one for "native and coloured children." Lamb hoped that the Army might send British boys to Nel's Rust. Some Dutch farmers wanted British boys as farm laborers.

Lamb had discussed his thinking on "group settlements" with South Africa's Prime Minister Hertzog, ex–Prime Minister Smuts, and with Sir Charles Coglan, the Premier of Southern Rhodesia. On Rhodesian migration, Lamb found that Southern Rhodesia's new post–British South Africa Company white settler government was just getting established. Instead of an aggressive immigration and settlement policy it was continuing the old policy that called for immigrants with capital resources of £1,500 to £2,000. Like South Africa, Rhodesia had an abundance of cheap native labor and did not share Lamb's perspective that "nothing can be of greater importance ... to the British empire in Central and South Africa than a large and steady influx of selected British folk." Lamb met Colonel Frank Johnson, the Army leader in Salisbury, whom he credited with replanting the British flag in Rhodesia after the Army had left the country in 1897 due to an African revolt in which Captain T. Cass was killed. Lamb then visited President Paul Kruger's house in Pretoria.

David Lamb was always a British imperialist who favored efficient management of the Empire. Looking back on the tour, he saw that "probably the most fruitful of our meetings in New Zealand" was with businessmen who understood the link between British workers' need for work and the dominions' need for workers. Otherwise he found "indifference ... to the claims of the workless in the homeland." At Flock House Orphanage he had seen "shrewd business management on the farming side, and the kindly disposition through the home itself."

Conservative British Prime Minister Stanley Baldwin had told the U.K. branch of the Empire Parliamentary Association that the Empire's essential problem was: "What can we do to prevent that aggregation of people into the towns which makes it so infinitely more difficult to maintain that standard of life which we would like to see people enjoy and the environment in which they could develop themselves to the best?"

Lamb's solution, after reading the records of more than 2,000 boys from ages 16 to 18 that The Salvation Army had sent overseas, was that the incidence of "town–drift had been practically nil." He gave the credit to Hadleigh training farms where the boys were "inoculated with the 'land sense' before they left England. The Empire had "an almost insatiable demand for such boys." They could be "quickly absorbed by thousands." Hadleigh was dealing with about 1,000 boys per year. In Lamb's judgment, the government needed 100 such farms.

In Australia, Lamb had found men and women in all parties grappling with combating "destructive communistic theories," which he failed to identify. Australians were sympathetic towards workers in the homeland, and they cheered when Lamb told them that the "Old Country" was "all right … going strong … paying our debts and other people's … balancing our budgets, etc." Debts had accumulated during World War I. The big problem at home was the lack of housing, which should stimulate the United Kingdom to look to the dominions. In the city of Westminster (in London) statistics showed 6,258 families of 1–8 persons living in one room, families of 1 to 11 living in two rooms, and 7,142 families of 1–12 persons living in three rooms. There were similar statistics for Glasgow.

In Canada the Lambs had visited every province except Prince Edward Island and talked with most of the provincial premiers and many ministers. Canadian conditions impressed him, but the question of population was "a momentous problem." Lamb claimed that everyone agreed that "British immigration is needed." Throughout their travels, but "especially in New Zealand and Australia," settlers referred to the "Old Country" as "home." The Lambs took this as an indication that their message of imperial solidarity was heard and applauded. They hoped that it meant support for further migration.

When the Lambs arrived back home in Southend, the Mayor presided over a civic reception in their honor. David Lamb claimed that "it has been said, and is probably true, that I have interviewed more of the Empire's Cabinet ministers than most men." The tour had "probably added a hundred ministers to the number." Among those who had gone to Waterloo Station in London to welcome them were G. F. Plant and E. T. Crutchley, the secretary and the finance officer of Britain's Overseas Settlement Department.

On the tour the Lambs had lunched with Lord Stonehaven, the Governor–General of Australia, and had tea with General Sir Charles Fergusson, Governor–General of New Zealand. They had interviewed Australian Prime Minister Stanley Bruce and New Zealand Prime Minister J. G. Coates. Due to the general election in Canada, most federal ministers were unavailable, and Governor–General Viscount Byng was on a tour of the provinces. American President Calvin Coolidge had received them at the White House and they had a long talk with Britain's U.S. Ambassador Sir Esme W. Howard.

Back in London the Earl of Clarendon, the Parliamentary Under–Secretary of State for Dominion Affairs and Chairman of the Overseas Settlement Committee, and Vice Chairman T. C. Macnaghten welcomed Lamb at the dominions office at Whitehall. The Prince of Wales invited him to St. James Palace.

Despite the large number of people in the press, in prison, and in the street, who approved of The Salvation Army's work, Lamb held that many were uninformed that the Army's migrants "are well above the average." They no longer fell into a group that William Booth had termed the "submerged tenth" that the Army was allegedly dumping in the dominions. Many citizens were surprised to hear Lamb say that "every able–bodied man and woman" who sailed with Salvation Army backing, "had a guarantee of work" on arrival. Many thought that the migrants were all Salvationists. And many were ignorant of the Army's social services in the United Kingdom. Many did not know that the migration and settlement work was quite distinct from reformative work at the women's rescue homes and the prison work.

Commissioner Lamb concluded his report to General Booth by asserting the value of emigration.

> The cessation of emigration in any appreciable numbers is only one contributing factor in unemployment, but it is an important one, since it operates by the presence of idle men who would otherwise be abroad and at work in some of our Overseas Dominions or dependencies, supplying us with the products of their labor, mostly foodstuffs and raw material, while goods manufactured here at home would have been required by those dominions and dependencies in exchange ... Emigration is not a panacea for unemployment, but it meets the dual test of labor absorption and creative value.[8]

Lamb placed overseas newspapers' editorial comments at the end of his report. The *Manitoba Free Press* had concluded that the migrants' "value to any country depends absolutely upon the worth and stability of the settlement involved." The London, Ontario *Morning Advertiser* agreed that the dominions needed "continual renewal in their population of British stock," and commended The Salvation Army for having "no axe to grind" and for being "an organization in which the public has generally confidence." The *Saskatoon Daily Star* stated that "the dominion is clearly entitled to exclude physical and mental defectives.

Within these limits, however, there seems no reason why Canada should not extend a general welcome to all and sundry." The *Montreal Gazette* chided the "Canadian immigration service in England as a first–class exclusion agency."

The *New Zealand Herald* supported Lamb's appeal to "New Zealand's duty of sharing fully in the Empire settlement scheme" and "his words of blame, direct and frank, are justified." The *Sydney Evening News* applauded Lamb for seeing that "it must be the absorbing power of the Overseas Dominions, and not the economic or social pressure at home which determines the flow of migrants." It noted that Australia also had a surplus of women, "120,000 more Jills than Jacks." The *Johannesburg Star* said that South Africa needed settlers more than other dominions if "the actual numbers of the white race of European civilization is to be established beyond all doubt, and if the country is to take the position it should do." The *Cape Times* observed that "until some British leader arises who has the sense to see that the whole British Empire is one magnificent field for human progress and prosperity [the] barren portions of the field will remain barren till they are fertilized by the addition of the men to develop them—and the women too—emigration for Great Britain's superfluous population will be an uninteresting, unpopular, dead issue."[9]

It may seem to be an enormous jump from a discussion of Lamb's tour of the British Empire, with a few stops in the United States, to problems in the internal workings of the international Salvation Army, but there is a link. In addition to talking with leaders of the dominions, the Lambs also spoke with Salvationists and likely sensed increased tension over the centralized nature of the Army with total authority resting in the hands of one man and one family in London. The tensions were not new. Their roots in the United States went back as far as the mid–1880s and led three of William and Catherine Booth's children to "leave the work" in 1896 and 1904 and settle in America.

A system of federalism called for in the United States and the overseas dominions was not new in the British Empire. It had begun in Canada in 1867 with a restructuring that put the dominion's government on a par with Her Majesty's government at Westminster. David Lamb had long realized that his emigration and resettlement program rested on the mutual acceptance of its benefits to Britain and the dominions. But The Salvation Army's highly centralized authority had not accepted a federated view of its internal governance. In 1929, under great stress, Salvation Army leaders would meet in London to produce a sea–change in the way the Army chose its general and in the international nature of its imperium. It was Commissioner David C. Lamb, the Army's leader with the greatest international experience, who would take the lead in proposing a first step towards a federal system of polity. It would bring Army leaders from all points on the compass into the decision–making process. But it would be only a first step. It would be a long time before further steps were taken, but they would come.

7

David Lamb's Role in the 1929 High Council that Deposed William Bramwell Booth as General

As a leading Salvation Army Commissioner, the first rank below the general in its military–diplomatic rank hierarchy, David C. Lamb was as interested in reforming The Salvation Army as he was in reforming the world. Gradually it had dawned on him and other senior leaders (seven London commissioners requested the meeting of the High Council in 1929) that General Bramwell Booth was becoming increasingly despotic and quite ill. It was also their impression that Booth had become more dependent on the counsels of his family and less interested in the advice of senior officers. This was particularly irksome to the Army's staff at International Headquarters in London.

By 1928 leaders in London, North America, and Australasia had begun to plot a change in the Army's constitution set forth in 1878 and 1904 Deed Polls registered with the British government. Lamb leaned in the direction of a "general in council" system patterned after the role of the British prime minister in a Cabinet form of government. It would also resemble a Pope in the midst of his curia or bishops in an ecumenical council.

Bramwell Booth met the senior commissioners' appeals with a defense of his father's 1878 Founding Deed. In that Deed Poll the founder and first general, William Booth, had given the general the right to choose his or her successor by placing that person's name in a sealed envelope to be held by the Army's solicitor. Upon the death of a general, the solicitor would open the envelope to reveal the name of the new general who would be the international leader of The Salvation Army until his/her death or incapacity or resignation. There was no retirement age. This was the manner in which Bramwell Booth had succeeded his father as general upon the founder's death in 1912.

In Bramwell Booth's case the likely successor was his eldest daughter, Commissioner Catherine Booth. William Booth's best biographer, St. John Ervine, held that the senior leaders "did not wish to have [Catherine] for their leader." In her mid–40s (born July 20, 1883), Catherine had been named for her grandmother and dedicated to work in the Army by her grandfather in an Exeter Hall celebration that would have been worthy of Queen Victoria's brood. She was the senior Booth of the next generation and as a commissioner she held senior rank. But Catherine was not the whole problem. Ervine claims that some leaders "did not, indeed, desire any woman or any Booth" to become general. That category would also include Bramwell's sister Evangeline, the Army Commander in the United States.[1]

With six other London commissioners David Lamb played a central role in asking the Chief of the Staff to call a meeting of the High Council in London in 1929. Following early American attacks on Bramwell Booth's autocracy and nepotism in the appointment and promotions of his children, there were also pleas for federalism in which each national unit in the Army would have some independence from centralized London domination. After initial attacks from North America in early 1928, Lamb became the prime organizer in London of clandestine moves that led to Booth's removal as the Army's second general in February 1929. St. John Ervine paid close attention to Lamb's description of the events that led to the removal. He made multiple references to Lamb's central role in the plot to depose Bramwell.[2]

In particular, Ervine pointed to Lamb's behind–the–scenes meetings with other London commissioners to plot Booth's removal and to the lead Lamb took in the movement to reform the Army's constitution by an act of Parliament in 1931–32. Most notably, Ervine cited a clandestine meeting of London commissioners, including Commissioner Edward J. Higgins, Bramwell Booth's Chief of Staff, away from the International Headquarters, where their designs almost certainly would have been uncovered and reported to General Booth.

Nine commissioners met secretly "in mufti," at the home of the Lambs' daughter, Mrs. Carton, at 35A Gloucester Road, Kensington, London, on March 5 and 9, 1928, nearly a year before Chief of Staff Higgins convened the High Council to depose Bramwell Booth. Conveniently Lamb lived next door to Mrs. Carton. According to Ervine, the London commissioners feared that Bramwell might "strengthen his dynasty by rewriting William Booth's Supplementary Deed Poll of 1904 that established a way to depose an incapacitated general and elect a new one.

Ervine wrote that several members of the Army's High Command had questioned the nature of the Army's government for at least a decade.[3] In fact, as early as 1878 a few brave souls had questioned the Foundation Deed in which the Booths overturned the 1873 Christian Mission constitution that established the mission's democratic conference system that mimicked other British Wesleyan denominations. Since the Wesleyan societies in Britain, founded by John Wesley, were not seen as churches, they had no bishops, unlike the Methodist Church in the United States. An annual meeting of ministers and lay conferees set the agenda for the Christian Mission, including the annual appointments of evangelists. The 1878 Foundation Deed, proposed by the Booths and a group of their most intimate supporters, had laid the foundation of one–man autocratic rule by William Booth and his closest advisors.[4]

Was it Lamb's leadership of what some saw as a "palace coup" that led a later general, Albert Orsborn, who had a high regard for Lamb, to refer to him as a Scottish "dirk" (dagger)?[5] Whatever Lamb's reason for taking the lead in this matter, Ervine surmised that the antagonism that soon developed between Bramwell Booth and his "high officers" was not based on "personal antipathy," This was a defense of Lamb's motives, but not necessarily his deeds. By 1929 he had spent more than three decades as a close associate and admirer of the Booths, and Bramwell in particular.

The Army's American commander, Evangeline Booth, had advised her brother: "If you would like to know the convictions of your leading officers" on altering the Army's government, "give them an opportunity to express themselves, making it clear at the same time that their present positions and future appointments would not in any way be affected by the views they hold?"[6] No doubt Lamb would have been delighted to voice his concerns to Bramwell informally rather than through a circular letter or in a memorandum from a secret meeting. Bramwell obviously took such secret acts to represent disloyalty.

But Ervine concluded that the decision of nine commissioners to sign a petition proved that Bramwell's "relations with them were more arbitrary than they ought to have been." Bramwell now knew that the Army's "Higher Command in Britain, no less than in the United States, was discontented." He quickly interviewed each of the nine commissioners, except his retired brother–in–law, Frederick Booth–Tucker. He promised them that he did not intend to alter the 1904 Supplementary Deed Poll to make it impossible for a High Council to remove an incapacitated general and choose a new leader.[7]

Just ten days later Booth learned that someone had sent the letter composed by the nine London commissioners and addressed solely to him to Salvation Army staff officers all over the world. This toughened his determination to stand his ground. On March 14, 1928, eight senior American officers sent the general a cablegram to support Evangeline Booth's call for "constitutional change."[8] On April 12, the general, feverish and depressed, left his International Headquarters office for the last time. A letter from Evangeline on April 9th argued that their father had impressed on them "the advantage of boards, of councils, and the value of the judgment and opinions of our leading staff." She asked Bramwell to trust the High Council.

In fact, Evangeline was wrong in her interpretation of William Booth's preference for a "general in council," as David Lamb envisioned the role of future generals in his plea for change. In fact the founder had quite intentionally given up the Conference Committee of senior members of the Christian Mission that had assisted him in decision–making prior to 1878.

That year he abolished the Christian Mission's democratic government and made himself the sole leader.[9]

Bramwell, in his response to Evangeline and other critics, persisted in his view that he could not consider any change in the Army's 1878 Foundation Deed that allowed him to name his successor. Neither did he intend to alter the Supplementary Deed of 1904 that established a High Council to determine whether a general was fit to continue in office. But it may have been too late to stop the reformers from requisitioning a meeting of a High Council.

While Bramwell's anxieties caused him to lose sleep, Ervine argues that there were only fifteen days during the period leading up to the meeting of the High Council in January 1929 when Bramwell was "not able to sign deeds" as the owner of all Salvation Army properties in the British Empire.

In June 1928, Chief of Staff Higgins had assured Mrs. Bramwell (Florence) Booth that six of the nine London commissioners who wrote to Bramwell had told him privately that they did not intend any further action. Higgins also claimed that he had written to Evangeline to "stop everything," and that she had agreed to do nothing "for the present."

Commissioner Higgins, as Bramwell's Chief of Staff, pledged himself to "stand for the General in all my actions." He stated that of the nine London commissioners, only Commissioners Booth–Tucker and possibly Henry Mapp would support Evangeline for general if the position were open. This indicates that Lamb was not a party to the American conspiracy to replace Bramwell as general with his sister. Yet Ervine argues that "there seems to have been underground communication between London and New York," although he gave no evidence to support this claim.[10] It appears that communications between London and New York were mainly through Commissioners Mapp and Booth–Tucker.

In November 1928 the situation came to a head. Chief of Staff Higgins was ready to act on a request from the London commissioners to call a High Council. On the 13th Higgins visited the Booths at their seaside home at Southwold, Essex, to inform Florence Booth that he would likely summon the High Council if the necessary seven commissioners asked him to do so.

Bramwell Booth was sleeping under the influence of a narcotic at the time. The family feared that he was dying. When Higgins told them the reason for his visit Florence asked that their eldest daughter Catherine, likely Bramwell's chosen successor, be present when Higgins told them that he could not defer calling the High Council. He expected to receive the request from seven requisitioning commissioners at any moment. Bramwell's nurse, Brigadier Bertha Smith, took Higgins to the General's room. Ervine reported that the Chief of Staff believed that "he had seen his General alive for the last time." Bramwell laid "unconscious in his bed." This sight assured Higgins that it was time to issue a summons for the High Council to meet. When he relayed his impression to the London commissioners, they feared that Bramwell's choice as successor would claim the office if they did not immediately send Higgins a requisition to call the High Council to London.

The seven London requisitioners met at about 9 a.m. on November 14 after being informed by Commissioner Hurren of Chief of Staff Higgins' concern. Following their meeting Commissioners Lamb and Hurren presented the requisition to Higgins. Higgins appeared relieved, according to Hurren. The requisitioning commissioners were Hurren, Lamb, Hoggard, Mapp, Jeffries, Simpson, and Wilson. On the November 15, after conferring with the Army's solicitor, Higgins told Mrs. Booth: "I have no options but to dispatch the necessary cables and notices and this I am doing to–day."[11]

David Lamb's role in removing Bramwell Booth from office continued when the High Council convened at the invitation of Chief of Staff Higgins in January 1929. Given Lamb's close working relationship with Bramwell since he had joined the Army's International Headquarters staff in 1888, it may appear strange that he took such a prominent role. Was there a point at which Lamb had a change of heart as he reflected on the Army's despotism? Could it have been his association with outside political leaders in Britain, Europe, North America, Australasia and South Africa that caused him to see the Army's polity in a new international light?

In 1904 William Booth had sought Prime Minister William Gladstone's advice on the stability of the Army's polity. Gladstone expressed concern over the system of replacing a general who was unable to bear the load of office. Was it Bramwell's tendency toward anxiety as he grew older that made him a despotic disciplinarian? Or was it his nepotism that upset Lamb as the general's children moved ahead of older leaders? Or had there been some personal slight? Or maybe it was Lamb's positive urge to see a more consultative, business–like system of leadership.

Without a personal diary or correspondence that opens David Lamb's mind it is impossible for an historian to know his thought process in 1928–29. As a 30–year veteran of the London staff he no doubt saw The Salvation Army as a personal treasure. But whether for personal or political reasons, there can be little doubt that he took the lead among the London commissioners who asked the Chief of Staff to call a meeting of the High Council of Army leaders.

The Council would consider whether 73–year–old Bramwell Booth was mentally and physically fit for office. The seven requisitioning commissioners were joined by eight retired commissioners in signing a pamphlet that they sent on December 8 to explain "The Why and Wherefore of the High Council of The Salvation Army, 1928–29."[12]

On November 26 Bramwell recovered sufficiently to begin to sign legal documents. On December 30 his physicians advised his wife to tell him that the High Council would soon assemble. The Booth family began to fight back in the pages of *The War Cry*, the Army's official organ, which was owned by the General and served as his voice.

While William Booth's biographer, St. John Ervine, held that the requisitioning commissioners "had sadly mishandled their case, and had caused onlookers to wonder how Bramwell Booth could have kept his Army marching with the help of such incompetent commanders," he nevertheless defended "men such as David Crichton Lamb and Samuel Hurren," who presented the requisitioning petition. Their case was for a modest democratizing of the Army through the appointment of the General by the High Council. This they preferred over the Foundation Deed's formula of a General writing the name of a successor and placing it in a sealed envelope. They were certain that the name in the envelope was that of Catherine Bramwell–Booth, whom the senior commissioners did not want.

On January 6, as High Council members arrived in London, Bramwell Booth offered to "place the administration in the hands of a council" composed of the chief of staff as president, Commander Eva Booth, Commissioner Catherine Booth and "probably two commissioners of IHQ" This was a step in the direction of Lamb's dream of a "general in council," and was certainly better than Bramwell's alternative choice to resign and appoint his successor. But it was not acceptable to the High Council. At this late date they were looking for a permanent, not a temporary solution, to The Salvation Army's governance problem.[13]

When the High Council convened on Tuesday, January 8, 1929, there were 64 members present. They needed a three–fourths majority to depose Bramwell Booth as general. If 17 leaders opposed his removal, he would remain as general. Four certain votes against removal would come from his wife Florence, his daughters Catherine and Mary, and his sister Lucy Booth–Hellberg. Four international commissioners would almost certainly oppose: John Beauly Laurie; Theodore Kitching; John Cunningham; and Allister Smith. Two commissioners leaned towards Bramwell: Albin Peyron of France (his daughter had married Bramwell's son Wycliffe); and American Samuel Brengle. After the High Council elected a president, Commissioner James Hay of New Zealand, a vice president, Lt. Commissioner William Haines from London, and a recorder, retired Commissioner John Carleton, it sent a message of sympathy to Bramwell and got down to business. Fortunately for historians, the High Council meetings at Sunbury Court, a Georgian mansion the Army had purchased for the training of officers, was, as Ervine wrote, no more able to keep secrets than the British Cabinet during World War I. Thus Ervine pieced together a record of events and had them read and approved by participants on all sides.[14]

No doubt Commissioner Lamb was the choice of the seven requisitioning commissioners to place the resolution before the High Council to remove General Bramwell Booth from office.

Commissioner Wilfred L. Simpson seconded the motion. The resolution read:

> *That this meeting of the High Council of The Salvation Army, deeply regretting the necessity, doth hereby, in exercise and furtherance of the powers and duties conferred on the council by the provisions of the Supplemental Deed Poll of July 26, 1904, adjudicate William Bramwell Booth unfit for office as General of The Salvation Army and remove him therefrom.*[15]

But on Wednesday, January 9, before the Council voted on the motion, they passed a resolution, moved by Commissioner Mapp, to ask General Booth to "retire." They chose a committee of seven to visit him to propose a retirement package. Bramwell would keep the title of General and the honors that came with it. The committee included the Council president and vice president and five members that Bramwell would not see as enemies: Commissioners George Mitchell, Samuel Brengle, John Cunningham, Gunpei Yamamuro, and Colonel Annie Trounce. Yamamuro had written the only published biography of Bramwell. Brengle was a friend.

On Thursday morning, January 10, 66 High Council members signed the letter asking Bramwell Booth to retire. Seven declined to sign: Mrs. Booth, daughters Catherine and Mary, sister Lucy, and Commissioners Laurie, Kitching and Allister Smith. Three who were seen as sympathetic to the General signed the petition: Cunningham, Peyron, and Brengle. The delegation offered the retirement proposal to Bramwell at Southwold on the morning of Friday, January 11. Bramwell asked for time to think about the proposal. On the way out of the house the committee asked Catherine Booth to influence her father to retire.[16]

Tuesday, January 15, Florence Booth informed the High Council that the General refused to resign. In his response Bramwell agreed to "leave the final choice of my immediate successor to the commissioners of The Salvation Army." But he also raised the possibility of a lawsuit if they did not comply with the 1878 Foundation Deed, the deed that allowed him to name a successor. Thus the letter was at odds with itself. The Council refused to hear from Bramwell's attorney, William Jowitt, K.C. Bramwell's possible appeal to law courts turned Commissioner Brengle against the Booths' position.

On Wednesday morning, January 16 a vote on the David Lamb motion to declare Bramwell Booth physically incapacitated and to remove him as General was finally taken. Fifty–five voted to depose, and eight voted to retain Bramwell as General. Besides his family, elderly international commissioners who formed Booth's most intimate circle outside the family, Commissioners Cunningham, Laurie, Kitching, and Smith, voted to permit Bramwell to continue as the Army's general.[17]

To keep the High Council from electing a new general on Friday January 18, the Booths carried out their threat to go to court. Another of Booth's lawyers, Wilfrid Greene, K.C., applied to Mr. Justice Eve for an injunction to halt the Council's proceedings until Monday based on two points. First, Greene held that the 1904 Supplementary Deed was not valid because a charitable trust trustee could not alter the trust at will, as William Booth had done. Thus Bramwell was asking a judge to hold William Booth's 1904 action invalid. Second, Bramwell had not been allowed to put his case before the High Council, and the Council had considered no medical evidence as to his fitness.

The High Council and many Salvationists resented this appeal to law. Many must have found it strange that Bramwell was questioning his father's right to draw up the 1904 Supplementary Deed. Chief of Staff Higgins attacked Bramwell's position on grounds that he had accepted the office of General based on the terms of both the 1878 and 1904 deeds. Evangeline excoriated her brother for "hauling his brethren into the secular law courts."

On January 29 Mr. Justice Eve held that the High Council had acted within its rights to assemble as it did. And the General's condition "was a matter for the High Council alone." However, Eve held that the Council had made a mistake in not giving the General or his agents time to present his case. Therefore, the Council could not act on the David Lamb resolution that it had already passed until they had given the general a chance to present his case for continuing in office.[18]

The High Council did not reconvene until Wednesday, February 13, when Commissioner Lamb moved a new resolution to "adjudicate William Bramwell Booth unfit" based upon his "state of health." Lamb then gave a speech and moved that the Council listen to Bramwell's counsel, William Jowitt, before a vote was taken.

Mr. Jowitt spoke for two hours and read a letter from Bramwell that argued: "We ought to find a better way than that of separation." Sir Thomas Horder, Dr. E. Wardlaw Milne and Dr. John Weir gave medical testimony and presented a certificate that held that "the General is recovering steadily from a very severe illness." In six months he could be fully recovered. G. A. Pollard, a former Salvation Army commissioner and Maurice Whitlow, an ex–officer and journalist, testified to Bramwell's mental capacity. Jowitt asked for an adjournment of the Council's decision for three months. If the General was still sick at the end of that time, he would retire and the Council could choose his successor.

Commissioner Hurren proposed that the Council investigate this compromise by asking those who represented Bramwell to authorize Jowitt's offer. If they did so, Hurren would propose that another deputation visit Bramwell at Hadley Wood to gain his formal agreement. Ervine holds that the Booths were unprepared for this offer and "fumbled" the opportunity. Commissioner Mapp argued against the Hurren proposal, holding that the Council could not remain in session for an additional three months and thus the compromise was impractical. The compromise did not carry the support of either the Booths or most High Council members and was set aside.[19]

The High Council's election of the new General on February 13 had six nominees, four of whom refused to run for office: Commissioners Catherine Booth; Hay; Hurren; and Charles Rich. The last two candidates were Chief of Staff Edward J. Higgins and Commander Evangeline Booth. In her speech to the Council Evangeline Booth announced governance reforms that would lead to a succession of short–term generals. Higgins made no promises of reform, but agreed to appoint a Commission to study reform. Higgins won by a 42 to 17 vote.[20]

Why was David Lamb not a nominee, given his leadership of the requisitioning commissioners and his international experience? First, it was highly unlikely that a social commissioner would be elected General, given the Army's view of itself as having an essentially evangelical soul–winning message. Also, there is little evidence that Lamb was a charismatic platform performer who could galvanize the Army into action. Still he had gained the recognition of his colleagues and was at the peak of his career in 1929. William Bramwell Booth died on June 16, 1929, three months after the High Council had removed him as General.

8

David Lamb and the Salvation
Army Act, 1931–32

etween the end of the High Council on February 13, 1929,
and the completion of the British Parliament's work on
writing reforms into The Salvation Army Act of 1931–32,
David Lamb was an advisor to the new General, Edward J. Higgins. Lamb's internal advice was for the General's ears only;
thus there is no record of what it was. The Salvation Army Act
primarily aimed at transferring the Booth trusteeship to the
Army's new trustees.

In 1928, as pressures on his regime were increasing,
Bramwell Booth had appointed the next General to be the executor of his estate. His estate included the transfer of Salvation
Army property as the new General's personal property. But after
the High Council deposed him, Booth added a codicil to his will
and substituted for the name of the next general, whom he had
expected to appoint, the names of his wife Florence, his daughter Catherine, and his solicitor Frederick Charles Russia Sneath
as trustees.[1]

But the Booths' attorney, Sir William Jowitt, advised them in
1929 not to engage in further litigation. Therefore, on the advice
of Jowitt, who was by then Britain's attorney general, Catherine
Booth met with negotiators for General Higgins and concluded
a tentative informal agreement that read: 1) The Bramwell–
Booths would agree to give faithful service in the Army. 2) The

next High Council would open the sealed envelope with the name of Bramwell's chosen successor; and 3) if the Council saw fit it could follow its dictates. For their part the Bramwell–Booths would not oppose: 1) transfer of property to a trustee company; 2) the election of future generals by a High Council; or 3) setting an age at which generals would retire. But negotiations ended when Higgins insisted that all such changes could only be sanctioned by Parliament. Thus the trusts remained in the control of Bramwell's executors for nine months after the meeting between Higgins and Catherine Bramwell–Booth, without injury to the Salvation Army.[2]

On January 22, 1930 the Army's solicitor, William Frost, burned the unopened sealed envelope that contained the name of Bramwell Booth's designated successor. General Higgins, Chief of Staff Mapp, and Commissioners Laurie, Blowers, Sowton, Unsworth and Kitching were present for the event. Bramwell Booth had signed the envelope on March 14, 1928, as rumblings from the Army's senior leadership began to be heard in London. Frost submitted a memorandum of destruction of a document to the Supreme Court of Judicature on January 22.

It is uncertain what role international commissioners or the High Council played in the design of The Salvation Army Act that the British Houses of Commons and Lords passed in 1931. The measure transformed the Army in Britain and Northern Ireland from an organization solely owned by the general, as it had been under the Booth family from 1878 to 1929, into a custodian trustee company with the status of a charitable trust. The Army would hold its international properties in a number of national corporations that conformed to laws of the nations in which it operated, rather than in the name of the general or his designee as sole international trustee. The High Council would elect generals. The House of Commons deleted from the bill a provision that set the age at which a general would retire. That was for the High Council to decide. Parliament also declined to establish an arbitration committee to settle internal Salvation Army disputes and deleted a clause that increased the powers of the Chief of Staff.

General Higgins and a Select Committee of the House of Commons prepared the legislation. Lamb's work was, as usual, behind the scenes. No paper trail of his influence on the wording of the act survives. This was primarily a matter for the Army's solicitors. The Booth family, who saw Higgins and the seven London commissioners led by Lamb as traitors who had attacked Bramwell when he was too ill to combat their charges, opposed the Salvation Army Act. Their opposition gained the support of many Salvationists and two members of Parliament who were friends of the family. George Lansbury and Frank Smith tried to move the legislation in the direction of the 1878 Foundation Deed Poll, but to no avail.[3]

David Lamb's post–High Council efforts were mainly to lobby for his own view of the direction The Salvation Army should take.[4] He filed a petition against the Salvation Army bill, as did Catherine and Florence Booth, and a group of soldiers and officers who opposed the Army's appeal to the government for an act to establish its legitimacy. The petitions differed, but they all agreed that the Army must be kept outside the realm of secular state control. Commissioner J. Allister Smith testified before the House of Commons Select Committee that shaped the act and argued that:

> *the General of The Salvation Army is not only the General in virtue of his people wishing him to be the General, but by Divine right, if I may call it so, by Divine inspiration; and I think we ought to be very careful, as Salvationists, in interfering with any of his prerogatives. That past history of the Army shows that God's blessing has been upon it as it is, and we ought to make haste slowly in making any alterations.*

St. John Ervine found that General Higgins' views were on both sides of the argument as to the source of a general's legitimacy. Before the House of Lords he was "sympathetic with the divine authoritarians," represented by Allister Smith. But before the House of Commons "his sympathies were all for the democrats."[5] The new general and David Lamb, his international social commissioner, could not have been of one mind on Salvation Army polity, since the General himself was of two minds.

Ervine, attempting to unravel this muddle, concluded that there were in fact three schools of ideas on Salvation Army governance. The first school, represented by Edward Higgins, favored "absolute and unrestricted autocracy," only modified by the right of the High Council to choose a general. The second school, led by Evangeline Booth, wanted the general to be controlled by "a sort of Senate," which sounds like David Lamb's "general in council" idea. The third school, with Lamb as its champion, wanted to limit autocracy, but would give a general the last word in making policy.

To put it simply, as Ervine put it, David Lamb wanted the Army to work in the same manner as the British government, where "the prime minister has the last word in a Cabinet meeting and is ultimately responsible for the policy of the government."

As for Edward Higgins, Ervine wrote that at his reception meetings, where Salvationists saluted his rise to the seat of power, "he claimed to be spiritually autocratic, but temporarily [sic] democratic." Ervine, possibly mirroring Lamb, wondered how Higgins' division of the spiritual and temporal work of the Army would relate to its spiritual and social divisions.

Bramwell Booth and David Lamb held that spiritual work and social services were twin means of the Army's program of "wholesale salvation." As Ervine put it, Bramwell saw "the soldier who collected premiums for life assurance policies was doing the will of his Father in Heaven as much as the soldier who strove with sinners at the penitent–form." After Higgins became general, Ervine found him to be "as autocratic in temper, and harsher in practice, than it was under his predecessors."[6] This comment may have been the result of a biographers' tendency to embrace his subjects as heroes, or it could have been the candid outsider's view of a non–Salvationist. It may well have been contradicted by the majority of Salvationists.

9

1932–1941: The End is Not Yet— David C. Lamb's 50 Years in The Salvation Army—Still a Mover and a Shaker, but in New Fields

In January 1933, at age 66, Commissioner David C. Lamb celebrated 40 years in London as a member of the International Headquarters staff. He had been a Salvationist for 50 years, serving most of those years at IHQ, except for a brief appointment in South Africa. That year General Higgins relieved Lamb of his international social secretary title and responsibility. In its place Higgins gave Lamb continued oversight of several social service departments, as chair of a social council, and a member of the finance councils of the men's and women's social work.

Higgins' most interesting appointment made Commissioner Lamb the director of the International Headquarters intelligence department. As Lamb looked backward, he was being asked to look forward. This department, first proposed in 1890 in the book *In Darkest England*, collected and collated social reform ideas from secular and religious sources for The Salvation Army to use in its work. In 1933 the British home office and local government board had begun to index their intelligence data, collected in white papers and blue books. This would give the Army a variety of sources from which to choose novel ways to dispense its social services.

Prior to 1933, David Lamb had been absorbing and broadcasting ideas from government white papers and other secular sources while he actively managed the Army's international social programs. In writing *In Darkest England and the Way Out*, Frank Smith and the Booths had envisioned an intelligence department as the beginning of what would ultimately become a "kind of University," where the "accumulated experiences of the human race will be massed, digested, and rendered available to the humblest toiler in the great work of social reform."[1]

It may have been Frank Smith's association with the Fabians that led him to this line of thinking. This element of the Darkest England plan had not been fully implemented in 1890. Here was a unique opportunity for Lamb to do the social planning he greatly enjoyed. He would no longer be responsible for direct supervision of the Army's international social service enterprise. It must have been a relief to take this new "think tank" role.[2] There is no evidence that he took the change to be a demotion. In fact, it is possible that he proposed the new arrangement.

Commissioner Lamb had publicly celebrated his "spiritual jubilee" of 50 years as a Salvation Army officer at Goldsmith's Hall, London, on October 24, 1932. An effervescent optimist, he addressed this audience of dignitaries with a message of gratitude and named four influences on his life. First, spiritual books had encouraged his devotion to Jesus Christ. His second debt was to economists, including Henry George, the American socialist and land–for–the–masses single–tax advocate, who was also a major influence on Frank Smith. Third, he had not forgotten his roots—Aberdeen friends that included the Urquharts chemistry shops and the public dispensary where he trained as a chemist.

His greatest gratitude was for advice that Catherine and William Booth had given him. Catherine had told him to "never reduce your expenditures, raise your income." William's advice was to "stick to the lowest Lamb. You see if you raise the bottom the whole superstructure rises."[3] Lamb testified that for fifty years he had been "deeply conscious that the real battle is with inherent evil rather than with social conditions, and I have endeavored to work in the knowledge that spiritual values—the unseen and the eternal—transcend all others."[4] In this he shared the vision of his mentors: William, Catherine, and Bramwell Booth. To them, compassion was the heart of the Christian message and a love for all must be expressed in a "wholesale salvation" with spiritual and social dimensions.

Looking Backward: 40 Years of Social Change, 1893–1933

On January 13, 1933, Commissioner Lamb celebrated "Forty Years of Social Change" during his time in London with a broadcast from the British Broadcasting Company headquarters. It had been 40 years since William and Bramwell Booth had appointed him as director of the Migration and Settlement Department at The Salvation Army's International Headquarters in London.

Lamb recalled that the Booths had sent him on a "pilgrimage of the streets of London" soon after he came to the city from Scotland in 1888. There he found "hundreds of men and some scores of women, homeless, hungry, dirty, despairing, huddled on the steps of buildings, beneath railway arches, in stables, in vans, even in dustbins." Others "sprawled in a sullen stupor on the seats of the Embankment." And still more were "huddled in squalid hovels, in vile tenements, in underground dens" seeking protection from the weather.

In the 40 years since that walk, he claimed that "slum areas have been reduced in extent, and the numbers of the homeless poor in mid–winter have fallen from nearly 3,000 to about 80." Lamb listed The Salvation Army's response to these needy souls. Mainly they needed "food and shelter," which the Army had been providing since the London dock strike in 1888–89.

Among other social changes he listed were teashops, libraries in villages, recreation facilities, cinemas, radio, telephone, cigarette smoking, chocolate and sweets, dog racing, professional soccer, women justices of the peace, changes in dress and working hours, and the disappearance of shoe–blacks and crossing sweepers. But he concluded that "conditions today in some of our industrial centers are a blot on our Christian civilization."

Charles Booth published his *Life and Labour of the People of London* in 1903, the year Lamb began his Migration Department.

Life and Labour had found that "Comparisons with the past are absolutely necessary to the comprehension of all that exists today; without them we cannot penetrate the heart of things." But Lamb was a disciple of the practical emphases of William Booth who taught him that: 1) poverty was not a crime or disgrace; 2) "by raising the bottom of the social edifice the whole structure would be raised;" and that 3) it was not enough "to succour the victims of poverty and hardship; the evils themselves must be attacked and subdued." In 1933 the Army controlled islands in Sweden and New Zealand "to which inebriates can retire for treatment," and it operated leprosy hospitals in the Dutch East Indies and India.

Lamb cited recent social changes: "the loss of nearly one million men in the Great War;" and "emigration of at least twelve million men, women and children." Yet convictions for drunkenness had not increased with the growth of population, but had fallen from 200,000 to 50,000 a year. And the prison population had sunk from more than 32,000 to less than 13,000. Much of this was due to the fact that the courts were putting offenders on probation rather than sending them to prison, a policy that had begun in 1887 for young first offenders. In 1901 and 1907 British law extended the policy to all classes of offenders and established the rule of restitution. Lamb favored another reform, the end of imprisonment for debt that was still in vogue in 1933.

In 1893 London had been full of common lodging houses. Yet there were homeless people in the streets. And there were 28 Poor Law authorities administering "casual wards and supplying beds." But the casual wards were scattered all lover greater London, with no regard to where the homeless needed them. By 1933 The Salvation Army alone had 6,000 beds, and Rowton Houses and the London County Council had about 7,000. After 17 years of pleading by the Army, in 1912 the local government board had set up one authority in London "for the relief of casuals," and provided for cooperation between the police and voluntary societies. By 1914 the government had reduced the number of wards from 28 to 12, and beds from 1814 to 834, which were seldom occupied in one night. The local government board had set up a clearing house on the Embankment where outcasts were taken care of. In 1897 a law required "the cleansing of verminous persons" in lodging houses, and The Army provided "fumigators for the destruction of vermin" in its shelters.

The Army also challenged methods used by the London Health Authorities. Instead of scattering the homeless who were using lodging houses that had been cleaned, the Army proposed that lodgers be kept under surveillance for a few days. Slum areas, where disease ran rampant, had been cleared by the authorities in the area west of the law courts and replaced by "the splendid thoroughfares of Kingsway and Aldwych."

In 1893 80 percent of the children of the poor were "hungry–looking, poorly clad and poorly shod." In 1933 Lamb estimated that only four per hundred, rather than 30 per hundred school children were "flea and bug–bitten." The infant death rate had fallen by over fifty percent, and the life span had been extended by 15 years. Working conditions for men had "changed greatly," and the "standards of comfort" for working girls had "soared." But "older men in industrial centers ... have nothing to do."

Lamb said that there was "less open solicitation of prostitutes" in 1933 as opposed to conditions in early 1885 when W. T. Stead launched his "Social Purity Crusade" that convinced Parliament to raise the age of consent from 13 to 16 years. In 1912 Parliament legislated that men and women convicted of living on a prostitute's wages would be flogged. Lamb claimed that "within a few months ... more than 2,000 of these 'bullies,' male and female, left the country." And The Salvation Army had fought for matchbox workers, who were likely to contract "phossy jaw" from phosphorous matches. Due to agitation by *The Star* workers wages rose and the home office regulated factory conditions.

Speaking for himself, Lamb said that he had "always regarded the English abhorrence of Poor Law relief [welfare] as an asset in the formation of the English character." In the place of the dole, Lamb held that a balanced social system should provide "appropriate work for all able–bodied men." The "means test" of 1933 had replaced the "destitution test," under which all furniture but the barest necessities had to be removed in order to receive the dole. In 1893 "an able–bodied widow with one child would not [ordinarily] receive any relief." In 1933 they received 15 shillings a week.

On health matters, Lamb saw the move from a "destitution" test to a "means" test as a "peaceful revolution," conducted in 1892 to 1902 by local government board orders. A sick poor man was now to be admitted to an infirmary even if he received "an allowance from his benefit club." Order, neatness, and skilled nurses had made infirmaries more attractive.

On emigration, Lamb claimed that prior to 1933 "at least 200,000 British emigrants had moved to the dominions with the Salvation Army's assistance, although in 1933 emigration was "largely suspended." He was still convinced that "organized settlements" would prove to be "a substantial contribution to the solution of the unemployment problem." Under the Army's approach emigration was more attractive than it had been in 1883.

In 1933 Lamb still saw unemployment insurance and public assistance as "a dope" that drugged recipients and lulled the conscience. Nearly three million able–bodied men and women were "maintained in idleness," and "nearly half a million of them [were] continuously out of work for one year or more."

Unemployment and educational expenditures were his principal areas of disappointment. Migration was still the answer to the problem. "Work is the great antidote for the world's economic and social ills and the working man calls out in vain for it." As he saw it, there were tens of thousands of families in Britain "who would go anywhere to work and gladly adventure in any well–considered plan that gave assurance of continuous employment for a few years and the promise of ultimate independence."[5]

The Second High Council, 1934
David C. Lamb: A Candidate for General

In August 1934 the second High Council met in London, following the announced retirement of Edward J. Higgins as general. Commissioner David C. Lamb, as was rumored before the conclave, was one of the nominees to become the fourth general of The Salvation Army. The year was one of several landmark honors for Lamb. King George V had decorated him as a Commander of the Order of St. Michael and St. George (C.M.G.). Aberdeen University had conferred on him an honorary doctorate of laws, LL.D. And now he was nominated to be General along with: Chief of Staff Henry William Mapp; Commander Evangeline Booth, who, if elected, would be the first American citizen to be General; Commissioners Catherine Bramwell–Booth, Samuel Hurren, James Hay, and John McMillan. The last two nominees declined the nomination.

When 47 councilors met at Congress Hall, Clapton, David Lamb came prepared with a "Private Memorandum" of "some provisional rules for procedure" that he had composed in August. He had alerted the leaders of a need for rules when they met in a Conference of Commissioners in November 1930. Since the new High Council had no rules, he had drafted "provisional rules for procedure" for their consideration. The rules were as minute as: "Every member shall stand up when speaking, and shall address the president," and "each teller [would] be sworn to secrecy." A sample of his mental process may be seen in his concern about "how the fractions are to be counted" when a vote required two–thirds or three–fourths. The closest higher number would be the rule. No doubt the rules Lamb proposed would be recognized in embryo by subsequent members of High Councils.[6]

For the business of the 1934 High Council, Lamb proposed that the Chief of Staff, Commissioner Mapp, take the chair until the Council chose a president. The Council elected Commissioner Karl Larsson, a Swede, to preside. It took five ballots to elect a general by the required three–fourths margin. The first vote was reported to the President, who read the candidates' names in the order of their polling. On the second ballot Evangeline Booth was a strong first and Henry Mapp second. On the third and fourth ballots Mapp lost votes to Booth. On the fifth ballot Booth won the necessary three fourths with 32 votes. Mapp was second with 9, Catherine Bramwell–Booth had four, Samuel Hurren 2 and D. C. Lamb 0.[7]

Curiously, of the five candidates only Commissioners Bramwell–Booth and Hurren mentioned reform in their speeches to the High Council. Hurren asked each candidate to assure the Council that a referendum would not be made to alter the general's age of retirement. This meant that on Christmas 1938, five years hence, when Evangeline Booth would be 73, the age at which commissioners retired; she would not be required to retire if there was still no mandatory retirement age for generals. When Lamb addressed the Council he did not rehearse his plea for the General to work in council with senior officers.

Why did Lamb get no votes on the final ballot? First, there is no indication of how well he ran on earlier ballots. Second, compared to the Chief of Staff and American Commander, he had a tiny personal contingent on the Council; there were few commissioners from the Army's social side. The vast majority of members held their commands on the Army's spiritual side.

Outgoing general Edward Higgins later expressed a view that many likely held. He said that in his reflective moods:

> I fancy (am I correct?) that sometimes I detect that in our social service work [there is] an absence of spiritual effort which has made the Army's social work the wonder of the world. I know that in some countries governments are introducing methods which often run across some of our principles, but I say without hesitation where this is the case I would prefer to do without social work than try to run it without God and religion.[8]

Although Lamb had an international reputation, none of the commissioners answered to him. Third, there is no evidence that he had the sort of platform presence and charisma that were expected of generals. Salvationists liked to be stirred by the evangelical prose of great orators. While Lamb was occasionally a good speaker, he was not one to play to the emotions with stirring phrases. Lastly, it may well be that Lamb was seen as politically too far to the left for those who saw the Army in military, even monarchist terms. Lamb had many secular friends on the Labour/Socialist/Fabian side of the political spectrum.

After 1878, when it formally adopted its military form of government, The Salvation Army had wrestled with the issue of autocracy versus reform that would give it a less despotic polity. The Booths' biographer St. John Ervine favored autocracy over Lamb's "general in council" idea. Ervine held that if Lamb's council was not the High Council composed of all commissioners from all over the world, then it would be a British and not an international Council. This would produce stern repercussions in North America and elsewhere.

Ervine saw chiefs of staff as the logical successors to generals, and proposed that in the case of a general's "unexpected death," the chief should automatically succeed, as American vice presidents succeed presidents. For this reason, it followed that the chief should also be elected general. A chief would be a "business man," a sort of chief operating officer (COO) in modern parlance, and the general would be a "platform figure," as Bramwell and William Booth had been. There was a question as to how well a "business man" chief of staff might perform as a "platform" general.

Ervine, who published his biography in 1935, held that "democratic government of The Salvation Army is impossible." In this he disagreed with United Kingdom Attorney General William Jowitt's report to the House of Commons on the Salvation Army Act of 1931. Jowitt asked for a vote by rank and file Salvationists to elect a general. Frank Smith, M.P., had supported that democratic idea. Ervine commented that "democracy cannot operate in such a society as The Salvation Army; it can only destroy what autocracy created."[9]

Since this was the stance taken by most Salvation Army leaders, its soldiers (members) have continued to stand in the same subservient role to the hierarchy as they did in the days of the Booths. Only senior officers have gained a greater say in its international governance. This is particularly true in the United States where the Army's income derives largely from United Appeal, public philanthropy and government support for its social programs, and much smaller amounts from its own members. Lamb's push for more participation did not gain support from senior leaders until the end of the 20th century.

10

David C. Lamb, 1934–39,
On the Road to Retirement

During the five years prior to his retirement in 1939 at age 73, Commissioner Lamb became nostalgic. But he was also a vigorous exponent of his social philosophy in various publications and at numerous public occasions where he addressed primarily secular audiences. As he looked backward with gratitude he was always making assessments of both The Salvation Army and the international situation and how they could each improve in the future. In a 1933 essay he had focused on the fiftieth anniversary of his October 21, 1882 Christian conversion in a Salvation Army hall in Aberdeen, Scotland. He wrote the essay for the New York edition of the Salvation Army *War Cry*. In a second essay he discussed his 40 years as an officer in the Army's social wing, from 1892 to 1932.[1]

David Lamb recounted the honors he had received in 1934 and afterwards. Most impressive were secular honors that recognized his social reform work for the British Empire. Such honors had been bestowed on only a few Salvationists. In 1934 King George V put Lamb on his birthday list for his work on emigration and Empire settlement and gave him the title of "Companion of the Most Distinguished Order of St. Michael and St. George (C.M.G.)." On April 4, 1934 Lamb was one of five men who received the honorary doctorate of laws (LL.D.) from one of the leading institutions of higher learning in Scotland, the University of Aberdeen. Prof. Gray, promoter in law, said that "in honoring the Commissioner, the Senatus Academicus desired to Honor the great institution which he represented."[2] In 1939, Lamb became a Fellow of the Royal Empire Society (F.R.E.S.). On his retirement as a Salvation Army officer in 1939, retiring General Evangeline Booth conferred on him the Order of the Founder (O.F.), the Army's highest honor.[3]

It is the judgment of Commissioners Harry W. Williams and Arch R. Wiggins that Lamb would have received a knighthood if he had not been a Salvation Army officer. Army regulations did not permit officers to receive any titles at the risk of offending Salvationists outside the empire.

David Lamb on the Economic Value of Teaching the Unfit

As David Lamb looked backward, he also looked forward. In September 1934, immediately after the High Council in August, he addressed a meeting of the British Association for the Advancement of Science at a Salvation Army citadel in Aberdeen. His title was a new one: "The Economic Value of Teaching the Unfit." But since many thought that the Army was transporting the "submerged tenth" to the dominions in its emigration program, it was a topic that Lamb had often addressed informally when speaking to overseas audiences. The last time the British Association had met in Aberdeen was in 1885, and Charles Darwin's theory of the "survival of the fittest" was a topic for debate. But already, Lamb claimed, Darwin "had begun to think he had assigned too little importance to the modifying factors of use and disuse, environment, and so on." According to Lamb, "the survival of the 'unfit' is now [in 1934] being quite seriously discussed." In Lamb's view, "the unfit ought to be educated more than they are at present."

Lamb cited Sir Arthur Keith, rector of Aberdeen University, who had given as his 1931 inaugural address: "The Place of Prejudice in Modern Civilization," and dealt with "War as Nature's Pruning Hook." Keith held that "modern civilization has wrecked nature's original scheme." He held that "in the real

Garden of Eden the prehistoric world, nature had arranged to serve her own particular purpose—the production of new and better breeds of men." Keith concluded that, "Mankind is more in need of a racial physician than in any of its previous maladies." Lamb broke ranks with Keith's assertion that "'Nature keeps her human orchard healthy by pruning. *War is her pruning hook.* We cannot dispense with her services.'"

Instead Lamb argued that: "We must dispense with war as a pruning hook," since "the strongest ... are slain in war." He agreed that a certain number are "misfits." But who are they? They are those who, for whatever reason, "are a charge on the public or charitable funds." He saw them in four categories: 1) the "mentally deficient, feeble–minded, idiots, half–wits, lunatics," and placed their number at 505,000; 2) the "blind, deaf, dumb, cripples, diseased," whom he estimated at 380,000; 3) the "poorhouse and workhouse inmates, prisoners, the unemployable, etc., 410,000; and 4) "those reduced in moral stamina, and in general health by long periods of unemployment or under–employment," about 200,000.

This was the language of at least one element of social science in the 1930s. Lamb agreed and disagreed with its stipulations, and to his credit he was willing to assert his Christian principles in a secular meeting. As we had stated earlier, he saw the prison population decreasing, convictions for drunkenness declining, but there were increases in what the times termed "certified lunatics" and suicides. He asked: "What has science done?" He hoped that "out of chaos and darkness a new creation may come; that the evolutionary idea which Darwin and others saw at work in the natural world may be not far apart from what, in the spiritual realm, we call growth in grace."

Lamb had seen growth in The Salvation Army and its social services spanning four decades. But he also saw its rough beginnings. In 1860 Catherine Booth began preaching, and in 1861 the Booths left the Methodist New Connexion and went on their own as itinerant evangelists. In 1862–65 they faced hardship—William had no vocation and his wife was over–employed, supporting their growing family from her income, as she did for most of the rest of her life. Then in 1865 William rediscovered the "joy of service" in London's East End.

Lamb asked: Was there such a thing as a "combination of Calvinism and Darwinism," of "election and selection." What Lamb knew was that "I am a humanitarian and an individualist, and a creationist, and I submit to you that it is a moral wrong to maintain able–bodied men and women in idleness for long periods, and I submit further that what is morally wrong cannot be economically right." He saw work as "the great antidote for the world's economic and social ills."

He argued that even "unemployables" did not want charity. They wanted "training that will make them useful citizens," that gave them the "self–respect that comes from labor." He wanted to know of "the possibilities of educating the unfit," but concluded that "our humanities are not spiritually effective." He asked: "Have we lost the power to cast out devils? Have we lost the art of spiritual healing?" He held that the "Christian ethic is the answer to the problem … Spiritual influences, properly directed, with an educational bias, may have a definite economic value." He asserted that "applied Christianity is good and profitable economics."[4]

Lamb loved addressing public audiences. In September 1936 he addressed The British Association for the Advancement of Science in Blackpool, England, on a subject he knew best: "The Social Work of The Salvation Army," with the Lord Mayor presiding. In September 1937 he addressed the Nottingham Meeting of the British Association on "Impacts: Spiritual, Economic and Social," with the mayor of Nottingham presiding.

In 1937 Lamb wrote an essay on "The Challenge of the Christian Ethic in Social Services," published in the *Liverpool Quarterly*. His thesis was the theme of his life: "the social service inspired by the Christian faith may be the highest form of worship. I refer, of course, to *personal* service. But I do not overlook the fact that the Christian ethic may manifest itself in communal service and in the decisions of public authorities which will govern the community." It was not a theme that all Christians embraced. Many held that true worship took place only in a proper Christian sanctuary with proper prayers and hymns and preaching. In fact, not all Salvationists adhered to Lamb's credo of Christian ethics.

As examples of Christian ethics in practice David Lamb cited the need to deviate from the "law" of *Orders and Regulations* when mercy was called for. He mentioned the Army's shelters for the homeless in winter, maternity hospitals for unwed mothers and married mothers as needed, rooms for young working women in cities, crèches for children of working mothers, industrial and land settlements for criminal tribes in India, hospitals for the blind and lepers in the Dutch East Indies, sanatoria for the treatment of tubercular patients in Japan, and dispensaries in many lands that needed them. Social service meant meeting the whole need. He had no patience with those who nit–picked at the failures of social institutions. He noticed that "the reputations of workers and institutions are often made by the way that the most difficult cases are handled."[5]

In November 1937 Lamb addressed the Empire Club of Canada in Toronto on "Population Problems." He introduced himself by saying that he divided The Salvation Army and the world into "those that talk and those that work," and "I belong to the workers and I don't find talking easy, as those on the other side, but on occasions like these I have standing instructions from my children to this effect: 'Now, Father, not too high, not too low, not too fast, not too slow, and for goodness' sake not too Scotch.'" Then he mentioned that his friend George Bernard Shaw had told him "that he had learned the art ... of public speaking at The Salvation Army." He'd gone to the Army's open air meetings in his early Socialist days to "gather up what the Army left. I don't know what he did with it, but still the Army marched off and he was left. Then he started coming early to see how we got on and he told me that the fellow who talked of himself and of his own experiences was the man who gripped the crowd."

First, Lamb noted the movement of racial groups, mainly blacks moving northward in North America and southward in Africa, but he drew no conclusions. Then, before talking about the politics and economics of population he noted that the "Salvation Army doesn't know anything about politics." The speech itself was a choppy, hodge–podge of accumulated economic, political and social opinions, many of which he had previously exploited in England, but now he was in Canada. A man on the move, social leader or evangelist, has the luxury of repeating himself.

He had come to the tentative conclusion that "the fittest do not survive." Why? War "destroys the best of the race." The "increase in the number of the dependent part of the population—other than the unemployed"—was a sure sign that in large numbers the unfit did survive. He had long held that "unemployment lowers the physical, spiritual, and moral standard of people maintained in idleness," and that the "unrestricted growth of our great cities inevitably creates living conditions in which people cannot be 'A1.'" He was appalled by the "slaughter on the roads," an "evidence of lack of control and disregard for courtesy."

He held that "economics is like science, unethical and immoral. No one understands them; at least no school of which I have yet heard commands general respect." Yet he drew his evidence from economic statistics and as a chemist, challenged science from the inside. During the depression 25 to 30 percent of workers had been thrown "on the scrap–heap of industry." That moral wrong could not be "economically right or politically sound." Britain had spent £2 billion "on the endowment of idleness," and Canada had not offered "to take these people, take them and make something out of them ... I don't know where you Canadians have been. Surely you have been looking to the Americans." It cost £2,000 "to maintain a family in idleness, but only £800 to £1,200 "to settle a family on what I regard as a somewhat satisfactory economic basis, and the land available for settlement is limited."

Then Lamb turned to "political power." Some political parties do not want immigration until "the unemployed in the dominions are absorbed." Some see development of the dominions' resources as a way to solve the unemployment problem. Both agree that they do not want immigrants dumped on Canada. They do not want to do anything that "would aggravate the unemployment problem." And they agree that "any new movement should be so regulated in respect of racial origins that there would be no danger of the Canadian standards of living being adversely affected ... or her ethical standards lowered."

But Lamb was inclined to embrace an old, well–tried colonization principle, "namely the bringing together of idle lands, idle capital and idle labor." And he proposed taking the "long view." To cut the "endowment of idleness" costs and devote at least half of that money to "migration and settlement" made sense to him. But this was a matter for the Canadian people to decide. He suggested that the driving principle behind their decision might well be Jesus' words: "Do to others what you would have them do to you, for this sums up the Law and the Prophets" (Matthew 7:12). Lamb said that he found eight of the nine Canadian provinces were "prepared to encourage a selected British immigration."[6]

In May 1938 Lamb outlined in The Times of London The Salvation Army's work for "the Homeless Poor: London Streets Fifty Years Ago." He was reacting to a London County Council report on the homeless and Lamb wanted to provide a historical background for what he had to say. He commended the council for its work, but called for more access by the poor to the services the city was now providing.[7]

In August 1938 Lamb addressed the British Association for the Advancement of Science in Cambridge on "Outcroppings." The mayor of Cambridge presided. Even when Lamb spoke in Salvation Army corps auditoriums, as he did in Aberdeen, Nottingham, and Cambridge, he liked to include secular audiences and have a political leader in the chair.

On October 24, 1938 a luncheon at the Goldsmith's Hall in the City of London, honored David C. Lamb's 50 years since his conversion at a Salvation Army penitent–form in Aberdeen. David and Minnie Lamb received the guests together. British Prime Minister J. Ramsay MacDonald had agreed to preside, but was unable to attend. In his place, Secretary of State for Dominion Affairs J. H. Thomas chaired the luncheon. The archbishop of Canterbury's secretary, the Rev. Alan C. Don, said grace. Messages from the Duchess of York, the Dowager Countess of Airlie and the "Fricokers" came from Lamb's home county of Angus. This was one of a series of "testimony meetings" that had begun the day before with a "breakfast with London's homeless poor."

Minnie Clinton Lamb, J.P., "Promoted to Glory," April 22, 1939

On November 2, 1938 David and Minnie Lamb celebrated their 50th wedding anniversary. Among the 600 guests were

George Lansbury, M.P., now retired from the House of Commons, the cabinet, and leadership of the Labour party; Thomas Lamb; and Professor Herbert Spencer, the Social Darwinist. Appropriately, the London Angus Association sponsored the event for the couple who had been married in Glasgow. The site was the Royal Scottish Corporation, Fetter Lane, E.C. The sponsors gave Minnie Lamb a check "for her charitable fund." During their 50 years together the Lamb's were "comrades–in–arms" in the best of traditions in The Salvation Army. Their work, ideas, and companionship reinforced each other.

Just six months later, On April 22, 1939 Minnie Clinton Lamb died suddenly while she was visiting her family at Trebetherick, Daymer Bay, near Wadebridge, in Cornwall. Obituaries gave her home address as Kirkden, Chalkwell Ave., Westcliff, Essex, the county where the Lambs had lived since their appointment to The Salvation Army industrial colony at Hadleigh. She was 75, and had been a Salvation Army officer for 57 years. Newspapers noted that during her first year as an officer in 1882 "a mob" had chased her through the streets of Perth and she "had to be sheltered by the police."[8]

As early as 1907 the home of David and Minnie Lamb, known as "Lamb's House," was a headquarters from which she, with the support of her husband, carried on local social philanthropies in addition to her Salvation Army work. While a local newspaper stated: "Col. and Mrs. Lamb have no official Salvation Army responsibilities in the neighborhood," by 1907 Minnie had opened a day nursery for working mothers at 369 Leigh Road and had become president of a committee of eight local women that raised £1,000 for a suitable location for a children's home that would be turned over to The Salvation Army in due course. She frequently wrote articles about her social enterprises in Southend, Essex,[9] including a 1935 series of ten articles for the *Sunday Post* on hard cases she had worked with during her career in social service.[10]

As one obituary put it, Minnie Lamb had an "enthusiasm for humanity." For twenty–four years she served as a Poor Law guardian and probation officer for Southend, and represented The Salvation Army at the county court of sessions, the petty sessions police court, and the Rochford police court. A reporter noted that her local work kept "DCL in close touch [with] the poorer classes and their needs. She has championed the cause of the injured and vehemently dealt with the evildoer."

A list of her labors of love included many of the philanthropic enterprises of her day. In addition to being a police court missionary, she was a justice of the peace; chairman and secretary of the Boarding–out Committee; president of the Samaritan League; and "first visitor" for the Poor Law board under the Infant Life Protection Act. She was a member of the board of management of Lock Hospital in London; and a member of the council of the Lunacy Law Reform Society. She attended an international prison conference at Prague. As for honors, in 1937 Queen Mary received her at Marlborough House. At the November 1938 celebration of their 50th wedding anniversary the Lambs received many letters, including one from the London Council of Social Services.

Along Minnie Lamb's High Street funeral procession route to Leigh Cemetery, thousands of friends paid their respects, including Salvation Army officers, children from her Millfield children's Home, and men from the Army's Land and Industrial Colony at Hadleigh. Commissioner Catherine Bramwell–Booth conducted the service and her mother, Mrs. General Bramwell Booth, was also present.[11] Beginning in 1927, when Bramwell Booth approved a biography of Minnie Lamb, David Lamb pushed the Army's literary department to have it written, but to no avail. The project died in the 1950s. There has been no biography of either David or Minnie Lamb, just biographical sketches.[12] While this book does not pretend to be Minnie Lamb's biography, it does contain a bit of her life as the companion of David Lamb and an ardent worker for social reform.

Order of the Founder, October 31, 1939

October 31, 1939 David Lamb added another set of letters behind his name. General Evangeline Booth, on her last day in office and in the presence of all the commissioners in the United Kingdom and their wives, members of the international staff, and many high ranking retired officers, conferred the Order of the Founder, O.F., and decorated Lamb with the corresponding insignia. The ceremony took place at the William Booth Memorial Training College at Denmark Hill, Southeast London, The Salvation Army's temporary International Headquarters (IHQ).

Lamb's response was a tad strange. He had a tendency to give unexpected responses. As a man who loved honors, he said that he had not sought this "signal honor." "Indeed the General knows my feelings, and how all values have profoundly changed for me this year. But it would be idle to suggest that it does not give me great pleasure to receive this decoration, and I know the General has real pleasure in bestowing it. I have asked for very little for myself from any general: I have asked for and expected much for the Army. Apart from asking for permission to get married I have no recollection of ever requesting any great personal favor, and my request to get married must have made a great impression at Headquarters for it was readily granted and I was married a few days before my 22nd birthday. But then, as we know, Army marriage is not entirely a personal affair!"

This autobiographical speech was revealing. He noted his previous honors, including the "Companion of the Most Distinguished Order of St. Michael and St. George" from King George V. He mentioned for the first time that "a higher Order was mentioned to me on at least three separate occasions, and an emissary of the British government once came to IHQ, urging me to accept it. But headquarters frowned upon the idea, and my wife would have none of it although she confessed once that she would have liked for about ten days to have moved about in Southend in her uniform as Commissioner Lady Lamb, and put some of the snobs in their places! (My wife was a commissioner in her own right by virtue of an appointment she held as a justice of the peace)." He mentioned his honorary LL.D. (doctor of laws) from Aberdeen University. "The *Cap* with which the heads of those so honored are tapped, is made from an old pair of breeks—'trousers' to you English—which John Knox wore."

As for the Order of the Founder, Lamb stated that William Booth was "a great individualist," and that he himself had not been an organization man—"being something of a heretic." "I have been in a good deal of hot water, but always in a good cause." He opposed "glorifying the state or the organization and placing it above the individual." Rather, he saw himself "as being a bit troublesome to my leaders." But when General Bramwell was chief of staff and I was troublesome, he seemed to make occasions and to give me opportunities of expressing myself." The Founder had told him: "You get the people converted, Lamb, and the Army can look after itself."[13]

The Royal Tour, 1939

David Lamb seldom missed a chance to comment on a public event into which he could plant his imperial and Christian philosophies. In 1939, as war was breaking out in Europe, the British king and queen traveled to Canada. Lamb was thrilled by the enthusiasm of the Canadian reception at a time when the "Old Country" was under stress. He followed the progress of the Royal train as it crossed Canada and applauded the Statute of Westminster that had given British and Dominion Parliaments equality in all matters of domestic and foreign affairs. He saw an "inspiration to spread the British race, to populate the vacant areas, firstly with British stock then with the assimilable types of settlers from other countries." He was pleased with the King's Empire Day broadcast that embraced a "perfect truth" that: "It is only by adding to the spiritual dignity and material happiness of human life in all its myriad homes that an Empire can claim to be of service to its own peoples and to the world." He was thrilled to hear two Salvation Army bands playing the national anthem in Manitoba, and know that their Majesties had visited Salvation Army maternity hospitals in Halifax on the Atlantic and Vancouver on the Pacific and Toronto's Grace Hospital. Of course Lamb put in a plug for emigration to the dominions.[14]

11

1940–1951: David C. Lamb in Retirement—The Best Years of His Life?

E ven though at age 73 David C. Lamb was on the verge of retirement in January 1940, General George L. Carpenter asked him to continue at the International Headquarters as a director of The Salvation Army Assurance (insurance) Society.[1] Fifty years earlier Lamb had supervised the signing of a contract to take over an insurance company that the Salvation Army had received from the Wesleyan Methodists as a legacy to the Booth family, and then Lamb participated in its reorganization. The company was intended to provide a means by which poor folk could bury family members. Such benevolent insurance companies were common at the time, often under the control of ethnic groups or fraternal brotherhoods.[2] By now Lamb had become a fellow of the Royal Empire Society, F.R.E.S.

World War II and Post–War Planning

As early as February 1940 David Lamb was looking forward to the post–World War II "problem" and its solution. There was only one problem, as Lamb saw it: "to find work for unemployed men and women." Once again he was moving into the political (at least the governmental) arena. When peace was declared, as he saw it, military organizations would come under civilian control, except for defense forces. The minister of labor would be in charge, with an advisory council "until all the men and women affected are absorbed into the normal life of the community." The armed forces would become "an army of construction," and "every man and woman will be under orders to do something."

There would be "three channels" to gain employment upon discharge: 1) the Government Labour Bureau; 2) local and state governments and voluntary associations that engaged in settlement work; and 3) people of independent means with their own businesses, or with friends who will find work for them. A settlement board and repatriation authority would examine schemes submitted by voluntary agencies and local and state governments and finance ways to execute the schemes they approved. Those wanting to go overseas would choose the locale, but the dominions would have the last word on immigrants. The Salvation Army International Headquarters issued Lamb's scheme, which was marked "confidential until Wednesday, 21 February 1940." It was copyrighted by David Lamb of 23 Canonbury Square, London.[3]

In July 1941 Lamb's friend, George Bernard Shaw, dropped off a copy of his play *Major Barbara*,[4] with pictures, at Lamb's home in London. Lamb wrote a "thank you note" and termed the book "just splendid!" but he warned "GBS" to watch out "if you should chance to meet one of our bandmasters of the West of London, you will find him in a truculent mood!" One picture showed an Army bandsman throwing wine on the fire—"which a well–saved bandsman would promptly do"—but Shaw must understand that "bandmasters are responsible for the spiritual well–being, as well as the musical efficiency of their bandsmen."[5] It is difficult to know what Lamb meant by this unless he thought that it might be taken for the bandsman's own bottle that he threw.

Shaw knew Army bands and defended them against public criticism. In 1905 Bramwell Booth had invited him to make a "technical criticism for private circulation" of a December 7 Salvation Army band festival. Several bands performed, including the International Staff Band. Shaw's report of March 31, 1906 assessed the skills of the bands and arrangers frankly and constructively. He did not like "florid scoring" for euphoniums. He preferred "broad simple chords," since "exercises are not music and should be kept out of the public performances of the band." Bands should strive to make an emotional effect. "It should be possible for a blindfold [sic] critic to say which was the Salvation Army band and which was the professional."

General Booth had the report put in a sealed envelope and the Army did not publish it until December 3, 1960, fearing that it would upset bandsmen. Shaw provided a progress report on Army bands in 1922. His coy comment was: "Very smart, both playing and uniform; but not a man of them saved. Quite secular in tone." Brindley Boon, in his history of the International Staff Band, wrote that "the secrets of this second commentary have been safely guarded." At a national band concert in 1930, Shaw said: "I consider that Salvation Army bands are among the best. Because of their fervor the Salvationists get more real music out of their instruments than many professional bands."

In October 1941 Shaw offered high praise. "Had the Albert Hall, the B.B.C. Orchestra, and The Salvation Army's International Staff Band been within Handel's reach, the score of 'Messiah' would have been of a very different specification. The music would not and could not have been better, but the instrumentation would have been much richer and more effective."[6] The Fabian/socialist, music critic, playwright, had become David Lamb's friend out of a shared love for music and drama and social reform.

On the Road Again, 1941–1942: Canada and the United States

During World War II David Lamb was a member of the Empire Settlement Committee for Ex–Servicemen. With their support he toured North America and made four round–the–world voyages. After his last retirement from The Salvation Army in 1941, at age 75, he made two extended goodwill tours of Canada and the United States. In his late 70s he wrote and spoke as a senior statesman of The Salvation Army, but also as an international social reform and peace advocate. His first articles were on "The National Unit in Peace and War" and "Co–operation in Commerce." In November 1942 he spoke on a "War of Ideas–the

'Jury.'" During the war he wanted to "rally men of every country and class in support of the common ideals of western Chris-
tendom"—and he wanted to snatch "security" from the jaws of
"aggression." In his judgment the Anglo–American alliance had
to produce "national unity in peace and war" and this included
"cooperation in commerce."[7]

At the end of Lamb's two years of touring North America, Major Gladstone Murray, director–general of the Canadian Broadcasting Corporation, wrote to Clement Atlee, then the Secretary of
State for the Dominions in Winston Churchill's national unity
(Tory–Labour) government. Murray's letter to Atlee praised
Lamb's work: "I write to call your attention particularly to the
distinguished work which Commissioner David Lamb has been
doing on this continent. He certainly earned his C.M.G. in double
measure."[8] Murray regarded Lamb as one of the top British
propagandists in Canada's mid–West and urged Atlee to "keep
him in the United Kingdom for as short a time as possible."[9]

During the tour Lamb had a check–up at the Mayo Clinic in
Minnesota in May that "revealed the need for an early and serious operation," which Dr. Charles Mayo performed. While Lamb
was "lying critically ill in St. Mary's Hospital," his youngest
daughter Janet (Mrs. Ronald Carton), came from London to be at
his bedside. She remained with him for several months. He did
not mention the nature of the illness or the operation.

He was traveling on his own expense, "under no obligation
to anyone, nor is anyone but myself responsible for the views I
express." When he stopped at his sister's home in Detroit he had
three shillings, and six and a half pence. When his sister learned
that he planned to "hitchhike" across America she gave him $50.
But he "incurred no debts," no doubt because he had "Army
friends and others" who looked after him.

In his luggage he carried his identity card, a gas mask, his
C.M.G. insignia, and his Aberdeen LL.D. gown, which he used
to entertain his audiences. He had lost his O.F. decoration when
The Salvation Army's International Headquarters was destroyed
in the German bombing in May 1941. Audiences saw him as
"something of a hero" due to his two years in London's blackout
and air raids and his crossing the Atlantic on a ship. On the tour
he traveled 12,000 miles by road, rail, air and sea, with extremes
of temperature as low as 25 degrees below zero and higher than

100 degrees in the shade. In addition to visits to Canadian cities he had seen on previous tours he visited 24 American cities: Boston, Newport, New York, Washington, Ann Arbor, Dallas, Waco, Corpus Christi, San Antonio, Oklahoma City, New Orleans, Atlanta, St. Louis, El Paso, Tucson, Los Angeles, San Francisco, Seattle, Tacoma, Spokane, Portland, Duluth, St. Paul, and Northfield.

He talked to mostly secular audiences, counting the United Clubs' luncheon in Oklahoma City, with 753 present, as "among the most outstanding of these." His Los Angeles Breakfast Club speech was attended by 400 and was broadcast, but he spoke for only eight minutes since he had to share the podium with "Babe Ruth," the "darling of the gods" in the United States "where all is baseball." He spoke at Episcopal churches in San Antonio and Tucson, and at Northfield College, founded by Dwight L. Moody. He had interviews with judges, editors, and university presidents and faculties. He met The Salvation Army's six commissioners who had oversight of 6,000 officers in 3,000 centers in the United States and Canada.

As he had already revealed in his speeches and writings in Britain, he was deeply concerned about a depression that would almost certainly come at the end of World War II, as it had after World War I. He had discussed the problem with "orthodox and unorthodox economists" like Montagu Norman, governor of the Bank of England, and George Bernard Shaw, Socialist and playwright, etc. His plea was that economics be influenced by the Christian ethic of the golden rule. Otherwise his topics came from his pamphlet, "War of Ideas." As a member of the New Commonwealth he proposed their two–plank program of: 1) a court of equity; and 2) an international police force. He also pushed his own view that "restitution and reparation are in the Divine order of things and that there can be no satisfactory settlement of the world's miseries if they are ignored."[10] He wrote these letters and others in this period of his life largely for family and friends and they were thus more folksy and intimate.

Salvation Army Matters, 1941–1946

Lamb kept one foot in internal Salvation Army affairs. In December 1941 he wrote a private note to General George L. Carpenter, who had been elected to office by the 1939 High Council and served to the end of the war. Lamb assumed that due to the bombing of the Army's Victoria Street headquarters in May 1941, "all papers I left at IHQ on Saturday afternoon last are, or may become a total loss." Thus there was no record of his correspondence or management of the migration and settlement department due to the bombing. Fortunately Lamb had moved some papers to his flat at Canonbury Square, but papers "for proposed biographies were ... at IHQ," data that cannot be replaced.

But his "notes of High Councils, and the Commissioners Conference," and the "matter for an Official History of the Emigration Department" that had been put in order by Colonel Hancock, was also likely lost. Matters that concerned him most were: 1) A history of the first and subsequent High Councils; 2) an official history of the migration department since 1903; 3) a book on social problems requested by General Evangeline Booth, designed for libraries; 4) a case book "written from a study standpoint—Bramwell Booth's idea; 5) publication of some of his articles "for Staff Officers, and our more intelligent Locals;" 6) a biography of Mrs. Lamb; and 7) "My own Biographical Notes."

He offered to reduce his staff to two–thirds of what it was years ago. He preferred to maintain an office in his flat at Canonbury Square "rather than set up an Establishment at Sunbury," where the Army was moving its headquarters outside London. Major Wynn was helping Lamb list "contacts I have made and expected to make" so that "when I passed on or off, the Major and the Histories in question" could be merged with public relations or with the secretary's staff of the General or Chief of Staff, so that the contacts would not be lost.[11]

Throughout this period Lamb pestered the Army's Literary Department under Colonel Carvosso Gauntlett's direction, to carry out Bramwell Booth's directive to produce a biography of Minnie Lamb. Just before Bramwell had sent Literary Secretary George Carpenter to Australia in 1927, Carpenter had "commissioned Major [Leal] to write this biography," and "she had made a start on it but then was appointed to full time work for Mrs. Bramwell Booth." Now Major Leal, who had come into the Army through Mrs. Lamb, was ready to write the book if General Carpenter agreed and if David Lamb would turn over all of the material he had kept on his wife. But while Leal loved Minnie Lamb, she was no fan of David's, whom she saw as having a "craze for personal publicity." But she assured Gauntlett that "I should like very much to write her life. If D.C.L. can post me all available data. You may be quite sure he has plenty!"[12] This saga of Minnie Lamb's biography continued past David Lamb's death into the late 1950s, with no result.

On August 15, 1945, David Lamb wrote a family letter from the home of his sister, Mrs. Jessie Robertson, and her two daughters, at 14042 Strathmoor Avenue, Detroit. As usual he was spending a great deal of time on the road. He had met the mayor of Victoria, British Columbia, who had arrived in Canada 40 years ago as a member of one of The Salvation Army's "Conducted Parties." He was now the father of six, with four boys in the Canadian Navy, and a grandfather of seven. Lamb had met an "old Salvationist," who had emigrated to Ontario after learning the farming trade at Hadleigh. He and his wife had nine children and 22 grandchildren and "many great—grandchildren. At Hadleigh his wife had assisted Mrs. Lamb in the "Darning and Mending League of Women" for the 300 resident men of Hadleigh. Such large numbers of progeny could only cause Lamb to think of how many Canadians had descended from his Army–sponsored migrants.

Lamb was in San Francisco when the United Nations Conference opened and he spent more than two weeks there "making informal contacts with delegates, secretaries, pressmen and others," during which he addressed a public meeting chaired by Salvation Army Commissioner W. H. Barrett. Lamb gave them a dose of Scottish history to show them that he sympathized with the small nations at the conference. From 1314, when Scotland won independence from England at Bannockburn; to 1603–5 when Scotland joined England in a United Kingdom; to 1745 when "Bonnie Prince Charlie" led his Highlander troops to London; and when the Stuart dynasty ended at Derby.

At a service at Grace Cathedral at the close of the British Commonwealth of Nations Memorial Service, Lamb had what he termed a "bad moment" and choked during the singing of "God Save the King" and was unable to join in till the last line as he thought of London, Edinburgh, Capetown, Rhodesia, New Zealand, Australia, and ships at sea. The recessional was: "God of Our Fathers."

In Southern California Lamb met Colonel Dr. William Noble of India who had been born and received his early education in Aberdeen.[13] At Santa Barbara he met Mrs. I. Murphy who had cared for him at the Mayo Clinic three years earlier as he "lay for a whole week unconscious." He spent a night at a "guest ranch" where he discussed the "merits and demerits of Herefords, Aberdeen–Angus, etc." It had been 42 years since his first visit to North America. Yet he managed transportation, accommodations and traveling alone.

In Los Angeles he visited the offices of the three great railways on his list: Union Pacific; Santa Fe; and Southern Pacific. He said that "as usual I made my approach in an expectant spirit and lo and behold within one hour I got all I wanted." In Denver he called at The Salvation Army Headquarters and introduced himself. He made a lunch appointment with the divisional commander's wife, whose parents he knew years before in Canada. He then called on the mayor for a helpful talk, then at the *Denver Post* where he met Lord Lyluph Ogiluy with whom he chatted of Angus, Cortachy Castle, and Airlie Castle. They had been born within a few miles of each other. And so it went from stop to stop, meeting friends, hitchhiking, and making contacts.[14]

On November 30 he followed up his September letter with a "postscript" catalogue of the important people he had met in the United States, particularly in Washington. He dropped by the U.S. Chamber of Commerce offices, the National Geographical Society, and the London *Times* where he discussed Anglo–American relations with correspondent Sir Willmott Lewis and his assistant Frank Oliver, " a well–informed American." He met the representative of the Southern Rhodesian government, B. F. Wright, and was a guest at a Siamese reception to honor the King of Siam's birthday. He went with a German–American to the National Cathedral to commemorate the "Battle of Britain." He had lunch at the capitol with Chaplain to the Congress Dr. Montgomery. In Washington he stayed at the Evangeline Residence run by Major and Mrs. Purdom.

At Harvard University he lunched with a member of the faculty prior to a "long talk" with President Conant concerning the "soul of America" and "post–war problems," two of Lamb's favorite topics. At a dinner in his honor attended by 180 "leading citizens," Alan Forbes presided. Lamb talked for an hour on Anglo–American relations. He discussed "World Problems" with the *Christian Science Monitor* editor, Canaham. Colonel and Mrs. Stretton set up Lamb's meetings with Salvation Army offices and the public.

In New York, "as in every other city, the tune 'Take off your hats to London' brought an eager response." London had become England to many Americans. Yet, "England is still a bogey to a very great number of Americans, who honestly believe we still live under the feudal system." Those who knew better often used the word "British" and avoided the word "English," which caused Lamb the Scot "considerable mortification" when an editor published a letter Lamb wrote and referred to Sidney and Beatrice Webb's seminal work as "The Breaking of the *British* [rather than the *English*] Poor Law.*

Commissioner Lamb lunched with General Evangeline Booth (retired) and several commissioners and chief secretaries at National Headquarters. He was present when the U.S. National Commander, Commissioner Ernest Pugmire, presented a Bible to General Jonathan Wainwright, "as a momento of his deliverance after great suffering" from a Japanese prisoner of war camp.

At the invitation of the captain of the *Queen Elizabeth*, J. G. Bisset, Lamb returned to England on that ship in October. Passengers were restricted to $50 worth of food, but by the time the ship lifted anchor Lamb had passed that mark. He explained to the customs officials that after he signed the declaration he "had been asked to take parcels for others." They let him pass and even encouraged him to spend more. He did and he arrived in England with bacon, Carnation® brand milk, and a prayer: "(God Bless America)."

The food situation in England had worsened, but the war was over. There were no blackouts and no air raids or air raid alarms. Damage done in his own London borough during the 12 months he was away was "enormous." Re–housing the British people "is probably our greatest national 'headache.'" But for his 79th birthday on October 26, "thanks to friends in the States we sat down in the 'Old House' (my daughter Janet's home) to a

sumptuous repast—chicken and ham and cookies (i.e. fancy bis-
cuits), cheese, fruit juice, preserves, honey, etc., and tea with
cream!"

Within days he was back into his London routine: a meeting
with friends at the Council of the London Angus Association;
and a meeting of the Pedestrians' Association. In November he
met with the head office staff of the Salvation Army Life Assurance Society at its temporary headquarters in Reading. He was a
founder and director of the insurance company. Managing Director Commissioner Frank Dyer had sent him the invitation. After lunch he visited Reading University's principal, Sir Franklin
Sibly, and then the editor of the county newspaper, the chief of
police, and had afternoon tea in the mayor's parlor with the
mayor and his wife and a "small group of ladies." He spent the
evening talking with Commissioner Dyer on "a favorite topic,"
The Salvation Army's founder. He had accepted an invitation to
address the cadets at the Denmark Hill Training College.[15]

Lamb on Salvation Army History and
"the Next General," the 1946 High Council

In April 1946, for the *Spectator*, one of England's oldest, most
prestigious magazines, David Lamb wrote an article on The Salvation Army's post–war election of a new general on April 25 to
replace George Carpenter. Lamb began at the beginning, July
1865, to discuss how the Army got to 1946. He mentioned the
1870 trust deed that set out the doctrines and governance structure of the Christian Mission. William Booth had been appointed
General Superintendent for life, with sole right to govern, although "the Conference might, by unanimous vote, disqualify
him." Booth could nominate his successor, but 12 Conference
members could nominate candidates. The General Superintendent would be the person who received "the highest number of
votes—by ballot." The term was for five years, but re–election
was possible. Every ten years the Conference could consider
modifications. The Conference had to meet at least once a year.

In August 1878 the 1870 deed was annulled. A new deed allowed the General to resign, but the Conference could not remove him. And he was required to nominate a successor. In 1890

when the Army began to solicit large amounts of money from the public for the Darkest England scheme its one–man rule and sole trusteeship of property came under attack. In 1891 a new deed, affecting social operations, was drawn up and provided for the General to appoint a committee of outsiders, but William Booth maintained that one–man rule was the best government. Lamb pointed out that the 1878 deed left no room to deal with "calamity ... incapacity ... nor for heresy," as W. E. Gladstone told Booth at Hawarden Castle in 1896.

In fact, there was a "narrow escape" when a Fenian bomb near the Mount Pleasant (London) post office went off as William and Bramwell Booth's carriage passed on their way from IHQ to King's Cross Station. William knew that Bramwell's name was in the sealed envelope that carried the name of his successor. So he made drafts of a supplementary deed that would establish a High Council "for at least ten years" after the incident, and continued to consult lawyers and statesmen "in many countries." W. T. Stead went to Rome to see how the College of Cardinals elected the Pope. In 1904, after consulting constitutional attorneys, R. B. Haldane and H. H. Asquith, William Booth signed the supplementary deed. He remarked comically, "My death–warrant," and told Bramwell: "Think of it, Bramwell, back to committees and voting!" In 1929 the 1904 deed worked to call the High Council to elect Edward Higgins to replace Bramwell Booth as general.

In 1931 Parliament passed a Salvation Army Act that placed that power in the hands of a High Council. Lamb held that among the 1929–30 reformers the "legal element" prevailed. This gave the High Council of Army leaders in 1946 only one choice, "the High Council can do only one thing—elect a General." When that is done, the High Council is dissolved.

Lamb argued that the fixing of a retirement age of generals in 1931 had been a mistake. In the previous 17 years the Army had three generals. Two of them had their terms extended to increase continuity in policy. But he agreed with William Booth's dictum: "the work shall always remain under the direction and control of some one person [who] shall remain inviolate." Lamb held that over time "who is actually the General will become less and less important to the rank and file." Over time "local officers" and a "Census Board" had gained some say in the management of the corps. And on divisional headquarters a system of councils gradually evolved. Lamb observed that in the early 1890s, when the Booths issued orders and regulations for territorial commanders or commissioners, "they left the General and the Chief of the Staff alone without regulations or restraint of any kind. Ultimately, the Chief ... was specifically restricted in some matters reserved by the General for his own decision."[16]

Forty–eight officers from all over the world would comprise the High Council in April 1946. The voting would continue until one nominee had two–thirds majority. The present General would offer no counsel to the High Council. On May 9 the election began under the direction of David Lamb's friend, Commissioner Dyer, who was the Council's president. With 36 votes, the High Council elected Albert Orsborn as the Army's sixth general. Orsborn was the man who referred to David Lamb as the "Scottish dirk" (dagger).

Commissioner Lamb soon submitted a memo to Orsborn, "for the General's consideration." For his 80th birthday on October 26 Lamb, who had "not yet had any official retirement function," wanted the General to "sponsor one or two meetings in London about that time." He was aware that the general would be away, but that was no problem. "The London Angus Association (the Queen is our Patron)—(for years I was the Almoner for the Association)—is planning a special gathering of the (Angus) clans in the Conway Hall on the 30th October." "Outside" friends were setting up a luncheon that "you could sponsor (without cost to Army funds) in addition to some Army gathering." Orsborn agreed to apply for the Conway Hall and if Lamb had a committee sending out invitations "I might allow one of our officers to be a member of it. Beyond that I was sorry I could not go."[17]

Testimony to the Advisory Council Commission, 1946

On July 8, 1946, Commissioner Catherine Bramwell–Booth, Chairman of an Advisory Council Commission, wrote to Commissioner Lamb to invite him "to come and give us your mind" on the subject of an Advisory Council to the General, in terms of its "form, powers and processes." Chief of Staff Charles Baugh had set up the advisory group to fulfill General Orsborn's promise to the High Council that had elected him General.

A "general in council" was still a cherished idea of David Lamb's. It would conform to the organizational style of the cabinets of the British prime minister and American president. And it would allow a senior staff group to advise the General on a regular and formal basis. Lamb responded immediately to the Commission Secretary Colonel W. Rushton with copies of correspondence and memoranda that he had sent to "Commissioners and Territorial Commanders before the meeting of the High Council." Lamb said the materials had convinced Albert Orsborn to embrace the idea. The original date of Lamb's memo on the topic was June 26, 1939, the occasion of the 3rd High Council.

Lamb offered three suggestions: 1) "The desirability of divorcement ... of the Legislative from the Executive (The Advisory Council is a thinking body);" 2) "The importance of a world outlook;" the Council's personnel should not have departmental or territorial responsibility; and 3) "Any lines drawn now for procedure would/should be very loosely drawn" to allow for trial and error development.

Lamb commented on the Army's government and an Advisory Council to the General. 1) The "primary object of the Council idea is to aid the General." 2) "The Council should also do some thinking" on its own and not just when the General requests it. 3) "The Council may seek information anywhere, any time (directly or through the chief of staff)." 4) "A few highly trained, experienced Staff Officers would be more desirable than several ... inexperienced." 5) "The Secretary to the Council should be an officer of high rank with assistants who know languages." 6) The advisory group could consult "experienced men of affairs like: Lord Hankey who organized the first secretariat of the British Cabinet; Field Marshal Lord Milne who "was chief of the staff of the Imperial British Army." On the secretary for war's council there were "three professional soldiers and three civilians;" and Sir John Anderson, a former Chancellor of the Exchequer who had given the Romanes Lecture at Oxford on "the Machinery of Government in May 1946."[18]

On August 16, 1946 Chief of Staff Charles Baugh wrote to Brigadier Frederick Coutts regarding a suggestion by Colonel Gauntlett that Coutts write a biography of Mrs. Commissioner Lamb. Baugh understood that Coutts had expressed a "willingness to do this." General Orsborn "will be glad for you to undertake this work, and Commissioner Lamb is being informed accordingly." They hoped that Coutts would be able to "alternate this book with other more urgent departmental matters," such as "the need of the International Training College for Bible lessons immediately." In late 1948, Lt. Colonel Coutts told Chief of Staff John Allan that he "was so occupied with departmental work that I could not make further progress with this biography." In September 1955 the Army contracted with Lt. Colonel Unsworth to write the biography in six months for £1 5 shillings a week, but in October the literary secretary wrote that he had "informed the General" that "Katherine Lamb has certain details and Miss Lamb's policy is just not to answer letters." The General, now Wilfred Kitching, said to "Let the matter drop." Kitching wrote to Mrs. Brouen (Lamb's daughter), to tell her that "under the circumstances, we could do nothing in the matter."[19] That was the end of the case of the authorized, but unfulfilled biography of Minnie Lamb.

On November 1, 1946 David Lamb celebrated his 80th birthday with a public gathering, as he had proposed to General Orsborn. A luncheon party at the Savoy Hotel on November 1 was presided over by British Prime Minister Clement Atle. It is difficult to recall a Salvation Army event at which the head of the British government was in the chair. Prime Minister Ramsay MacDonald had agreed to preside at an event honoring David Lamb's conversion and 50 years as a Salvation Army officer, but the prime minister was unable to attend. Lamb expressed his debt to a "kind friend who has made [this celebration] possible," but he did not mention a name. He addressed those attending as: Mr. President, your Grace, my Lords and Gentlemen," only the last of these titles could likely fit a Salvation Army representative. One wonders how many of Lamb's Salvationist colleagues agreed with Major Leal's estimate of him as being publicity crazy, the problem of prophets and promoters in their own land.

Lamb's remarks were unusually brief. He recalled his first voyage—in a family wash–tub launched by his two older sisters. The mill dam served as an ocean in the garden of his home in the village of Friockheim in County Angus. He was four years old and "still unbreeched." His next adventure was spiritual, "struggling with the doctrines of predestination and free will in his teens. He decided to "associate predestination with hard work, undertaken of my own free will." At 15 he made his first contact with The Salvation Army in Aberdeen, and in spite of "some rough passages," he had spent his life in its service.

Since his official retirement in 1941 he had traveled to North America as an "unofficial ambassador of goodwill," to cement "our continued cooperation" on which so much depends. He had visited university principals and faculty members, newspaper editors, governors of states and provinces, mayors of cities, captains of industry and finance, and "leaders of thought in all walks of life." He had not neglected those who were "off the beaten track."

While as an old man David Lamb dreamed dreams, he said that he was "still young enough to see visions." His vision had six points.

First, he saw "that love and fear (and not hatred) are likely to continue to be the two great driving forces in human affairs and that in the Atlantic Charter and the San Francisco Conference we have the bases upon which permanent world peace could be firmly established; but the men in the street must get on with the building until the war drums throb no longer."

Second, Lamb saw that "Christianity cannot be nationalized; and I do not forget what Christ said on one occasion, 'And other sheep have I that are not of this fold.' Things of the spirit … know no national frontiers nor can their influence be restrained by tariff walls. While we may now see greater armies and greater navies than our own, I believe we can still give the world leadership."

Third, Lamb saw that "personal service will still give the greatest satisfaction in life, enriching at once the individual and the commonwealth. I believe that the people, content with some measure of simplicity in the amenities of a very complex civilization, may, in the long run, win in the race of life."

Fourth, he saw "a need for a more robust expression of our Christian faith," that "we have had enough ... of the 'gentle' aspects. We could do with a quickened sense of original sin and the depravity of the human heart and less, by way of excuse, of heredity and environment; a dangerous heresy (inherent in the German philosophy) which, in my view, was a very considerable factor in making for the world what we have had. I think that our faith must be a constant challenge to the existing order of things."

Fifth, he saw two things that disquieted him. One was deaths on the road, and the other was traffic congestion.

Sixth, Lamb was surprisingly optimistic for an octogenarian, for he saw in the future "a better world. The world is better than it was sixty years ago and the next sixty years are going to show still greater progress. The law of sacrifice is the law of life, and I believe that youth will ever respond to the call for sacrifice and adventure; only thus can we hope to survive."

He concluded with a word on behalf of small nations of the world, and his brief for Scottish history. Then he mentioned an experience he had in Chicago when, "at the point of a gun in my ribs, [he was] robbed of all my belongings," including a list of contacts that he had recreated to replace the list he had lost when German bombers attacked The Salvation Army's International Headquarters in London in 1941.

He told of his experience at the Mayo Clinic in Minnesota that he had not previously discussed, but where he had been unconscious for over a week. He now mentioned that his "youngest daughter, Mrs. Carton, flew from London to collect my ashes; suffice it to say that the said ashes are now talking to you in London." Despite such incidents, his immediate plans were to leave in December as an unofficial ambassador on a goodwill tour "of South Africa, Southern Rhodesia and, probably some of the lands which lie to the north of the Zambezi." The primary problem of the future was "how to plan society and at the same time preserve the rights of the individual."[20]

12

The Final Chapter 1947–1951

In the post–World War II period Commissioner David Crichton Lamb was a gray–bearded sage who increasingly focused
on "Today's World Problems," a theme that obsessed him. He
spoke and wrote on the subject in Britain, North America, Australia, New Zealand, and Southern Africa. From the commence-
ment of the Cold War soon after World War II to his death in
1951, he worried about Anglo–American relations, much as he
had worried during the war about the English–speaking allies'
future relations with Germany. Now, with his insights lost on
many of his contemporaries, he was deeply concerned about
Anglo–American relations with Russia. The *San Francisco Chronicle* reported the 82 year–old "optimist" saying that: "Russia is
right when she says that the U.S.A. and Britain are 'scheming together,' but Russia is wrong when she thinks the scheme is
against her." He agreed that there was conflict between Com-
munism and Democracy. But he claimed that "it is economic,
[and] will never be physical, and the outcome will be achieved
through the hardly painful process of evolution."[1]

The Salvation Army Migration Program, Australia, Canada, New Zealand, 1937–1951

Although The Salvation Army's migration program was still
operating after the war, Lamb seldom mentioned it. He had

moved on. Migration was only one of many fascinating topics for his mind to ponder. The Canadian *War Cry* reported that by 1937, when the 1922 Empire Settlement Act was renewed for another 15 years, "the Army had transferred more than 25,000 people under its provision. No other voluntary agency had achieved anything like it. Less than 15 percent of these had previous Salvation Army connections. Indeed, by the outbreak of the Second World War a quarter of a million people had been transplanted overseas by what had become the largest voluntary emigration agency in the world and less than one percent had turned out to be failures."

Australia was in the lead in submitting proposals under the new migration legislation. Canada, the gem of the Army's migration program, had taken in another 25,000 immigrants since 1922, but by 1937 Canada had other "social and industrial difficulties." By 1952 Australia was taking the lead in immigration. That year the first of several conducted parties of selected boys sailed for Australia. After training at an Army farm at Riverview, Queensland, the Army found them employment on farms. This program lasted into the 1960s. Between 1966 and 1976 The Salvation Army's London office received 4,000 applications from men, women and children for emigration. Out of that number the Army sent 2,072 to Australia, Canada, New Zealand and South Africa.[2]

In New Zealand, by 1932, when the Army closed its migration department there, the Army had transported more than 800 youths to the colony and had "placed in farm jobs" according to historian Cyril R. Bradwell. Again, "only one percent of the youths proved unsatisfactory." Bradwell discussed David Lamb's connection to the 1948 centennial anniversary of the 1848 Otago settlers. The originators of New Zealand's Otago settlement were part of an evangelical group with social concerns in Dunedin. Members of the group had asked William Booth to help them with the "rescue of perishing souls in this respectable and highly favored city." Enclosed with the plea was a draft for £200. Three women signed the request: Miss Arabella Valpy; Mrs. Caroline Valpy; and Mrs. Rachel Meadows.[3]

Estimates of the total number of emigrants sent overseas by The Salvation Army's emigration department that David Lamb founded in 1903 range as high as 300,000. Since the records at the emigration program's headquarters and the International Headquarters were destroyed in 1941, this is an approximation of the number. In most cases the reported number must have come from Lamb's memory.[4]

Lamb in Rhodesia, 1947

In the post World War II period David Lamb's interests extended to what later became known as the Third World, which was breaking its ties to Europe after the war. In 1947 Lamb visited Rhodesia for several months, partly to visit his siblings who had settled there in 1893. His two brothers, James and George, and a sister Mary, settled in Rhodesia three years after Cecil Rhodes had named the Shona and Ndebele territories for himself. James and his wife had trekked up from Johannesburg, South Africa, to the land ruled by Rhodes' British South Africa Company (BSAC) through an arrangement with Queen Victoria and her government in London.

During his visit Lamb linked up with newspaper editors and wrote candid articles for the *Rhodesia Herald* in the capital of Salisbury in Mashonaland and the *Bulawayo Chronicle* in Matabeleland. His choice of topic was his search for "Rhodesia's soul." He was candid in his opposition to the national lottery and gambling, but tackled the issue of racial discrimination only as a part of other issues, such as the way the lottery was administered. A native was not permitted "to have his 'flutter,'" even though he had been "granted political equality." It is unclear what Lamb meant by "political equality," since Africans had no right to vote or run for office in national elections in the white settler colony until they fought an independence war and gained majority rule in 1979–80. Africans had their own "bigger and bolder" lottery from which Europeans were excluded, thus copying South Africa's apartheid system of racial separation.

Lamb argued that Africans could develop "a superior civilization" if they deplored the "something for nothing" idea of gambling. While Lamb was careful not to offend Rhodesia's white minority, he also condemned Salisbury's Native hospital and its "painful overcrowding." And he "doubted the wisdom of sending natives to prison for breaches of pass laws and such–like offenses." He hoped that returning servicemen and women from World War II, to whom the government had given land near the Native reserves (what Americans termed Indian reservations), might carry "the torch of our Christian civilization amongst the natives of this great Dark Continent."

He told a reporter in Bulawayo, the second major city, that Rhodesia was "a happy, care–free land of ease and plenty," and a little "happy–go–lucky." The reporter became defensive. The rest of the article reads like an interview of the reporter by David Lamb. The reporter saw Rhodesian pleasure–seeking not so much as a means of ignoring Rhodesia's problems as it was a way of gaining respite from constantly meditating on them, in particular the "racial issue." The reporter argued that there was "a growing volume of liberal–minded opinion." Lamb asked "whether the white man would survive—the white man with his western civilization, carrying the burden almost if not quite, beyond him." The reporter laid the problem at the feet of the native's "urbanization and industrialization." He claimed that Rhodesians were thinking about the "structure that is to be erected on the constitution which gives equal political rights to all races." In the end the reporter was satisfied that Lamb "chasteneth us because of his love for us, and we will not let his words pass unheeded."[5]

1948–1949

David Lamb wrote a "Family News Letter" that covered the year from July 31, 1948 to July 31, 1949. During this period he visited family in England's West Country (Bristol) and Scotland (Edinburgh and Glasgow), and toured Canada (from Halifax to many of the cities he had previously visited), and the United States (from Detroit mostly to western cities and Indianapolis, Pittsburgh, Washington and New York). His purpose was to talk to everyone he could about: 1) no more world wars; 2) constructive elements he saw in the Atlantic Charter, United Nations, a Western European Union, a North Atlantic Pact; and recent disputes that could lead to war (Indonesia, Palestine, India).

He would also discuss: British economic recovery; isolationism in the United States—"dead but not buried;" Russia—"the U.S. and U.K. must have patience with Russia, be realistic—but there may come a time when patience wears thin." Lamb also found "widespread interest in the working of Britain's National Health Service.

What was the prime reason for his visit to the United States? With a twinkle in his Scottish eyes he told American audiences that he had come: "To try to keep you Americans humble ... You have twisted the British lion's tail for many years—now let us pull a few feathers out of the American eagle; not from the tail (that would spoil her beauty), but from the wings, so that she won't soar too high."

He had a lesson for the Americans since, "America is now going to 'police the world.'" Britain, not a bit jealous, would sit back and watch. The president of a large Midwestern university disagreed and argued that together the United States and United Kingdom "are to police most—and keep the peace." Lamb would also tell Americans that the war debt was not Britain's debt to America, but America's debt to Britain.

As the Director of the Salvation Army migration and settlement department for many years, he felt that he could claim credit for a half million of Canada's population, but he was revising that estimate upward when three of the Army's immigrants told him that they had 22, 41, and 24 descendants. He had made contacts with fellows of the Royal Empire Society in Canada, and the English–Speaking Union in the U.S.

As for the physical "results" of his tour, he estimated that he had traveled 18,000 miles to 30 centers, slept in 20 hotels and spent 48 nights on trains and boats, met 20 editors and 10 university presidents responsible for 5,000 faculty members and 80,000 students, spoken at more than 20 public meetings, and eaten lunch, tea, and dinner with groups from 6 to 60. As for spiritual results—"God gives the increase." He listed 20 newspaper headlines from his interviews—mostly on his optimism at age 82. He concluded that: "My lines have fallen to me in pleasant places."

The rest of the letter dealt with news of his far–flung family of whom there were 50 in Southern Rhodesia, more than 100 in North America, more than 100 in Scotland, more than 70 in England, "with units in Australia, Africa, China, and elsewhere." He had begun his "Family News Letter" in 1914–18 as he traveled during World War I. It was now going to the third generation of

Lambs, for whom he was providing an excellent genealogical treatise on the location of their relatives.

How did he keep going so strong at 82? An unknown correspondent in the House of Lords, Westminster, sent him this poem to provide him with an insight into his philosophy of life:

Age is a quality of mind.
If you have left your dreams behind
If hope is lost
If you no longer look ahead
If your ambitions' fires are dead
Then you are old!

But if from life you take the best
And if in life you keep the jest
If love you hold.
No matter how the years go by
No matter how the birthdays fly
You are not old![6]

Each lengthy "Family News Letter" written in Lamb's retirement years kept his children and many relations aware of his ventures and fulfilled the role of a lone parent. In late September 1949 he wrote the last letter in this series after his return from North America, where he once again had used his sister's home in Detroit as his base.[7]

In 1949, at the age of 83, Lamb addressed the British Association for the Advancement of Science at the Newcastle–upon–Tyne City Temple. The meeting was chaired by the BAAS president. Lamb made his usual plea for goodwill toward Russia and a deepening of Anglo–American relations. He assured the audience that he had not lost his belief in original sin and a need to believe in the devil.[8] Lamb was a member of the BAAS that had been founded in 1831.

In early 1951 David Lamb made his last "Unofficial Goodwill Tour" to New Zealand and Australia. He followed his usual pattern of discussing world problems with university principals, newspaper editors and professional societies. Australia's governor general received him, as did governors of states. He enjoyed a cabinet luncheon at which the prime minister, the Rt. Hon. R. G. Menzies, presided.[9]

13

David Crichton Lamb
"Promoted to Glory" July 7, 1951

David Crichton Lamb, F.R.E.S. (Fellow, Royal Economic Society), LL.D. (Doctor of Letters, honorary), C.M.G. (Company of the Order of St. Michael and St. George), O.F. (Order of the Founder), died at age 84 on Saturday July 7, 1951, while he was visiting his eldest daughter, Catherine Stewart, a county welfare officer, at the Cogswells, Tytherton Lucas in Chippenham, Wiltshire. Lamb's physician was Lord Hodder.

By the time of his death Commissioner David C. Lamb had visited the United States, Canada, South Africa, Rhodesia, Japan, Korea, Russia, China, Australia, and New Zealand. On October 12, 1951, the estate of David Crichton Lamb, of 23 Cannonbury Square, London N1, was registered at London's probate court by Harold William Martin, solicitor. David Lamb's effects amounted to £4,988 9 shillings and 3 pence, approximately $25,000.[1] His wealth was in his faith, his love for life and ideas, and his family.

Obituary Notices

The *Times* of London, Britain's newspaper of record, pointed to "two monuments" of Lamb's devotion: "enthusiasm and gifts of organization," that had made their mark on 1) the social work of The Salvation Army and the valued "migration and settlement within the Empire of over 200,000 persons." It pointed out that he had crossed the Atlantic "in war–time in a convoy" at age 75. At 25 he had been the Army's chief secretary in South Africa, after which he soon became governor of the Land and Industrial Colony at Hadleigh. During his time as The Salvation Army's international social secretary there was a "great increase" in its "farm and city colonies, shelters, homes, summer colonies, and other centers for aid and reclamation." Because of his expertise in these social programs he was often consulted by Royal Commissions and public bodies, organizations, and individuals.

The *Times* pointed to Lamb as one who listened to "men whose confessed iniquities would scarcely be believed," yet they "sought him out and found in him a helper and a friend." He wrote on "a diversity of imperial and social themes." He never had "office hours." He and his wife had a rule "that the door must never be shut and that none who came to it in distress should be turned away."

Early in the war, at age 75, he began a series of goodwill tours of the United States to "strengthen the ties" with Britain. His tours "won him an immense circle of friends and a remarkable influence in all walks of life." Since 1941 he made half a dozen prolonged tours of the United States, Canada, South Africa and the [two] Rhodesias, Australia, and New Zealand."

The *Montreal Daily Star* reported that on Lamb's last visit to Montreal "the physical vessel that held the torch was wearing thin. It was no surprise to read that he had died, filled with years and achievements; and his great host of friends in this country—from coast to coast—will miss the fire and sparkle of his visits." The report praised his "interest in British emigration" which it attested to "the Army's belief that many a man will fulfill himself if he can be only given a fresh start."

A final eulogy came in 1960 from Lt. Commissioner Arch R. Wiggins, who described Lamb as a "good looker," with a "carefully trimmed beard." He was of "medium height and carried a noble head on a shortish neck, supported by unusually broad shoulders. His step was sprightly almost to the end. He was not ... a clear public speaker so far as an English congregation was concerned. He spoke in the broadest Scottish dialect and his sentences were shot at you like pellets from an air gun." Wiggins said that "David Lamb was a greatly trusted henchman of Bramwell Booth and in his day was 'a mighty power in the land.'"

This observation makes it clear how difficult his role in the removal of Bramwell Booth must have been for David Lamb. Lamb left four living children: Catherine; Meta (Brauen); Janet (Carton); and Alexander.[2]

Memorial Services and Tributes

On Wednesday July 11 Lt. Commissioner Owen Culshaw, tThe Salvation Army men's social secretary, led the graveside funeral service for the family at Leigh–on–Sea, where Lamb was buried by his wife and eldest son, David, who had died in early manhood. His youngest son, Patrick, was killed in action at Bethune in 1918. They sang, "O God of Bethel, By Whose Hand," "The Lord's my Shepherd," and "Thou Wilt Keep Him in Perfect Peace." There were about 20 members Lamb's family present.

Commissioner Frank Barrett led a well–attended memorial service at the Southend–on–Sea Salvation Army citadel, near the Hadleigh farm in Essex where the Lambs lived most of their lives. Many civic leaders were present. The mayor of Southend read the lesson from Revelation, chapter 21. The children of Millfield sang "Our Blest Redeemer," and an officer from the Migration and Settlement Department, Major Fred Taylor, paid a tribute to the man with whom he had worked since 1903.

Mrs. Carton, the Lamb's youngest daughter, spoke for the family: "All my life I was able to spend more time with my father than the others. When I first went to work [at the *Times*] we traveled daily to London." Later they shared a flat and after her mother's death he moved next door. "We never feared his wrath, only his disappointment." Theirs was a happy childhood, "in the rather tumultuous but stimulating atmosphere of a home that was the refuge of all in trouble, but that was crowned by the essential goodness and nobility of the two who presided over it."

Her mother was "so mercurial, so vivid, so intuitive, so quickly moved to tears and to laughter; my father was balanced and judicial and calm, reasoning things out and usually coming to the same conclusions that she had reached by swifter means hours before! ... His desk was always meticulously neat, hers a hopeless confusion ... And he was always trying to divert and amuse her when the troubles of the world seemed to weigh her down." On one occasion he brought her a check for £1,000 from Canada for Millfield. After she died "he never came back to live in the house at Westcliff."

"Death came to him so kindly and swiftly. The Tuesday before he died, July 3rd, I went with him to the dinner to General Eisenhower at Grosvenor House." He went to Wiltshire on July 4th for a short holiday. After going out to see the sunset he went to his room and sat down in his chair. The doctor came when they saw that he was quite ill. He died in a few minutes.

The Salvation Army Chief of Staff Commissioner John J. Allan conducted a memorial service at the Regent Hall, Oxford Street on July 18. The International Staff Band played. The large congregation included Salvationists of all ranks, representatives of public life and organizations to which Lamb belonged. Princess Alice, the Countess and Earl of Athone, and the Lord Chancellor were there. Tributes were paid by the Rt. Hon. L. S. Avery and Commissioners Frank Dyer and Owen Culshaw. Colonel Dray read a letter from the British Prime Minister, Clement R. Atlee, who termed Lamb "an unofficial ambassador of goodwill" and "a good friend." Dray also read messages from Lord Athlone and General Orsborn.

At noon on July 24, the Rt. Rev. Bishop Michael Bolton Furst, K.C.M.G., D.D., the Prelate of the Order, conducted a memorial service in the chapel of the Most Distinguished Order of St. Michael and of St. George in St. Paul's Cathedral. The prime minister was represented by D. W. S. Hunt. The men's choir led the singing of the Twenty–third Psalm and the poetic prayer, "God Be in My Head, and in My Understanding." The congregation sang, "How Sweet the Name of Jesus Sounds in a Believer's Ears," before the "final prayer for the King, the Grand Master, the Prelate, the Chancellor, and all other Officers and Members of the Order." Bishop Furst led the congregation in "humble supplication and thankfulness for the life and work of Commissioner Lamb."[3]

The Importance of David Lamb's Ideas and their Historical Relevance

Two ideas particularly dear to David C. Lamb became historically–charged issues after the chronicle of his life ended in 1951. They were: 1) in the 1970s–90s, out of Lamb's dream of sending young men and women to the colonies to find a new life, a child abuse and record–keeping scandal erupted in Britain and the dominions that concerned the treatment of British children sent to Canada, Australia, and New Zealand by voluntary agencies, including The Salvation Army, prior to 1963; and 2) there was a call for reform of The Salvation Army's international organization that was reminiscent of Lamb's "general in council" system in place of decision–making by one person at the top.

Frederick Coutts, among others, has argued that ideas are precious commodities that must be embraced by their fortunate recipients and nurtured until they come to full bloom. Ideas, not facts, are the prompters of historical investigation. And the rare breed of the seminal idea will live on far beyond the chronicles of their favored recipients. David Lamb had two revolutionary seminal ideas, not in the sense that he was the only one who received these ideas, but because he nurtured them as the focus of his life and work for a half century, after which they had a life of their own well beyond his passing. These two ideas are the principal reason for writing about Lamb's life and times. Henry R. Winkler, emeritus president of the University of Cincinnati, claimed that he had two "seminal" ideas in his lifetime, one of which he nurtured into a doctoral dissertation.

David Lamb's two seminal ideas, as discussed in this biography, were: 1) the migration of British citizens to colonies of the British empire for the sake of relieving Britain of the scourge of unemployment that had led The Salvation Army to publish its Darkest England plan in 1890; and 2) the internal revolution in the Army in 1929 by which he and a group of collaborators brought to a close the 65–year rule of the Booth Dynasty in the Christian Mission and Salvation Army. This led to gradual moves in the direction of a more collaborative form of leadership.

Following Lamb's death in 1951, events occurred that had obvious connections to his ideas in the fields of migration and Salvation Army reform. The after–life events were extended versions of his ideas. Whether he would have seen them as fortuitous outcomes or not is beyond our ken. No doubt his efficient soul would have been troubled by record–keeping problems and child abuse accusations in the migration program. He would likely have been pleased by reforms in the international administration of The Salvation Army that included greater involvement of women and Third World representatives in the Army's international administration.

Epilogue A:
Investigation of the Child Migration Programs of Voluntary Organizations

David Lamb was an organizer and enthusiastic advocate of The Salvation Army's program to train boys at the Hadleigh farm in agricultural and technical skills before the Army transported them to farms and training centers in Britain's dominions, mainly Canada, Australia, and New Zealand, and Southern Africa, but not the United States. The Army was not alone in supporting child migration quite apart from supporting migrating families and single adults. It had a keen interest in "older boys" and girls who could be easily transferred to new lives in the dominions.

In 1998 the British Parliament asked The Salvation Army and other voluntary organizations who had sponsored child migrants to respond to questions from the Select Committee on Health. The organizations included: Barnardo's; a Roman Catholic Child Welfare Council of the Catholic Emigration Society (1903) and numerous Catholic religious orders; the Children's Society; Fairbridge; the Family Care Society (Belfast); NCH Action for Children; and the Child Migrants' Sending Agencies Group. This is by no means a complete list of voluntary agencies involved in child migration, but it represents many leaders in the field. There were also a number of government agencies in Britain and the dominions that were involved in the program.

In the late 20th century there was an attack on the way the governments and voluntary agencies in 1880–1960 had handled their migration records. Some irate migrants even accused the agencies of a "cover–up" of child abuse in foster homes and training centers. This led the Canadian Department of External Affairs and Immigration to study its records,[4] with similar inquiries by the Australian and New Zealand governments and hearings before a Select Committee on Health of the British Parliament.[5]

The Salvation Army emigration program began with the first party of migrants in 1905 and slowed to a trickle prior to World War II. Other organizations had begun earlier and extended to 1963. The point of the governmental investigations at the end of the 20th century had to do with three issues: 1) there was a record–keeping problem in terms of the treatment of children sent to foster care or to orphanages; 2) the degree to which children were abused; and 3) the extent to which agencies kept records of family connections in Britain.

Major Ray Oakley, director of The Salvation Army's Social Services Department, testified for the Army in the Parliamentary hearings. He explained the history of the Army's overall family migration program for Canada, Australia and New Zealand. As for children, he noted the concern in the "receiving countries" that the Army would export "waifs and strays" from England and dump them on colonies. Thus the Army "had to vet their health, the moral quality of their character and even then obtain the approval in the main of their parents." But in all of this, in England the Army's "records are greatly hampered by the fact that our headquarters were bombed in the Second World War." But Oakley assured the committee: the Army in "the receiving countries have very detailed records and those are available" in materials he submitted to the committee. Oakley pointed to the Army's Missing Persons Bureau as a source of family records that could link the children, now adults living in the dominions, to their British parents or relatives. He claimed an 85 percent success rate in making family connections.[6] While the numbers of boys and girls the Army sent to Canada and Australia were significant, it had sent only 29 to New Zealand. Oakley made no mention of records of child abuse while children were in the Army's care or supervision.

Other agency representatives, when questioned by the Select Committee's members, admitted to abusive behavior and misjudgments, including attempts to cover up problems. For example, Committee Chairman David Hinchliffe asked Canon Christopher Fisher of the Roman Catholic Church: "How can you deal with a former child migrant and explain why he or she was in the position they were in because their father was a priest?" A witness the previous week had charged that was a reason "certain people believe there has been a certain degree of cover–up ... by the agencies in general because of a concern about some very difficult parts of our history." Fisher responded indirectly by concluding that: "I do not think any of us would support such a scheme today," and proposed that responsibility for that misguidance ... has to be shared by the government."[7]

Barnardo's representative, Mr. Roger Singleton, after noting that his agency had sent 151 boys who were 14 to 17 years of age to Canada in August 1882 and 1883, and 72 girls in 1883, and a total of 30,000 children between 1882 and 1939 when the government ended the scheme. The purpose was to "save" the children "from the poverty and degradation of slum life" and give them "healthy fresh air and wholesome work." Like The Salvation Army, Barnardo's visited the children in their foster homes, but unlike the Army, Singleton admitted that "there clearly was some abuse of children and efforts were made to counter such concerns as early as 1889." Records had been shipped back to England after the closing of the program in 1960.

Singleton pointed out that in 1956, when many adults were tracing their roots and experiences of abuse in orphanages, the British Secretary of State for Commonwealth Relations had appointed a fact–finding mission to go to Australia and "collect information on the arrangements for the reception and upbringing" of child migrants. The mission's leader, Mr. J. Ross, had reported that "many children who are in children's homes in the United Kingdom would have much better prospects in Australia, if they are carefully selected and [were] of suitable ages." He was "very impressed by the thoroughness with which the interests of child migrants are safeguarded and by the standard of care available." His group concluded that "the child care system in the United Kingdom has for many years been vulnerable to infiltration by people who wish to abuse children." Yet

Barnardo's Roger Singleton acknowledged that he was "constrained from apologizing by the requirement of insurers."

Conclusions to be drawn from this large record are beyond the scope of this work, and David Lamb did not acknowledge cases of abuse. Yet there can be little doubt that the toll of abuse could well have remained with some children throughout their lives. As for record–keeping, Ray Oakley acknowledged The Salvation Army's problem. World War II bombings had destroyed records in Britain, but there were records in Canada, Australia, and New Zealand. As for genealogical searches for family "roots," a craze from the 1950s to the end of the 20th century, the Army had an international Missing Persons' Bureau network equipped to provide information that was important for general family histories and for medical information.

Epilogue B:
Alterations to the Salvation Army Organizational System—a "General in Council"

Ideas are indeed precious commodities, but as living entities they change their form over time. Part of the problem David Lamb and others saw in a Booth dynastic autocracy was solved by the Salvation Army Act of 1930–31. By this act of the British Parliament a Salvation Army general could no longer choose a successor by placing a name in a sealed envelope to be opened by the Army's attorney at the time of the general's death. And the Booth family voluntarily agreed to relinquish their ownership of Salvation Army property in the British Empire as a family trust.

The issue of the General as the Army's sole decision–maker and owner of Army property was left for Army leaders to decide at a future date. As discussed above, when Albert Orsborn took office as general in 1946, he established an Advisory Council Commission, chaired by Commissioner Catherine Bramwell–Booth, to study the idea of a senior advisory council to advise the General. That commission asked David Lamb, by then retired, to give expert testimony in which he restated his idea of a "general in council."

Lamb's interest in The Salvation Army's organization at its London International Headquarters may have begun soon after

William and Bramwell Booth appointed him to the IHQ staff in 1888. But there is no evidence of a desire to see it altered until the late 1920s, by which time Lamb was a senior commissioner and a member of the 1929 High Council. In that role he had become a prime mover in deposing Bramwell Booth as general and removing the Army from Booth family ownership.

Lamb's desire for administrative reform continued after the 1929–31 period, when he had begun to advocate for a "general in council" form of senior leadership. The generals' consultations with leaders may have improved after the passage of the Salvation Army Act and elections of Generals Evangeline C. Booth in 1934 and George L. Carpenter in 1939. But there was little formal organizational change until 1946 when General Orsborn promised the High Council that, if he was elected General, he would set up the Advisory Council to the General, the nature of which he would explore with his senior staff. Orsborn thus set up a committee to propose a plan.

Orsborn's Advisory Council continued, with refinements, until July 2001, when John Gowans, following his election as General, replaced it with a new body, the General's Consultative Council (GCC). A GCC sub–committee on Appointments and Promotions (APC) advises the General on persons the General proposes to promote to the Army's senior ranks and to place in its highest commands. The General is not present for the meetings of the APC, which is chaired by the international secretary for personnel. This committee has no power to propose persons for appointments or promotions, unlike the appointments committee of the Christian Mission, the Army's name from 1865–1877.

Eva Burrows, who was the General from 1986–1993, established an International Strategic Planning and Management Council in 1990. At the time the Salvation Army was facing a financial crisis due to President Gorbechev's "glasnost" policy that allowed the Army to open its work in the Soviet Union. It became apparent that the Army needed a new structure that ensured international ownership of the organization by the global Salvation Army.

General Gowans' new GCC, after 2001, would increase membership of the High Council to nearly 100 members. It also would include spouses of the Army's commissioners. The former "Mrs. Commissioner" would now hold the rank of commissioner and her vote would be equal to that of her husband, a privilege already attained by single–women commissioners. The General now presides at the GCC meetings that occur about four times a year. All IHQ commissioners are eligible to attend, and about eight non–IHQ members (different each time) attend. The agenda and minutes circulate to all members of the High Council, including those unable to attend.

General Burrows had appointed a two–year study of the Army's management headed by Commissioner John Larsson, and advised by the Coopers and Lybrand consulting firm. One outcome was changing the name of the Strategic Planning and Management Council to the International Management Council (IMC). This group, composed of all IHQ commissioners, meets monthly. The General attends the meetings and "will often take decisions 'in council,' but will equally often defer decisions until he/she has had time to reflect on the recommendation received from the council. Strictly speaking the IMC is an advisory body—but in practice it is as near to DC Lamb's idea as we have got."[8]

Overall, General Larsson, the Army's world leader at the time of this book's publication, states that the trend has been "towards greater consultation rather than towards the David Lamb 'general in council' concept." Larsson holds that the Army's system is different from a prime minister or presidential cabinet form of polity. In those systems members speak for their governmental departments and participate in decision–making, but the final decision is made by the prime minister or president. But whereas Larsson finds the International Management Council is more in line with what Lamb proposed, "the General's Advisory Council and the new General's Consultative Council are advisory, not decision–making bodies."[9] Lamb would not have disagreed with the Army's new organizational model that leaves the General with the final word after consultation with senior leaders.

Salvation Army property, owned by the Booth family until 1930, "both real and personal including shares in some of the Army's commercial undertakings," are now held by a new body, The Salvation Army International Trustee Company. The company's board of directors is chaired by the chief of the staff, the Army's equivalent of a company's chief operations officer. The Army created this corporate trust under the Companies Acts of 1985 and 1989. The corporate trust permits the London head-quarters to control some Army assets internationally, as well as all British assets. The General is not a member of the board but may attend. The board's members include appointed Salvation Army commissioners, officers of lower ranks, and non–officers with financial and managerial expertise. The company has no as-sets or liabilities of its own, but controls Army assets as a trustee.

On the advice of Coopers and Lybrand, with the concurrence of Army leaders, the management structures for the Interna-tional Headquarters and the British territory were separated. Britain was constituted as a territory on an equal footing to those of other countries in the Army's international domain. It would have its own executive council. The Army commissioned further studies of middle management and the United Kingdom terri-tory's structure.

For an historian the issue of change in Salvation Army ad-ministrative structures has do with why change occurred in the 1929–31 period, again in 1946, and at an accelerated pace of shared leadership and corporate responsibility after 1990, during the tenures of Generals Eva Burrows, Bramwell Tillsley, Paul Rader, John Gowans, and John Larsson. While "what happened, when and how," explains the nature of change, it does not explain "why" the Army's generals and other leaders decided that in these intervals the Army was ripe for change. Nor does it tell why and how they devised changes that were congruent with man-agerial styles in government and corporations in each time period.

Nor was it new for the Army to call on managerial and fi-nancial consultants to assist in devising modifications in its ad-ministrative structure and management style. William Booth had frequently called on outside evaluators to advise the Army on its management, finances, and objectives. While the answer to the "why" question may still be obscure in many cases, we must try to unearth motives that led to the creation of new schematic designs in the post–World War II era, and tie those changes to the ideas promulgated by David C. Lamb.

First, since World War I The Salvation Army has become less and less a mirror of the British imperial model that William

Booth used to devise its initial international structure after Booth's Christian Mission adopted a new military form in 1878. Most of Europe, and The Salvation Army as of 1929, gradually removed their monarchs from dynastic control.

After World War II, Anglo–American governments sealed an alliance that David Lamb applauded on his tours of North America and the British Commonwealth in the 1940s. The two nations and their overseas political and economic colonies, dominated an increasing number of nations in the United Nations, the North Atlantic Treaty Organization, and Southeast Asia. But in the 1950s the British Empire and those of other European nations were shrinking. Asian and African colonies were declaring independence from what one Indian Salvation Army officer termed, "Our father who art in London." The new world order called for independence—self–rule and self–sufficiency. The center was no longer in unquestioned control.

While the Army's generals and international staff continued to be mostly British in the 1950s and early 1960s, rapid change by the late 1960s motivated High Councils to elect generals from Europe, Australia, Canada, and even the United States, as well as two from Britain. By 2005 all international secretaries at the Army's International Headquarters were commissioners from areas they served and understood from the inside: Africa; the Americas and Caribbean; Europe; South Asia; the South Pacific and East Asia. The Army had become "federal" in nature and more congenial to the organizational style of other international bodies, while it maintained its military form and leadership by one General.

A striking example of this new independence movement in the 1970s and 1980s was a "Soldiers' March" on The Salvation Army headquarters in Harare, Zimbabwe in 1981. A soldiers' (lay person) committee chaired by Sergeant Major Jonah Blessing Matswetu opposed two actions by General Arnold Brown in London. The first was the sale of Pearson farm to a white commercial farmer. The farm had been given to the Army by Cecil Rhodes in 1891 to develop a school and a mission for the spiritual development of Africans. Second, the soldiers' committee disagreed with Brown's decision to suspend the Army's membership in the World Council of Churches (WCC), an organization that had supported the independence movement by the Zimbabwe Patriotic Front. A soldiers' protest march by about 200 Salvationists was a graphic illustration that the General's will was no longer taken as the voice of a "father who art in London."

In 1979 an International Conference of the Army's leaders had met in Toronto, two years before the Harare soldiers' demonstration. At that conference leaders from the Third World, where two–thirds of all Salvationists lived, temporarily convinced Canadian General Arnold Brown not to remove The Salvation Army from the World Council of Churches (WCC). Asian and African leaders were joined by a majority of those from Britain, Europe, Australia, New Zealand, and South America, in opposing the Army's withdrawal from the WCC. Even North Americans who had served as educators, physicians, and administrators in the Third World were convinced that the Army should continue membership in the World Council, a policy Army leaders in North America had strongly opposed.[10] If the "father" was no longer in London, it was clear that he had not moved to New York or Washington.

Financial crises around 1990 and investment problems in Britain in 1993 led to public pressure on the Army to add "outside" experts to its financial and management boards and to put the British territory on the same ground as the rest of the Army's territories. British charity commissioners asked the Army to account for how it managed public donations to its social programs, something Commissioner Frank Smith had proposed to William and Bramwell Booth in 1890, and something the Booths had done in that period in response to public accusations of scandal. The Booths separated Darkest England social program funds from donations to the Army's evangelical work, but they did not agree to separate the accounting department that was responsible for the funds into two departments.

Since 1990 there have been increasing pressures from governments, particularly in the United States where the Army receives significant government funds, to allocate support only to organizations that do not proselytize for their religious beliefs or discriminate in hiring practices against certain groups, whether on the basis of sexual preference, ethnic, or ideological, that are protected by law.

General Paul A. Rader, in office from July 1994 to July 1999, dealt with the criticism of the Army's financial management by meeting the demands of the UK charity commissioners. Rader negotiated new Articles of Association for the Salvation Army Trusts in the United Kingdom, one dealing with the UK territory, and one with the international funds: SATCO; and SAITCO respectively. It was the UK charity commissioners that insisted that non–executive "experts" from outside the Army's management system be made members of each of the boards of each of these trusts. This in turn led to the Salvation Army's alterations in its "temporal" affairs.[11]

These are a few of the possible reasons for "why" The Salvation Army has made alterations in its international management since World War II. A future historical question may ask why change has not occurred in lower levels of the Army's system. Why have soldiers (lay members) seldom participated in its international decision–making apparatus? St. John Ervine argued that a military body could not sustain such radical change. But The Salvation Army is not a real army. Soldiers in armies are not expected to donate money or raise their children in the ranks. It is true that in many countries, including the United States, Salvation Army soldiers are not the Army's principal financial donors, but neither are its officers.

Yet in the Third World, the Army has put pressure on its soldiers to make their church self–sufficient. Will this pressure on the Army's poorest members extend at some point to its better–off American soldiers? And will self–sufficiency in its spiritual branch extend to self–government? It is intriguing that soldiers in Zimbabwe are more inclined to indicate their rights to participate in decision–making, something that has had little impetus in the United States. Why are America's Salvation Army soldiers not as central to the management of the Army as those in other lands?

Frank Smith, M.P., during House of Commons discussions of the 1931 Salvation Army Act, proposed that soldiers participate in the elections of the Army's General. He received no support from David Lamb for that idea, and in recent decades, to my knowledge, no one has revived the idea.[12] Why has the Army not discussed a broader participation of Salvationists in its management? That is a question for another historian at another time.

Endnotes for David C. Lamb
Biography

Notes to Introduction

1. Robert Sandall, *The History of The Salvation Army*, Vol. III, 1883–1953: Social Reform and Welfare Work (London: Thomas Nelson & Sons, 1955): 155–58 gives a brief overview of Lamb and his emigration department from 1903 to 1934.

2. The 19th century was the age of British imperialism and an imperial mindset infected social, as well as political institutions, including churches. I use the term "Christian imperium" to place The Salvation Army in the context of its time. An imperial mind–set led the Army to use military ranks, jargon and regulations, patterned after the British Army, and to spread its work across the British empire and beyond.

Notes to Chapter 1

1. See "Forfar" and "Arbroath" in *AA Illustrated Guide to Britain* (Basingstoke, Hants., 1977): 498–500. I consulted this guide for locations and descriptions of British towns. On the Stone of Destiny see Magnus Magnusson, *Scotland: The Story of a Nation* (New York: Atlantic Monthly, 2000): 81, 654, 187–90. Magnusson states that a 1988 U.S. Senate Resolution declared that "the American Declaration of Independence was modeled on that inspirational document [Declaration of Arbroath]." The Declaration declared that Edward II. of England had committed cruelties that resemble the charges that the American Declaration of Independence writers leveled against George III.

2. David Brown, "The Morrisonian Church," 1999, *www.google.com*.

3. Anabaptists of the Reformation Era broke with other Protestants by asserting that baptism of believers must replace Roman Catholic infant baptism. Some Anabaptists were pacifists, but all argued for strict discipline and democratic congregational rule.

4. Americans generally use the word pharmacist for this profession.

5. Walter L. Arnstein, *The Bradlaugh Case: A Study in Late Victorian Opinion & Politics* (Oxford: Clarendon Press, 1965).

6. Norman H. Murdoch, "Evangelical Sources of Salvation Army Doctrine," *The Evangelical Quarterly* (UK), 59 (July 1987): 235–44; *Origins of The Salvation Army* (Knoxville: University of Tennessee, 1994): "Evangelical Alliance," 45–66. The Booths' broad view of theology in the early years of their East London mission became more Wesleyan after 1875, in particular their emphasis on the doctrine of holiness.

7. Lamb's conversion story comes from four sources: *The War Cry* (Apr. 13, 1889); Commissioner David C. Lamb, "How Was I Converted?" *The War Cry* (New York) (Oct. 7, 1933): 13; "Commissioner David C. Lamb Answers Last Command," *The War Cry* (Aug. 4, 1951): 12; Lt. Commissioner Arch R. Wiggins, "A Mighty Power in the Land: David C. Lamb," *The War Cry* (Oct. 29, 1960): 2.

8. William Booth's title as leader of the Christian Mission was "General Superintendent." When the mission became a "Salvation Army," evangelists became lieutenants, captains, majors, colonels, and commissioners; Booth was the general.

9. A Horbury Bridge, West Yorkshire Anglican curate composed "Onward Christian Soldiers" in 1864 as a children's procession. It was one of many martial hymns in the 19th century. During the anti–Vietnam War struggles of the 1960s and 1970s some churches removed martial hymns from their hymnals. Tom Aitken notes that others altered the words to: "Onward Christian pilgrims, Working hard for peace, Day by day we're praying, That all wars may cease." Hymns fit the culture of the times in which they are written. See Ian Bradley, *Abide with Me: The World of Victorian Hymns*, pp. 84, 100, 104; Gordon Taylor, *Companion to the Song Book of The Salvation Army* (London: The Salvation Army, 1989): 149.

10. Robert Sandall, *The History of the Salvation Army*, vol. 2, 1878–1886 (London: Thomas Nelson & Sons, 1950): 61–2, includes David Lamb in a list of six men and women officers that William Booth regarded as being from "the dangerous [middle] classes." One was his future son–in–law, Frederick de Latour Tucker. Booth told Tucker to "go among my people and find the dark side as well as the bright, and then … we will see." Sandall lists 22 men of a lesser class, who attained the rank of commissioner, but he mentioned only two women: Adelaide Cox and Mildred Duff, both of whom Booth assigned to social and literary work deemed proper for women of their class.

11. "David C. Lamb Officer Sheet Profile," Salvation Army Archives, London. The profiles serve as chronological guides to David and Minnie Lambs' appointments, ranks, and other career information.

12. "Staff Captain Lamb," *The War Cry* (April 13, 1889)

13. A song–evangelist, like warm–up acts for vaudeville headliners, prepared congregations for the evangelists' sermons in the 19th century. Ira Sankey did this for Dwight Moody.

14. See the *AA Guide to Britain* for information on these towns.

15. Margaret Troutt, *The General was a Lady* (Nashville: A. J. Holman, 1980): 41–53.

16. "Minnie Clinton Officer Sheet Profile," Salvation Army Archives, London

17. Andrew Mark Eason, *Women in God's Army: Gender & Equality in the Early Salvation Army* (Waterloo, Ontario: Wilfrid Laurier University, 2003) does not mention Minnie Lamb, but he does evaluate the roles of officer–wives in the Army. I assess Catherine Booth's influence on women's role in "Female Ministry in the Thought and Work of Catherine Booth," *Church History*, 53 (Sept. 1984): 363–78.

18. "Staff Captain Lamb," *The War Cry* (Apr. 13, 1889)

19. Arch R. Wiggins, *The History of the Salvation Army*, vol. 4, 1886–1904 (London: Thomas Nelson & Sons, 1964): 226–35.

20. Brian Tuck, *Salvation Safari: A Brief History of the* Origins *of The Salvation Army in Southern Africa, 1883–1993*, 2nd edn. (Johannesburg: The Salvation Army, 1985): 6.

21. Tuck, 19–22, 46ff., deals with social services, but does not mention Lamb in that connection. He notes that Australian Salvationists began the Army's social work in Melbourne in 1883, before the Army opened a prostitutes' home in Whitechapel, London's East End, in 1884, when the Army also opened its Port Elizabeth home in South Africa.

22. Robert Sandall, *The History of The Salvation Army: Social Reform and Welfare Work*, vol. 3 (London: Thomas Nelson & Son, 1955): 11–19; 31ff, surveys Salvation Army work with prostitutes. In 1868, Mrs. Cottrill, a lay Christian Missioner, opened her home to prostitutes when they had no place to go. See Pamela J. Walker, *Pulling the Devil's Kingdom Down* (Berkeley: Univ. of California, 2001), for a superb study of the social context of the Army's rescue work in Victorian England.

23. J. Allister Smith, *Zulu Crusade* (London: Salvationist Publishing, 1945), for work among Africans; and Tuck, 30ff.

25. Norman H. Murdoch, *Like a Mighty Army: The Salvation Army as a Christian Imperium in Zimbabwe, 1891–1991*, a yet to be published ms.

26. For more on American Salvation Army farm colonies and Sir Rider Haggard's study of them for the British government see: Norman H. Murdoch, "Anglo–American Salvation Army Farm Colonies, 1890–1910," *Communal Societies* (vol. 3, 1983): 111–121.

27. Tuck, 48–49

Notes to Chapter 2

1. Norman H. Murdoch, *Frank Smith: Salvationist Socialist (1854–1940)*, (Orlando: The Salvation Army National Social Services, 2003): 24 pp.

2. "David C. Lamb Officer Sheet Profile," Salvation Army Archives, London

3. I compare Bellamy and Booth in "Rose Culture and Social Reform: Edward Bellamy's *Looking Backward* (1888) and William Booth's *Darkest England and the Way Out* (1890), *Utopian Studies*, 3:2 (1992): 91–101

4. "The City Colony, in London, Eng.," *The War Cry*, London (Mar. 2, 1895).

5. Bernard Watson, *Soldier Saint: George Scott Railton* (London: Hodder & Stoughton): 178, termed the illness of the imperturbable Lamb and other officers in 1901, a "nervous ailment." Commissioners Cadman and Pollard, and Colonel Lawley were also ill. Watson found that pressures on "key men" often showed itself in this "obscure malady ... as the strains of the war took its toll. *The War Cry* of the early 20th century carried alarmingly long lists of officers who died, were "promoted to Glory," and many paragraphs on sick officers. Watson stated, "Bramwell Booth's war was costly."

6. See Clark C. Spence, *The Salvation Army Farm Colonies* (Tucson: University of Arizona, 1985):108, for a study of the Army's three U.S. farm colonies. Spence discusses Sir Rider Haggard's *Report on the Salvation Army Colonies in the United States and at Hadleigh, England, with a Scheme of National Land Settlement* of June 1905.

Notes to Chapter 3

1. In March 1867 the British parliament passed the British North America Act that concluded work on an 1858 idea of a federal union of all British North America. The American Civil War, Irish–American Fenian attacks on Canada from the U.S. in 1866, and other causes gradually brought British, French, and Canadians from maritime and prarie provinces together in a confederation that (unlike the U.S. federation) allows for the possibility of leaving the union. For specifics on this confederation see: Ramsay Cooke, *Canada: A Modern Study* (Toronto: Clarke, Irwin & Co., 1963): 84–100; and Desmond Morton, *A Short History of Canada*, 2nd rev. edn. (Toronto: McClelland & Stewart, 1994): 84ff.

2. Spence, 2–3, cites 19th century farm colony sources: *An Account of the Poor–Colonies, & Agricultural Workhouses, of the Benevolent Society of Holland* (Edinburgh: Peter Brown & James Duncan, 1828): xi, xii, 1, 10, 145, 181, 187; Annet Royaard, "Farms for the Country's Poor: Experiments in Which Agriculture is used to Better Humanity," *The Craftsman* 25 (Nov. 1913): 169, 70, 171; J. Howard Gore, "The Poor Colonies of Holland," U.S. Department of Labor *Bulletin* No 2 (Washington: Jan. 1896): 113–17; Harold F. Moore, *Back to the Land* (Lon-

don: Methuen & Co., 1893): 16–20, 208–10; Louis Napoleon Bonaparte, *Extinction du Pauperisme*, in Charles–Edouard Temblaire, ed., *Oeuvres de Louis–Napoleon Bonaparte* (Paris: Libraire Napoleoninne, 1948): vol. 2, 251–304; *Chicago Tribune* (July 20, 1902; *Encyclopedia Britannica*, 14th edn. (New York: Encyclopedia Britannica, 1936) 9:80.

3. St. John Ervine, *God's Soldier: General William Booth* (New York: Macmillan, 1935): vol. 1, 34; Harold Begbie, *The Life of General William Booth: The Founder of The Salvation Army* (New York: Macmillan, 1920): vol. 1, 49; Frederick Coutts, *Bread for My Neighbour: The Social Influence of William Booth* (London: Hodder & Stoughton, 1978): 26

4. Murdoch, *Frank Smith, M.P.: Salvationist Socialist*, 5ff., for Booth's "change of heart" brought about by Frank Smith and others who had developed a social consciousness in The Salvation Army.

5. Spence, 3, cites: C. S. Orwin & W. F. Darke, *Back to the Land* (London: Swan Sonnenschein, Le Bas, & Lowrey, 1885); Moore, 137–43; Charles William Stubbs, *The Land and the Labourers* (London: W. Swan Sonnenschein & Co., 1884): 106–47; Robert England, *The Colonization of Western Canada* (London: P. S. King & Son, 1936): 59–62.

6. Spence, 3, names some North American settlements: Beer–Sheba, Kansas; Devil's Lake, North Dakota; & Cotopaxi, Colorado. See Isador Singer, ed., *The Jewish Encyclopedia* (New York: Funk & Wagnalls, 1901): 1:241–59; Samuel Joseph, *History of the Baron de Hirsch Fund* (Baron de Hirsch Fund, 1935): 8–9, 33.

7. Harry Williams, *Booth–Tucker: William Booth's First Gentleman* (London: Hodder & Stoughton, 1980).

8. H. Rider Haggard, *Regeneration* (London: Longmans, Green, 1910). I assess the failure of the three U.S. farm colonies in "Anglo–American Salvation Army Farm Colonies, 1890–1910," *Communal Societies*, 3 (Fall 1983): 111–121.

9. By "unique" I do not mean that Lamb's plan for moving entire families was the only such program. There were many religious and secular emigration programs that worked on the same principles as the one Lamb was using in the Army.

10. Frederick de Latour Booth–Tucker, "The Social Relief Work of the Salvation Army in the United States," in *Monographs on American Social Economics*, 22 (New York: The League for Social Work, 1900): 31; *Farm Colonies of The Salvation Army*, in *Bulletin of the Bureau of Labor*, #48 (Washington: Sept. 1903); *The Life of William Booth*, "Farm Colonies" (London: The Salvation Army, 1901): 53–58; *The Salvation Army in the United States* (New York: Reliance Trading Co., n.d.): 14; *Prarie Homes for City Poor* (New York: The Salvation Army, c. 1901).

11. Williams, *Booth Tucker: William Booth's First Gentleman*, 64, 120.

12. *The War Cry* ,London (May 13, 1905).

13. "Songs for Services on Board Ship," (London: Emigration–Colonization & Shipping Office), n.d. This publication listed the locations of branch offices of the Emigration Dept., in Bristol, Liverpool, Glasgow, Edinburgh, Aberdeen, and Belfast, as well as offices in Canada at Halifax, St. John, Quebec, Montreal, Toronto, London, Winnipeg, and Vancouver. The Army managed hotels in Canada at St. John, N.B., Quebec, Montreal, Toronto, and Vancouver. The Army's Lodges for Young Women were in: Halifax, Montreal, Toronto, Winnipeg, and Vancouver. This sheet listed pamphlets on: how to bring your friends to Canada; how the Army can help; and an announcement that the Army would send "Parties" to Canada every week in the Spring and Early Summer. It also included an ad for Mothersill's sea sickness pills for 4 shillings 6 pence a box .

14. Begbie, *The Life of General William Booth*, vol. 2: 317

15. "A Vice–Regal Opinion," *War Cry*, Toronto (6 May 1905): np.

16. Haggard, *Regeneration*, 81; Sandall, *History of The Salvation Army*, vol. 3, 358; quote from R. G. Moyles, *Blood & Fire in Canada: A History of the Salvation Army in the Dominion, 1882–1976* (Toronto: Peter Martin, 1977): 149

17. Moyles, *The Blood and Fire in Canada: A History of the Salvation Army*, Revised 2nd edn. (Edmonton, AB, 2004, 1977): 123–135. I depend on Moyles' excellent history for statistics and a background of Canadian social and political history as it regards immigration.

18. Moyles, 128

19. Moyles, 129–31

20. *The War Cry*, Toronto (Nov. 10, 1908): np.; "Salvation Army Plans in B.C.," *Colonist* (May 9, 1909): 10; "Army to Bring Many Settlers to the Coast," *Providence* (Jan. 22, 1910): 2; "Proposed Bringing Settlers to Island," *Colonist* (Jan. 27, 1910): 3; "To Meet Critics of the Movement," *Providence* (Jan. 20, 1910): 23.

21. E.M.C., "Colonel David Lamb," *Young Soldier* (Oct. 9, 1909): 3–6; see "A Prosperous Immigrant," *War Cry* (c. 1909). Lamb described a successful emigrant, Brother Walters, a builder who had landed in Canada with $24. By 1907 he had hired as many as 300 men to erect about 20 buildings worth $24,000. Three of these were Salvation Army citadels at Yorkville, Riverdale, and Toronto Junction. Walters was a bandsman at Dovercourt Citadel.

22. Moyles, *Blood and Fire in Canada*, is the authority on the Salvation Army's immigration program in the dominion. I appreciate his assistance in finding sources for this book.

23. "'A Foremost Place,' The Superintendent of Immigration Eulogizes the Immigration Work of the Salvation Army," *The War Cry*, Toronto (10 Sept. 1910): 8–9.

24. "Canada," *The Salvation Army Year Book, 1910* (London: Salvationist Publishing, 1910): 25.

25. During the time of Elizabeth I, England established Poor Law unions as local government agents to supervise the care of the poor; a law in 1834 established local guardians of the poor, a program that existed until the Labour government's social reforms of 1946–48.

26. "Land and Industrial Colony, Hadleigh, Esssex," and "Small Holdings Settlement, Boxted, Essex," *The Salvation Army Year Book*, 1914 (London: Salvation Army, 1915).

27. Murdoch, "Anglo–American Salvation Army Farm Colonies, 1890–1910," *Communal Societies*, 3 (1983):118.

28. "Look This Way!: Colonization," *The War Cry*, Toronto (June 27, 1908). Responding to requests from "soldiers and friends" who wanted land on which to "make a home for themselves," Canada's Commissioner Coombs announced: "A limited number of able–bodied men, experienced in bush or farm work, are wanted, with the ultimate idea of taking up a homestead." After six months their families, if they had any, could join them. The Canadian experiments in Boxted–type farms seem to have begun with these requests.

Notes to Chapter 4

1. Moyles, *Blood and Fire in Canada*, 134–35.

2. Increasingly in recent years, Salvation Army Training Schools have gained accreditation to offer degrees and certificates in various social and management fields.

3. Sandall, *History of The Salvation Army*, vol. 3, 74.

4. Murdoch, *Frank Smith*, 1–2

5. *The Salvation Army Yearbook, 2006* (London: The Salvation Army, 2005): 35, indicates that the Army had 107,726 (lay) "employees" and 17,295 "active officers" (clergy) in 2004.

6. Peter Seinfels, "Beliefs," *New York Times* (March 13, 2004, A12. In the late 20th–early 21st centuries discrimination in employment policies tends to be the focus of court decisions, which are critical of religious charities' insistence that employees abide by or propagate an organization's religious beliefs. A 1995 case, *Employment Division v. Smith*, concerned an American Indian claim for peyote use as a religious exercise in the state of Oregon. As Seinfels points out, "the larger question is

whether religious organizations with distinctive values can continue to share the provision of social services alongside the government."

7. See E. H. McKinley, *Somebody's Brother: A History of The Salvation Army Men's Social Service Department, 1891–1985,* for a superb survey of this church–state clash in Chapter V. The Years of Crisis: Service to Man, 1940–1960, pp. 115ff.

8. "Questions for W. Todd Bassett," *New York Times Magazine* (Feb. 15, 2004): 6; & "The Salvation Army's Goal," *New York Times* (Feb. 8, 2004): 14. See Stephanie Strom, "Salvation Army Receives a Gift of $1.5 Billion," *New York Times* (Jan. 21, 2004): *nytimes.com.* Commissioner Bassett told the Times that "Mrs. Kroc was comfortable with [the Army's] Christian roots and knew that each [community] center" built with her donation "would have a chapel or a place of worship on the premises ... She fully understood the importance of the spiritual life of a person and knew that was integral to the Salvation Army."

9. Daniel J. Wakin, "Charity Reopens Bible, and Questions Follow," *New York Times* (Feb. 2, 2004): *nytimes.com;* and Robert S. Schachter, Executive Director, New York Chapter, National Association of Social Workers, "The Salvation Army's Goal," *New York Times* (Feb. 8, 2004): 14

10. Roger J. Green, *War on Two Fronts: The Redemptive Theology of William Booth* Atlanta: Salvation Army, 1989): 95

11. "Salvation Army Rescue Work," *War Cry* (23 June 1888): 8; Major James Cooke, "To Field Officers and Slum Candidates," *War Cry* (19 July 1890): 13

12. Beatrice Webb, *Our Partnership* (New York: 1948): 400

13. Mrs. Lt. Colonel Carpenter, *Three Great Hearts* (London: Salvationist Publishing, 1921): 219 pp. is an exception to this rule. It has biographies of three male social officers: R. J. Sturgess; James Barker; and Frank Aspinall. Other social officers who have biographies were better known for their spiritual side work, e.g. Elijah Cadman and Edward J. Parker. When the Army's Literary Department discussed whether or not to commission a biography of David Lamb's wife, Minnie Lamb, in the 1940s and 50s, it worried about whether or not by that time the Lambs were sufficiently known to warrant a book. They are still largely unknown in 2005.

14. E. H. McKinley, *Somebody's Brother: A History of The Salvation Army Men's Social Service Department, 1891–1985* (Lewiston/Queenston: Edwin Mellen Press, 1986): 273, is a fine study, but its price is beyond the means of many Salvationists. Lillian Taiz, *Hallelujah Lads & Lasses: Remaking The Salvation Army in America, 1880–1930* (Chapel Hill:

University of North Carolina Press, 2001): has chapters on a "New Message of Temporal Salvation: Reinventing the Army at the Turn of the Century," and "Salvationism at the Turn of the Century: Refining Religious Culture, Reconceiving a Religious Market." Diane Winston, *Red–Hot & Righteous: The Urban Religion of The Salvation Army* (Cambridge: Harvard University UP, 1999) found that the Army's success in cities was due to adaptation that expanded its mission "to include humanitarian aid [in] social services" and fundraising to support social programs.

15. [Winifred Leal], *Dave, David Clinton Lamb: A Memoir*—Prefatory Note by David and Minnie Lamb (St. Albans: The Salvation Army, for private circulation, 1912): 83 pp.

Notes to Chapter 5

1. Frederick Coutts, *The History of The Salvation Army*, vol. 4 (London: Hodder & Stoughton, 1973): 32

2. David C. Lamb, "The Salvation Army in Cooperation with Governing Authorities," *The Officer* [n.d.], pp. 669–75, a paper read at an International Staff Council.

3. David C. Lamb, "Lecture on Emigration," *The Herald of Stars*, Jan. 10, 1915, p. 10; George Lansbury, "Life and Life More Abundant," Feb. 3, 1914, 97. See David C. Lamb, "Memorandum on Empire Migration and Settlement," Lectures at the Trades Union Congress & London County Council in 1924, 1930, Salvation Army Archives, London.

4. More recently termed an "addiction" by the medical and social science communities

5. David Lamb, "The Reform of Drunkards," *Herald of the Star* (February 6, 1917): 65ff.

6. "Comprehensive Migration Schemes: The Army and After–War Problems," *The Salvation Army Year Book, 1917* (London: Salvation Army, 1918): 13–15

7. "After–the–War Migration," *The Salvation Army Year Book, 1918* (London: Salvation Army, 1919):11.

8. In the 15th century, Britain appointed country gentlemen as "justices of the peace." They assisted itinerant jusrists. But over time, justices were commissioned to try many sorts of cases. Minnie Lamb was one of the first women to receive a J.P. commission under the Local Government Act of 1888.

9. *A Local Social Problem and Its Solution* (St. Albans: The Salvation Army, c.1911); Minnie Lamb Papers, Salvation Army Archives, London.

10. Eason, *Women in God's Army.*

11. On the 1925–26 World Tour: the Lambs also made personal visits to friends in Ocean Grove, New Jersey.

12. David Lamb, "A New Outlook for Unwanted Children and Widows with Families," *The Child* (March, 1923): 6 pages, Salvation Army Archives, London.

13. "The Army's Migration Work," *The Salvation Army Year Book, 1923* (London: Salvation Army, 1923): 9–12.

14. "Migration and Settlement," *The Salvation Army Year Book, 1924* (London: Salvation Army, 1924): 30ff.

15. Commissioner David C. Lamb, "Juvenile Migration & Settlement," *Edinburgh Review* (July 1924): 15 pp.

Notes to Chapter 6

1. David C. Lamb, *Our Heritage—The Empire: A report on some aspects of a tour of the King's Overseas Dominions undertaken chiefly in the interests of Empire Migration and Settlement, 1925–1926* (London: Salvation Army, 1925): 31 pp., Forward by Bramwell Booth

2. October 10, 1925 *War Cry* article "regarding Commissioner and Mrs. Lamb," attached to a May 13, 1946 letter from R. D. Hughes, Editor, *The War Cry*, New York, to Colonel S. Carvosso Gauntlett.

3. "The Salvation Army in Outline," *War Cry – Canada and Alaska* (December 26, 1925)

4. "Mrs. Commissioner Lamb Speaks Out: A Salvation Army Woman J.P. Talks to *The War Cry* on Several Live Topics," *The War Cry*, Toronto (Nov. 14, 1925): p. 4, at the Salvation Army Archives, Toronto

5. Moyles, *Blood and Fire in Canada,*134–49.

6. Mrs. Commissioner Lamb, J.P., "Some Impressions of Our Tour," in David C. Lamb, *Our Heritage—the Empire*, pp. 36–37, at the Salvation Army Archives, London.

7. Lamb, *Our Heritage—The Empire*, pp. 9–16 for David Lamb's evaluation of what he learned on the tour, at the Salvation Army Archives, London.

8. Lamb, "Report to General Booth," in *Our Heritage—Our Empire*, pp. 20–28, Salvation Army Archives, London.

9. Lamb, "The Overseas Press," in *Our Heritage—Our Empire*, pp. 29–32, Salvation Army Archives, London.

Notes to Chapter 7

1. St. John Ervine, *God's Soldier: General William Booth,* (New York: Macmillan, 1935): vol. 1, xvi, vol. 2, 959, notes gratitude to Mrs.

Bramwell Booth and Commissioner Catherine Booth, for making family papers available as they had done for William Booth's authorized biographer, Harold Begbie. The reliability of Ervine's work rests on the broad range of readers who reacted to his text: Edward Higgins; Evangeline Booth; Catherine Booth; Samuel Hurren; David Lamb, and George Carpenter. Ervine wrote from 1927 to 1933, at the time of Bramwell Booth's removal from office, and during the passage of the Salvation Army Act by Parliament. His adherence to truth, as seen from the outside, is superior to those who wrote with a bias, although he displays a certain sympathy for Bramwell Booth.

2. Ervine, 815–1139, provides an account of the 1929–32 era on which I rely for this study of David Lamb's role in The Salvation Army's reformation. Ervine cites Lamb on 834ff, 845, 898, 919, 924–5, 930, 945–7, 954–6, 959–61, 966–9, 973, 984, 997, 1007, 1010, 1014–15, 1017–21, 1128–39. Among more biased studies are: a pro–Booth family book by Frank Smith, MP, *The Betrayal of Bramwell Booth* (London: Jarrolds, 1929); and a pro–reformer book by F. A. Mackenzie, *The Clash of the Cymbals: The Secret History of the Revolt in the Salvation Army* (New York: Brentano's, 1929). When Smith was writing his defense of Bramwell Booth he was running for the House of Commons, his last and only successful run for that office. As a Member of Parliament, Frank Smith opposed the Salvation Army Act of 1931–32; it took power away from the Booth family. Smith's adopted daughter lived with the Bramwell Booths. Mrs. Bramwell (Florence) Booth would be at Smith's side when he died on December 26, 1940. Friendship was thicker than Smith's Socialist–democratic sentiments, leading him to disagree with Lamb's general in council views. But Smith went beyond Lamb and pushed for giving all Salvationists, including lay soldiers, voting rights in electing a general.

3. Ervine, 919, 924, explains that the British Commissioner, Samuel Hurren, drafted a formal protest against alteration of the 1904 Supplementary deed. Seven London commissioners and two retired commissioners signed and sent Hurren's protest to the general on March 6th. Those signing the letter were: Hurren; Lamb; Booth–Tucker, Ret.; Blowers; John Carleton, Chairman of the S.A. Assurance Society Board; Charles H. Jeffries; Henry W. Mapp; Robert Hoggard; and Richard Wilson, director of Salvationist Supplies, Ltd.

4. Arthur W. Watts, *Lion Hearts: Memoirs of the Christian Mission, Afterwards Known as The Salvation Army* (Gillingham, Kent, England, 1929: 10–15, 22–23. Watts was a young evangelist in the mission at the 1878 conference when he voted against the new deed that made William Booth general for life with a right to name his successor. Watts claimed

that he and some older evangelists opposed the change, but few had the courage to speak or vote their convictions. Murdoch, *Origins of the Salvation Army,* "Forming a 'Salvation Army,'" pp. 88ff.

5. For the etymology of the term "dirk" see: *Compact Edition of the Oxford English Dictionary* (New York: Oxford UP, 1975): 736. Albert Orsborn, *The House of My Pilgrimage* (London: Salvationist Publishing, 1958): 138, discussed the 1929–32 period as a "Constitutional Crisis." He held that most of the chief participants destroyed "most of the private correspondence." I have not found Lamb's correspondence in this period.

6. Ervine, 903, and 906. Bramwell was known to have consigned senior officers to "the freezer," appointments far from the Army's command center in London when he felt that he had lost a person's loyalty.

7. Ervine, 925, 926

8. Ervine, 930, 938. Commissioners Adam Gifford, Henry C. Hodder, Richard E. Holz, William Alexander McIntyre, John McMillan and William Peart, and Colonels Gustav Reinhardsen and Walter F. Jenkins signed the petition. Commissioner Samuel Brengle's name was not on the list. In May–June 43 "highly–placed" Australian officers signed letters to Bramwell asking him to agree to Evangeline's requests for a High Council. Commissioner Mapp of the London group was visiting Australia at the time.

9. Murdoch, 88–112, on William Booth's authoritarian despotism as these traits developed in the Army's military system after 1878. See Ervine, 931 for Evangeline's letter.

10. Ervine, 932–41

11. Ervine, 951.

12. Ervine, 955–57.

13. Ervine, 959, 968–71.

14. Ervine took information from books by polemicists F. A. Mackenzie, *The Clash of the Cymbals,* and Frank Smith, *The Betrayal of Bramwell Booth.* He also had access to Mrs. Booth's notes, and "verbal accounts" of High Council members. The recorder, Commissioner Cunningham, wrote no "detailed official report." Ervine was "baffled by the failure in the memory of persons present" and "by contradictory accounts of what actually happened." But his account is the most balanced and thorough report of the event.

15. Ervine, 973.

16. Ervine, 976–77.

17. Ervine, 981–88.

18. Ervine, 989–96.

19. Ervine, 996–99.
20. Ervine, 1000.

Notes to Chapter 8

1. "William Bramwell Booth Estate Record," at the Principal Probate Registry, High Holborn Street, London.

2. Ervine, 1004–5, does not list the names of the negotiators for General Higgins or the Booths.

3. Frank Smith, M.P. and George Lansbury, M.P. led the insurgents who supported the Booth family out of personal attachment. See Frank Smith, *The Salvation Army Private Bill: A Series of Communications addressed to Mr. Frank Smith, M.P., by Members of The Salvation Army Designed to Elucidate the Provisions of the Bill and Voice Objections to it* (London: Fleetway Press, Dec.1930): 16 pp.

4. Letter, Harry Williams to Norman H. Murdoch, Williams notes that while he was on the staff at the International Headquarters, Chief of Staff Arthur Carr showed him two items from a small "cache of private papers" in the possession of the General and Chief of Staff. One dealt with "the masterful way Higgins dealt with the Parliamentary Select Committee in obtaining the SA Act of 1931." Williams believes that "Lamb would have been in on this." The other paper gave the names of "the leading of the land—titles galore," who attended Lamb's retirement.

Letters, John Larsson to Norman Murdoch, Jan. 3, 2004; Laurence Hay to Norman Murdoch, Feb. 4, 2004, included several papers: John Larsson's comments on "Commissioner Lamb's long–time advocacy of a council to support and advise (and restrain?) the General of the day;" "An Extract from a Briefing Paper Prepared by Larsson for 2003 Commission on Membership of the High Council on 1929–31;" Laurence Hay's draft, "Advisory Council to the General, See General's Consultative Council," for an *Historical Dictionary of The Salvation Army,*" John Merritt, ed,.; and David C. Lamb, "Private & Confidential Memorandum: The Background of Councils & Committees," July 20, 1939, 25 pp., and Lamb's correspondence with a 1946 commission to "enquire into an Advisory Council," chaired by Catherine Bramwell– Booth.

5. Ervine, 1007–08. Frank Smith opposed deposing Bramwell Booth and represented ideas that were autocratic. Smith was clearly a Stuart–era monarchist when it came to the notion that The Salvation Army was God's imperial kingdom. Thus this socialism was somewhere to the political right.

6. Ervine, 1010–11.

Notes to Chapter 9

1. Booth, *In Darkest England*, 227–28; Sandall, 3:246–49, discussed the Army's leaders' interest in an Intelligence Department to study such contemporary reform ideas as model suburban villages, a poor man's bank, Co–operation in general, a Matrimonial Bureau, and Whitechapel–by–the–Sea for East Londoners' summer recreation.

2. I have not located Lamb's personal papers apart from letters he wrote to his family, and thus I cannot discuss his private attitudes. Germany bombed The Salvation Army Headquarters at 101 Queen Victoria St., near St. Pauls Cathedral, during World War II. The Army's Archives Department has recently moved and is not aware of who may now possess Lamb's papers (diary, letters, etc.), or whether they were destroyed by the family.

3. "Appointments and Promotions Affecting International Headquarters and Far East," *War Cry* (Feb. 6, 1932); *The Sunday Times* (March 6, 1932).

4. "A Spiritual Jubilee, Commissioner Lamb's Speech at Goldsmith's Hall, London, 24 Oct., 1932, printed for private circulation; one of a series of testimonial meetings. Salvation Army Archives, London

5. David C. Lamb, *Forty Years of Social Change*, reprint of a BBC broadcast address of Jan. 13, 1933, 16 pp., Salvation Army Archives, London.

6. "Private Memorandum from Commissioner Lamb, High Council—28 August 1934," Salvation Army Archives, London.

7. Ervine, 1013–17.

8. William G. Harris, *General Edward Higgins: Storm Pilot* (St. Albans: Campfield Press, 1981): 108

9. Ervine, 1018–23.

Notes to Chapter 10

1. David C. Lamb, "How Was I Converted? *War Cry*, New York (Oct. 7, 1933): 13 (also Feb. 6, 1932, p. 10); and *Forty Years of Social Change* (a Broadcast Address of Jan. 13, 1933)—a biographical sketch of Jan. 1892 to 1933 that he published at 23 Canonbury Sq., London, N1, at the Salvation Army Archives, London

2. From *With Flag Unfurled: The Salvation Army Aberdeen Citadel, 1880–1980* (1980); "Helper of Humanity: Commissioner David Lamb, LL.D., 'Capped' in Aberdeen University," *War Cry*, London (Apr. 14, 1934, Salvation Army Archives, London

3. *The War Cry* (Dec. 16, 1939)

4. David C. Lamb, C.M.G., LL.D., "The Economic Value of Teaching the Unfit," address given during the British Association for the Advancement of Science, Aberdeen, Sept. 9, 1934, Salvation Army Archives, London.

5. "The Challenge of the Christian Ethic in Social Services," *The Liverpool Quarterly* (1937)

6. David C. Lamb, "Population Problems," *The Empire Club of Canada Speeches, 1937–1938* (Toronto: The Empire Club of Canada, 1938): 111–123; David C. Lamb, "My Visit to Canada," *Empire Review & Magazine*, 67 (Jan. – June, 1938): 79–84. Lamb visited Montreal, Ottawa, Regina, Saskatoon, Edmonton, Calgary, Vancouver, Winnipeg, Toronto, Brampton, Halifax, St. John, N.B., then to New York via Montreal, Toronto, and Detroit. He met with the British High Commissioner and Governor–General. The tour ran from Oct. 16 to Dec. 15, 1937, Salvation Army Archives, Toronto.

7. David C. Lamb, "The Homeless Poor: London Streets Fifty Years Ago: A Record of Progress," *The Times*, London (May 24, 1938): 4 pp.

8. Obituaries: *The Times*, Apr. 18, 1939; *Sunday Times*, June 3, 1932; *Officer Review* (Spr. 1939); *The Times*, Apr. 18, 1939; *Sunday Times*, June 3, 1932; the *Sunday Standard*, Apr. 20, 1939; "An Indomitable Fighter: Mrs. Lamb 57 Years an Aggressive Army Officer, Called to Her Reward," *War Cry* (Apr. 22, 1939); Major Winifred Leal, IHQ, "Minnie (Clinton) Lamb," *The Officer* (Sept. 1939): 411–14: "Noted Salvationist Dead," [Scottish newspaper]; *Southend Standard* (Apr. 20, 1939); Salvation Army Archives, London

9. Minnie Lamb, *A Local Social Problem & Its Solution* (St. Albans: Salvation Army, c. 1911) Rochford Hundred, Poor Law Administration; "An Army Advocate: Mrs. Colonel Lamb's Experiences of Probation and Police Court Work," *Salvation Army Slum Brochure 102*, [n.d.]. an article in the *Social Officer* (Mar. 1899): 250–51, Salvation Army Archives, London.

10. Mrs. Commissioner Lamb, articles in *The Sunday Post:* "Broken Lives," (Sept. 1, 1935): 12; "Strangest Job I Ever Tackled," (Sept. 8, 1935): 14; "Secret I Could Not Tell Wealthy Heiress," Sept. 15, 1935): 14; "Strange Story of Two Wives," (Sept. 22, 1935): 14; "Her Confession Took My Breath Away," (Sept. 29, 1935): 14; "Widow's Vow Never to Speak Again," (Oct. 6, 1935): 14; "Mother Who Chose the Hard Road," (Oct. 13, 1935): 14; "I Fight for a Girl's Freedom," (Oct. 20, 1935): 14; "Three Women in a Strange Affair," (October 27, 1935): 14; "The Men from Devil's Island," Nov. 3, 1935): 14, Salvation Army Archives, London.

11. Obituaries: *The Times* (April 18, 1939); "Sudden Death of Mrs. Lamb," "Noted Salvationist Dead," [Scottish newspaper]; *Southend Standard* (Apr. 20, 1939); Salvation Army Archives, London.

12. "Her First Corps, Lt. Minnie Clinton," *All the World* (Jan.–Feb. 1897); Winifred Leal, "Minnie (Clinton) Lamb," *The Officer* Review (Spr. 1939): 669–75; "Mrs. Commissioner Lamb," *Social Officer* (May 1899): 250–51; Winifred Leal, IHQ, "Minnie (Clinton) Lamb," *The Officer* (Sept. 1939): 411–14; "An Army Advocate: Mrs. Colonel Lamb's Experiences of Probation and Police Court Work," *Salvation Army Slum Brochure 102*, [n.d.], Salvation Army Archives, London.

From 1927 to 1955 Army leaders discussed David Lamb's plea that they publish Minnie Lamb's biography. Literary Secretary Colonel Carvosso Gauntlett suggested two authors to Chief of Staff William Baugh: Mrs. Lt. Col. Rhou, Lt. Col. Unsworth, but Minnie Lamb's friend in the Literary Dept., Major Winifred Leal, O.B.E., of Tar O'Moor House, Woodhall Spa, Lincs. was the principal choice. Leal died in 1957 at Finchampstead, home of the Bramwell–Booths, without writing the book. The Army asked Frederick Coutts of "Red Tiles," The Mall, Park St., St. Albans, to consider the task. Coutts contacted Lambs' daughters, Mrs. Brauen, at Hill Lodge, Harmer Green, nr. Welwyn, in Apr. 1947, and Mrs. H. Day, 39 Heathville Rd., Crouch Hill, # 19. Letters at the Army Archives, London. In 1948 Coutts wrote: "I have often wondered why the Commissioner [Lamb] has not written a 'history' of The Army's Social Work." On Nov. 13, 1948, Coutts returned Lamb papers he had found: "Her First Corps;" "The Greatest Sinner I Ever Knew;" and "Forty Years of Social Change" and observed: they "will be required for the life of Mrs. Commissioner Lamb if this is ever handled." Coutts had met Catherine Lamb, a daughter who had been a Salvation Army officer. She received Lamb's papers when he died in 1951. In 1955 she lived at Trebetherick, North Cornwall. Where those papers are in 2006 is a mystery.

13. David Lamb, "Receiving the 'Order of the Founder,'" (St. Albans: Campfield Press, 1939): 14 pp.

14. David C. Lamb, "The Royal Tour," *Empire Review & Magazine*, July–December 1939): 9–13

Notes to Chapter 11

1. "Energetic Helper of Humanity: Commissioner David C. Lamb Retires from Active Service After Fifty–five Years Spent in Administrative and Executive Work," *The War Cry*, Toronto (Jan. 13, 1940): 7. The article mentioned that Lamb's eldest daughter, Major Catherine Lamb, was in charge of "Hope Town," the Army's Shelter in Whitechapel.

2. *The War Cry* (Jan. 1940); Robert Sandall, 3:262.

3. David Lamb, "The Post–War Problem & Its Solution," (St. Albans: Campfield Press, Jan. 1940): 2 pp.

4. Bernard Shaw, *Major Barbara: Definitive Text* (New York: Penguin Books, 1907), was produced as a stage play and "screened" by Gabriel Pascal in 1941. This version must have been what Shaw gave to Lamb.

5. Letter, David C. Lamb, to G. B. Shaw, of Ayot, St. Lawrence, Wellyn, Herts., British Library, G. B. Shaw Papers, 50522 f.393. Lamb commented on a copy of *Major Barbara* that Shaw gave him. Lamb wrote: "Dear G.B.S, ... "I can see in the years to come if I am spared much personal pleasure in turning over the pages of your kind gift, although one of my high moments (when Major Barbara stands by the riverside with her bonnet held by the strings) is not in the album. Perhaps it is better so! Trusting you and yours are well, Believe me, I am, Yours sincerely, David C. Lamb, Commissioner." The British Library, London

6. Brindley Boon, *Play the Music Play! The story of Salvation Army bands* (London: Salvationist Publishing,1966): 207–09

7. David C. Lamb, *War of Ideas–the "Jury,"* pamphlet distributed by D. C. Lamb, C.M.G., LL.D, O.F., of 14042 Strathmoor Ave., Detroit, Michigan, U.S.A., Salvation Army Archives, London

8. David C. Lamb, "Six Months (Nov. 1941–May 1942) in the U.S.A. and Canada, being a Summarized Report of a 12,000 Miles Tour," Detroit, Oct. 1, 1942, Salvation Army Archives, London

9. Letter, Gladstone Murray (Victory Building, Toronto) to Rt. Hon. Clement Atlee, P.C., M.P., Secretary of State for the Dominions, Whitehall, London, Aug. 11, 1943.

10. Lamb, "Six Months," 4 pp.; see: Lamb's address at the Methodist Church, Rochester, Minnesota, Nov. 22, 1942; "Christian Future is Visualized by Lamb for Wacoans," *News Tribune* (Jan. 22, 1942): 1; and "Report F," March 20, 1942. Salvation Army Archives, London.

11. D.C.L., "Private: Notes Re Work & Staff," Dec. 5, 1941, Salvation Army Archives, London.

12. Colonel Gauntlett to General Carpenter, August 17, 1944.; Major Leal to Colonel Gauntlett, August 14, 1944; Colonel Gauntlett to Commissioner Lamb, Sept. 5, 1944, Salvation Army Archives, London.

13. Fraserburgh according to Harry W. Williams.

14. David C. Lamb, "Family News Letter, the Last of the Series," (Detroit, August 15, 1945): 11 pages, Salvation Army Archives, London.

15. David C. Lamb, "Family News Letter, Private (Nov. 30, 1945): 6 pp., Salvation Army Archives, London.

16. David C. Lamb, "The Next General," *The Spectator* (Apr. 12, 1946).

17. Commissioner Lamb, "For the General's Consideration" (June 26, 1946); Albert Orsborn to the Chief of Staff, "Memo: Commissioner Lamb's 80th Birthday" (July 25, 1946), Salvation Army Archives, Loncon.

18. Correspondence between David C. Lamb and the Commission on Advisory Council, July 1946, Salvation Army Archives, London. See my correspondence with General John Larsson.

19. "Personal: Charles Baugh, Chief of the Staff to Brigadier Coutts, Literary Dept., Aug. 16, 1946; "Lt. Col. F. L. Coutts to Commissioner J. J. Allan," Nov. 10, 1948; "Literary Secretary to Colonel Pallant," Oct. 25, 1955, Salvation Army Archives, London.

20. "1866–1946 and after: Commissioner David Lamb to His Friends, at the Luncheon Party at the Savoy Hotel, November 1, 1946, The Prime Minister (The Rt. Hon. C. R. Atlee, P.C.) presiding" (London: 23 Canonbury Sq., 1947). Salvation Army Archives, London

Notes to Chapter 12

1. "An Optimist at 82: Commissioner Lamb, of the Salvation Army, Has Faith in the Future," *San Francisco Chronicle* (Feb. 24, 1949).

2. "How Some People Came to Canada," *War Cry*, Toronto (Mar. 6 and 13, 1976): 5 pp., Salvation Army Archives, Toronto.

3. Cyril R. Bradwell, *Fight the Good Fight: The Story of the Salvation Army in New Zealand, 1883–1983* (Wellington: Salvation Army, 1982): 96–97; for Lamb's visits to New Zealand pp. 54, 90, 96.

4. David C. Lamb, "One World," *War Cry*, Western U.S.A, (Feb. 4. 1949), gave the 300,000 emigrants figure.

5. David C. Lamb, "Rhodesia's Soul," *Rhodesia Herald* (June 10 1947); "My Search for the Soul of Rhodesia: The Quality that Shows Itself in Crisis," *Rhodesia Herald*, [1947]: 4; "My Search for the Soul of Rhodesia: Gradual Emergence from the Embargo," *Rhodesia Herald* [1947]; "A Kindly Critic," *The Bulawayo Chronicle* (June 10, 1947) Salvation Army Archives, London.

6. David C. Lamb, "Family News Letter," July 31,1948—July 31, 1949, Salvation Army Archives, London

7. David C. Lamb, "Family News Letter," Goodwill tour of North America, Dec. 1948 – Apr. 1949 (May 14, 1949), 23 Canonbury Sq., London, N1, Salvation Army Archives, London.

8. David C. Lamb, "Today's World Problems" (St. Albans: Campfield Press, Oct. 23, 1949)

9. "Sixteen Week Unofficial Goodwill Tour of Australia/New Zealand," *War Cry* (May 19, 1951)

Notes to Chapter 13

1. David Crichton Lamb Estate, at Probate Court Records, High Holborn, London, 1951, Wills and Admons.

2. "Commissioner Lamb" A Salvation Army Leader," *The Times,* London (July 9, 1951); "A Soldier of God," *Montreal Daily Star* (reprinted in the War Cry (Toronto), Aug. 4, 1951.

3. "Memorial Services, David Crichton Lamb, D.C.L.," prepared by the family; "Memorial Service to the Late Commissioner David Lamb, F.R.E.S., LL.D., C.M.G., O.F. conducted by the Chief of the Staff John J. Allan on July 18, 1951, at Regent Hall; Obituaries: "Helper of Humanity," *The War Cry* (July 21, 1951); "David C. Lamb, Promoted to Glory," *The War Cry* (July 14, 1951).

4. *Canadian Immigration Since Confederation and the Department of External Affairs,* unpublished guide created in April 1988 and revised in September 2000, Library and Archives, Canada.

5. "Minutes of Evidence," Select Committee on Health, United Kingdom Parliament, London: Stationery Office, 1997–98.

6. "Examination of Witnesses," Ray Oakley, Testimony before the Select Committee on Health, British Parliament, Wednesday, 11 June 1998.

7. "Examination of Witnesses," Chris Fisher, Testimony before the Select Committee on Health, British Parliament, Wednesday, June 11, 1998.

8. John Larsson to Norman Murdoch, June 2005; and "International Headquarters," *The Salvation Army Year Book, 2004* (London: Salvation Army, 2004): 41–46 for the functions of Councils and a listing of the IHQ departments.

9. John Larsson to Norman Murdoch, June 2005. I am grateful for General Larsson's help in laying out these changes in the Salvation Army's international management system, and that owes something to David Lamb's thinking in the 1929 to 1946 period.

10. Murdoch, "Like a Mighty Army: The Salvation Army as a Christian Imperium in Zimbabwe, 1891–1991," an unpublished manuscript in which I discuss the clash of American and Third World interests at the Army's Toronto Leaders' Conference in 1979. The victory of the Patriotic Front of Robert Mugabe and Joshua Nkomo in the independence war, and the killing of two Salvation Army missionaries by an unidentified band of armed men had upset the Army's American leaders who were putting pressure on General Brown to leave the World Council of Churches. Brown kept his High Council promise to consult with leaders before he made his decision. In the end his deci-

sion was to suspend the Army's WCC membership in 1981, an action that caused Zimbabwe Salvationists to march on the Army's headquarters in Harare, protesting the action.

11. I am grateful to Commissioner Dr. Paul du Plessis, who was on the scene at the International Headquaarters during this period, for the nature of these changes in Salvation Army administration.

12. Murdoch, *Frank Smith—Salvationist–Socialist (1854–1940)— Principal Idealogue of the Darkest England Scheme that Created Salvation Army Social Services*, Alexandria: Salvation Army, 2003.

Bibliography

Brigadier Susie Forrest Swift
Sister Mary Imelda Therese, O.S.D.

Autobiographical Accounts:

Swift, Susie Forrest, Brigadier Susie, "Autobiographical Account,"
   March 1893

_____, *Diary (1887–1897) [Salvation Army years]*, at Sinsinawa Do-
   minican Archives

_____, "Account of her Roman Catholic conversion," 1897

_____, "He was better to me than all my hopes." Undated Poem

_____, Susie. Swift, (Sister Imelda Therese), "The Conversion of Su-
   san Swift," [1902]

_____ (Sr. Imelda Teresa.), "Miss Susie T. Swift," in *Some Roads to
   Rome in America*, 2nd ed., Georgina Pell Curtis, ed. (St. Louis:
   Herder, 1910): 463–96, Dominican Education Center Library

_____, *The City of Peace: 7 sketches by converts to the faith* (Ireland:
   Catholic Truth Society of Ireland; also Barclay St., New York: Ben-
   zinger Brothers, 1897)

Articles, Hymn & Poems by Susie Forrest Swift & The Creative Works of Sr. Imelda Therese Swift at the Sinsinawa Dominican Archives:

Poems:
After 'The Necromancers'
Called of God
Christmas Footprints
Christmas Consolatory
The Desolate Place He Rebuilded
Does God Always Have His Way
I Shall See the King, Some Day of Days
Up Toward Jerusalem
Upon the Book and Picture of the Seraphic S. Teresa
Dominus Illuminatio Mea

Prose and Drama:
This One Love . . . and the Other, by Teresa Forrest
Gwen's Summer in a Convent, written March 27, 1900

Christmas children's play
In the Convent Chapel
The Boy Prisoner of Roca Secca & What Became of Him, *Sunday Companion* (1890)
The One Love—and the Other (about Kevin Douglas, a priest)

Hymn:
Mine to rise when Thou dost call me
Lifelong though the journey be;
Thine to measure all its windings,
Leading step by step to Thee" (Salvation Army Songbook)

Handwritten in light ink—will not copy as is:
Bloodroot—a poem
Was It Worth While, by Teresa Forrest, 145 W. 61st St, New York
Deus ex Machina by Tressa Copeland (likely a draft of a future piece)

Also in the Susie F. Swift folder at the Sinsinawa Archives:
Josephine's Victory by Sister Innocent of Jesus, Dec. 11, 1910
Archivist (S.M.B.) copied Swift's hand–written works and noted that the writing of Susie Swift and Imelda Therese "seem very much alike to me." Swift also wrote under pen names. She wrote her only hymn, "Mine to Rise When Thou Dost Call Me," when she was a Salvation Army officer.

Essays

Susie F. Swift, "A Modern Miracle; or, How Mrs. Carleton Was Healed by Faith," *War Cry*, London (24 Dec. 1887): 7
_____, "Child–World," The Conqueror, 4 (1895), 228–29 (picture), Major Swift's work as head of a new waif and stray program for London's "destitute" boys.
_____, "Glimpses of East End Life," *War Cry* (25 Dec. 1889): 17–18
_____, "Sociology and Salvation," *All the World*, 1 (Jan. 1890, 39–41; II., Mar. 1890): 110–13
_____, Hymn: #460, "Mine to Follow Thee My Savior," *The Song Book of The Salvation Army* (London: Salvationist Publishing, 1953): 322
_____, "Dominican Sisters of Cuba," *Dominica Yearbook*, 1910 (pictures)
_____, "If the Clouds of the Sunset Parted Wide," Poem for Mother's Feast Day, 1910

Primary Sources

Roman Catholic Baptismal Certificate:
"Susie Teresa, child of George Swift and Camelia Paine," born 10 June
1862, "baptized according to the Rite of the Roman Catholic Church,"
March 4, 1897 at St. Paul the Apostle Parish, New York City, by A.P.
Doyle; sponsored by Annie McGinley; attested by Joseph McSorley.

Adoption Papers:
Eliza Madeley, [Christobel Douglas Swift], 18 Oct. 1888, 12 Idol Lane,
London EC, Ranger & Burton, Solicitors

Obituary Notices:
"Death of Noted Convert: Sister Imelda Teresa, O.S.D.," *The Missionary*
(June 1916), Sinsinawa Dominican Archives
Mother Samuel, Letter to "Dear Friends," April 24, 1916; "Sister"
Samuel, an account of Therese's death to "dear Sisters," April 21,
1916, Sinsinawa Dominican Archives
"Sister Imelda Teresa Dead: Vassar Graduate Quit the Salvation Army
to Become a Nun," obituary in the Sinsinawa Dominican Archives,
possibly from the *New York Times*
St. Clara Convent, Sinsinawa, Wisc., "Sister Mary Imelda Theresa
Swift," *Obituaries* 1:164–165, Sinsinawa Dominican Archives

Articles About Leaving The Salvation Army

Adamson, Laurence P., "From an Ex-Salvation Army Officer, San An-
tonio, Texas," *Irish World* (April 27, 1897)
"Salvation Army Deserter: Brigadier Susie F. Swift Leaves to Join the
Roman Catholic Church," *Irish World,* New York (Apr. 6) credits
Mrs. Hawthorne–Lathrop for bringing about Swift's conversion.
Swift will assist the Paulist fathers with "charitable work in the
neighborhood. Sinsinawa Dominican Archives
"From Salvation Army to the Church," (picture, "Brigadier–Gen. Susie
F. Swift"). Commander Booth–Tucker "begged [her] to reconsider,
. . . but her mind was made up and nothing could swerve her."
"Christobel Douglas Swift," "a waif whom Miss Swift adopted"
greeted her at the pier. Christobel had been "baptized a Roman
Catholic in her infancy." Susie was the niece of the former Mayor
Swift of Chicago and valedictorian of her 1883 Vassar class. Sinsinawa Dominican Archives
"Salvation Lass to be a Nun: Will Enter Dominican Convent on Madison Avenue [Albany]." Swift said: "It was in my work in the auxiliary league that I was naturally forced to examine more closely the

grounds of my own faith, coming, as I did, in contact with hundreds of inquiries, and with ministers of all denominations. Before that I had been so busy at the work of the Salvation Army that I had little time for reflection. I had always regarded the army as a mission and not as a church or denomination. Of course, I had always been familiar with the main teachings of Roman Catholicism, but when I came to examine [them] I grew satisfied that Christ did establish a visible church on earth, and that the Church of Rome was that visible church. For that reason I embraced the Catholic faith." She had taken her first communion in Liverpool when she went to London to speak with Bramwell Booth. She joined the staff of the *Catholic World* magazine when she returned to New York. Now she was joining the Albany Convent of the Third Order of St. Dominic, established by Lucy Eton Smith in 1880. Mother de Ricci, who founded the congregation, died in 1894. Mother M. Loyola, O.P. succeeded her. Miss Swift expected to be a postulant for a one year novitiate before assuming the white veil. After a second year she would take the black veil. Five years later she would take perpetual vows. The Convent was a "hospital for sick souls." Christobel was at school in New Jersey. Sinsinawa Dominican Archives

Susie Forrest Swift Correspondence (1897, and 1912–15)

W. Bramwell Booth to "My dear Major," Mar. 16, 1897: "I offer no objection to your seeing Mrs. Drummond, if she can aid you in any way to a right decision. . . . I pray for you. I will do all I can for Douglas. She and I will have to make up to our Lord—if indeed we can—for something of what we [unintelligible] in you. In true sympathy thought with deep regret. Yours very truly, W. Bramwell Booth

W. Bramwell Booth to "My dear Miss Swift," Mar. 18, 1897, "I think in full reflection that I am right in urging upon you the wisdom of taking a little time for thought and prayer before you take any further steps. Will you go away with Staff Captain Douglas to the sea—to some quiet place and really reflect and we will join in earnest prayer for you. Douglas may know of some quiet spot—if you do not care for the sea—go to Harrowgate or Matlock. . . . The more I give this matter thought the more do I feel the danger you stand in of putting externals in the place of God. That is the root error from which all other of the errors of the churches have sprung. May God save you from it—pray. Yours very truly. W. Bramwell Booth"

John Walsh to Mother M. Bertrand, O.P., Dec. 29, 1898: Albany Convent, from St. James' Church, Baltimore

Mother Loyola to Susan Swift concerning vocation to Albany Dominicans re: Bishop withholding Susan Swift's permission to enter Albany order; Bishop's final permission for Susan Swift's entrance, given April 1898

Evangeline Cory Booth

Lawrence Abbott, *The Christian Union: a Family Paper,* NY (June 24, 1893)

Sister Thomas Aquinas

Anna, 943 Amsterdam Ave., New York City

Mrs. Alphonse Bechamp

Family Notes

George H. Swift, father—likely at the time of her conversion to Roman Catholicism,—"My darling Susie, I have received your notes, and they have pained me greatly; but yet I do not know that I can deny to you the same liberty of conscience that I claim for myself— Come home as soon as you can—There shall be no scowls, no frowns, nothing but love, not even argument—'Mawwer' and I had but one 'baby,' and though she is gone I shall hold on to our baby while I live—Your loving papa—GHS"

George H. Swift to "Darling Susie," Apr. 16, 1897, 1st National Bank of Amenia, George H. Swift, President, written after her Mar. 4 baptism & Mar. 14 first communion. "Your letter with check came today and I send you $10 bill enclosed—I keep the $9 for you and more with it at any time you want money—Don't be so independent that you won't take what you want from your old father. Come up as soon as you can. I have read Father Searle's letter, and return it. He talks like a good man. . . . I have known many good men among Catholics and their priests, and some bad ones. They are probably very much like men in Protestant denominations. . . . Your loving father."

George H. Swift to "Dear Susie," Feb. 8, 1899: Susie had entered the Albany convent Aug. 24, 1898 & would receive the Dominican habit on Apr. 30, 1899: "I never expected to see the opening day of my 80th year." Susie had sent "the children" [nephew George & niece Elizabeth] a kaleidoscopic change in the combination castor bottle, and stamps. "Fleury is in N. J. to have an operation performed."

George H. Swift to "Dear Susie," Mar. 22, 1899: "Yours received and as I had just recd. $3 or 400—I send you the $100 as requested at once. I shall not ever miss it." Mother Loyola had invited him to visit—"But I simply cannot! I should be grieving with 'Mawwa' all the time that I was there. God bless and keep you, and help you to do *His* will—Your loving father,"

Christobel Janicki, adopted daughter, b. 1883

Samuel L. Brengle, brother–in–law, and Mrs. Elizabeth Swift Brengle, sister

Mrs. Elizabeth "Lil" Swift Brengle to "My dearest Susie," Nov. 14 (n.d.): Sam [Brengle] "does not seem to have any definate [sic] appointment yet," but "takes the Holiness meeting every week at Arlington & addresses the cadets & does a NY meeting now and again." Mentions horse named "Pet," Elizabeth, Peggie, Madge, and Gertrude. Undated, c. at the time Lil had returned from a sanatorium; unsigned 2–pages, poor hand–writing: deals with "Papa's will: "$20,000 given outright to each of us, and the rest held in trust, so that we could never spend the principal." He said "'If you should marry, your husbands might turn out badly, & influence you to spend your money, & leave you in poverty. . . . And I feel that I ought to do as I believe he would do in my place,—keep that money *for you*. . . . I *knew* that you would *never* leave the convent. And I can never know that. I may believe it, but I can't know it. . . . I feel still that it is *his* money. And I am trying to do with all of it what I believe he would wish. It is all put away, rolling up, except that I am obliged to use some for the straightening of Eseth—not *very* much."

"Lil" to "Darling Susie," Aug. 12, 1912: from The Andrews, rates $100 & up, Minneapolis, Minn.: "Don't you worry about Eileen's [Douglas] heart." Richards and Rabe tend to dismiss seriousness of the condition. "I'm afraid you don't get all my letters. For I told you several things you don't seem to [?]. [He says] my eyes are 20% better. I've only been to him twice—don't need to go oftener. My eyes are all right . . . the drops I use them . . . Eileen's glasses enable her to do more work with less fatigue. . . . She has a rush order for 2 Xmas stories in six days! So it is well she can write! Dorothy A[?] came on Friday to stay on Sunday. She's the same sweet . . . charming girl as ever, only more so. I surely wrote you that Marian had a stroke of apoplexy last winter. She can use all her limbs again, but still walks with a cane. She is coming to Kent on Wednesday, and I'm so sorry that I can't see her! But we shall then be en route for Graves End [sic] meeting. That is all the address there is, Gaines, Michigan. You might add, Care of Holiness Camp Meeting." "The annual railway excursion to Lake George [Eva Booth's summer house] takes place while we are gone. I'd come up to see you if I could be home. When we get back, I shall have only a very little time to get E off to her school, and then I go to . . . Sam in Pennsylvania." "I have just re–read your letter of the 15th. Thank you very much for that *odertesenuel*. It suits G's copyright! Sam is going to look it up tomorrow or next day in N.J. . . . I truly don't think you need worry over my eyes. They go on all right. They seem better. The tests prove that they are better. And if not and if they grow worse, what matter." "And Eileen, . . . it's the hardest thing in the world to make her behave herself. She's doing fairly well now. . . . Darling. I can't pray for Father Doyle. I said all that about Jafee in a letter which you can't have received. I didn't know F. Doyle, but you believe he is in heaven. Very well—I accept that. Then the utmost prayer I could pray for him, as I think of God answered it, would only . . . I [unintelligible quote, probably Scripture]. It isn't that I don't want to! It is that I am certain that God couldn't answer any prayer I could make for the happy dead without blessing their happiness. . . . I talk to the Lord about her. I thank Him for her sweetness and goodness and sanctification, and that she is in his immediate preserve. They see His face. . . . It is as if I should send a penny to Mr. Rockefeller, to help him in hard places. I am so constantly interrupted that I can't write. I may as well stop. My family is too large! We expect to come home Sept. 3rd." "I'm always loving Lil"

Elizabeth Brengle, niece, on The Salvation Army Foreign Office IHQ stationery, London, n.d.: "Dear Auntie Susie," She describes her mother [Lil Brengle] who "seemed to feel she was being paralyzed and going to die, and wanted to get home while she could. Rabe and Allan and Duckworth all agreed that as long as there was her mental attitude there was no use having her at a sanitarium and it would be better to have her home with a [?] nurse. So George took the sleeper out to Clifton Springs Tuesday night—and yesterday morning he telegraphed that mother was better, and going to Castile. He took her out of course, and I expect he will be home tonight. He said in his telegram that mother might want me to be with her for a while after he got home, so it's possible I will be going out there Sat. or Sun. Mother was worse for a few days after getting to Clifton, but it seems very natural that she should be, and that she was just 'finding her level.' The doctors there agree with those here that—it is a deep seated nervous trouble—nothing cerebral whatever. They also took her urinalysis and found it is good as there is nothing to fear from that source." As for [Sam Brengle]: "Tuesday afternoon I went to see father and found him in fine condition. All his pains went on the eighth day, and he hasn't had

a sign of one since. They're stuffing him with junkel—& custard and such like edibles now and he's looking better already. Probably he'll have answered your letter [?]." [Note: This letter should probably go together with Mrs. Brengle's 2–page letter.]
George Swift Brengle, nephew, 1915

Notes from Friends

Mrs. B. Ellen Burke, Pres., *The Sunday Companion, Juvenile Weekly,* 256 Broadway, NY

Isabella Katherine Byles, 145 Park Ave., Montclair, NJ (see Mary Byles, RSCJ letter)

Mary Byles, RSCJ to "Dear Sister," Sept. 12, 1988, "enclosed snapshots of Sister Imelda, O.D.

Mrs. Campbell—friend, letters from Suzie

Sis. M. Celestine Church of St. Paul the Apostle, 59th & 9th Ave, NYC, 28 Oct. 1909 "My dear child"

Georgina Pell Curtis, editor of Susie's "Some Roads"

Jessie K. Dewell, Vassar, Secty. Treas. Class of '83, 232 Bradley St., N. Haven, CN

Eileen Douglas, adopted sister,

Fr. A. P. Doyle, O.P. Catholic Missionary Union, Secretary–Treasurer, St. Mark's Church & Editorial Dept., The *Catholic World Magazine & Missionary,* NYC

Very Rev. A. P. Doyle to "My dear Sister Imelda," Oct. 11, 1909 response to New Years letter: "What a pity your dad [never let you in on your] settlement."

Very Rev. A. P. Doyle, C.S.P., Secretary–Treasurer of the Catholic Missionary Union, to Most Rev. John Ireland, July 18, 1910, "Your Grace, Sr. Imelda Teresa, O.P. who presents this has been to the Mayor Broskins in Rochester. This explains her presence in St. Paul. While in your episcopal city she is desirous of meeting you and talking over some important matters with you. "I gladly beseach for her an attentive hearing. You will be pleased to meet her any how. A woman of more than ordinary religious character—an eminent convert with church and while a Dominican Sister has devoted herself in a notable way to the service of souls both in Cuba and in the United States, Sincerely yours in X, A. P. Doyle, CSP

Adelaide Drummond, obituary card in mail from Josephine Delmonico Russell, widow of James Edward Russell, Brooklyn, died Apr. 27, 1911 in her 84th year (picture)

Fr. Thomas Marie Gill, O.P., Dayton, Minn.—Lewiston, Me.

Mary G. Haines to "My very dear Miss Swift," Sept. 20, 1897: Haines tells of Salvation Army officers who had been offering opinions on why Susie left the work—due to fatigue, mental breakdown, or "the stupidity of H.Q. in meddling with A.W. [*All the World*]. Emma Booth-Tucker had asked about her and said, "Be sure to tell her that I love her very much and send her my best love." "She felt your leaving no less than Ballington's." Col. Cozens said: "She had worked so incessantly, and had had so little rest in all these years that it had undermined her health and had been too much for her." Haines felt that it was "the interference [that] was practically the charge of mental collapse under the pressure of onerous and continuous duties, though without the slightest trace of any ill will and with the deepest regret." "only one woman . . . has mentioned you in an unkind way. They speak of you with unbounded admiration for what you *were*." Brigadier Bown had gone home to England. Elma Vickery was married. Haines had been "comparing myself with the old M.H.[mission hall] prior to the S.A. Gain in some directions, loss in others, a distinct loss in reverence for *the Sacrament*—why can't there be a Church Army to call people to repentance in the SA manner and then to educate them gradually by Church rites, to teach them reverence and dignity and respect for law and order." [The Church of England has a Church Army.]

Mary Haines, Lorrele Mass., to "My dear Susie," Apr. 15th 1903, response to letter from Susie. Invitation to come to the 20th Vassar reunion by a classmate.

Isabel [Vertiley] to "My Dear Miss Swift," at 3803 Spruce St. Phila., Apr. 17, c. 1897–8: "We shall be most glad to have you as associate especially now, for we are in great need of thee. Will you please write to an old (I think old) lady named Mrs. N. E. MacKenzie, [in] Maxwell, Mississippi. She is a covert and I am sure you will interest her. Another member I should like to give you is a leper in the Johns Hopkins Hosp., Ward I. (Baltimore) Mrs. Sansone. She was born a Catholic but has been brought up a Presbyterian and unless she mentions it first, it would be better not to speak to her of religion as her letters will be read. The nurse at present in the ward for contagious diseases is a convert from a very rich and fashionable family in New England. It seems strange to me to think of her nursing a leper, as she was one of the laziest and most luxurious girls I ever knew. Please let me know if you find any difficulty with these cases, or write to my assistant who answers letters more promptly than I can do. Her address is Mrs. Marie Bouchard, 43 Vernon St., Worcester, Mass. Remember me to Fr. Doyle and Fr. MacVillian."

Florence A. Jeffrey, 492 Manhattan Ave., NYC, wrote from Brighton, Mass., Sept. 1, 1915 to request "a good short & concise Catholic Treatise on Psychology."

Bishop Jones, Puerto Rico

Dr. A. M. Jones, cause of death statement

Julia to "Dearest Sister" n.d.

Rose Hawthorne–Lathrop, Sisters of the Sick

Ella Leonard, Vassar friend, with Swifts in Glasgow

Sr. Mary Innocent of Jesus Papers, Albany Dominicans: card on Death of Mother M. Loyola of Jesus, O.P., Prioress Provincial of the Dominican Congregation of St. Catherine di Ricci, b. Feb. 8, 1854; Received the Faith, July 22, 1876; Professed in Religion, Oct. 12, 1886; Died, Apr. 23, 1904—"Merciful Jesus, grant her eternal rest. (7 years and 7 quarantines) Sweet Heart of Mary, be her salvation (100 days). May unceasing Adoration, Reparation and Thanksgiving be offered to the Sacred Heart of Jesus in the Blessed Sacrament of the Alter (40 days).

Mary E. McCall, Monsey, NY

Fr. McD—Bishop of B (godfather?)

Fr. John T. McNicholas, O.P., Holy Name Society

"Muggins," Salvation Army officer from Kingston House, Bath, Mon. mrg., "dearest Susie, I spent the whole of last evening over your letter to the Chief . . . some things are less incomprehensible to me now . . . you seem *now* to have stepped into the experience most people get when they claim to receive sanctification . . . this plunge has been to you the ladder by which you have climbed out of self into Christ only, but it's so remarkable that you have not found and climbed it before—its feet must have stood near you all your Army life, waiting to be used even there." Muggins wanted to see her off if she was sailing from Southampton. "Your letter made me want to put arms of comfort and love around you." "Your Muggins ever."

Sr. Mary Ellen O'Hanlon Papers, Sinsinawa (no pre–1913 letters)

Fr. Pardow, S.J.

Sr. Mary Raphael, Lanherne Convent, St. Columb, Cornwall, England

Josephine Delmonico Russell, widow of James Edward Russell, Brooklyn, NY, an invitation to Sister Imelda Teresa, to the marriage of her daughter, Isabelle Katherine to William Esdaile Byles, on April 20, 1912, at the Church of St. Augustine, 7th Ave & Stirling Place, Brooklyn

Mother Samuel, O.S.D., Sinsinawa Convent

Fr. Searle

Anonymous Paulist novice at St. Mary's of the Lake, Lake George, NH to "My Dear Miss Swift, July 20, 1898: He apparently knew of her conversion: "I wish I could make you realize all the enthusiasm your letter has aroused in me and in my fellow novices . . . Even before you became a Catholic many of us were praying for you. . . . Your heroism in going to stop with your family for so long on the way to Albany is quite beyond any of us. I would not dare to do it. In fact, I cannot imagine any more trying ordeal."
Sis. C. M. Thuente, O.P.
Fr. Van Rensselaer
James J. Walsh, M.D., 11 W. 74th St., NYC
AR. Wolfe, St. Mark's Church, Catonsville, MD, Oct. 14, 1909, "My dear Susie,"

Photographs

Sinsinawa Dominican Archives, Sinsinawa, Wisc.; Dominican Convent, Elkins Park, Pa., & The Salvation Army Archives, Alexandria, Virginia; & London, England
The Swift Family, circa 1898
George Henry Swift
Mrs. George Swift
Mrs. Elizabeth Brengle
Susie Swift
Susie Swift and Samuel Brengle
Susie Swift in Salvation Army uniform & Dominican Nun habit, 1898
Nov. 1906—possibly in Cuba with Christobel

Clipping File, Sinsinawa Dominican Archives

"Dominican Sisters of Media, Pa.," *New Catholic Encyclopedia*, 1967, 988
"Elizabeth Swift Brengle, Obituary," *The Castillian Castile*, New York, n.d.
"Mazie and the Major," in Susie Swift's 1913 Notebook
"Monastery of Our Lady of the Sacred Heart, 886 Madison Ave., Albany," *Catholic Directory*, 1899
Receiving House Girls Statements: Bk. I., London, "Miss Swift, Salvation Army Home of Rest," Gore
Rd., 22 Apr. 1887, 203; "Gertrude King sent to situation," 6 Feb. 1888; Miss Swift, Penge, 301a *Salvation Army Song Book*, 1899– refers to Susie as "Mother Superior of a convent"
"From Salvation Army to the Church"
"Salvation Army Deserter," New York, 6 April 1897

"Salvation Lass to be a Nun, Will Enter Dominican Convent on Madison Avenue"

"Susie Swift on Teresa of Avila," undated, 6 pages, 3 hand–written–3 typed. Note p. 4 description of S. Teresa's mingling of an active and contemplative life on the order of Swift's Salvation Army-Dominican experience.

"Brigadier Susie Swift, head of the Auxiliary League"

"To and Fro Through the Earth," *The Conqueror*, 5 (1896): 483

Walsh, Fr. John, "Sermon Delivered at the Profession of Sister M. Imelda Teresa, Apr. 30, 1900

War Cry *(London) articles:*

17 Jan. 1885, 3

"Miss S. F. Swift, editor of *All the World,* to be Staff Captain 23 Mar. 1889, 8

"Interview," 25 February 1893, 7

"In the Slums," H.453

"Eighteen Pence is Better than Nothing," H.210

War Cry *(U.S.) articles:*

"Swift Appointed to US with Adjutant Pease and Captain Elizabeth Clark," 4 Apr. 1896, 14

Report of 1896 resignation, Apr. 1897

Secondary Sources

Bras, Sr. Benenuta, "Susie Swift," Sinsinawa Dominican Archives, Nov. 1986

Clark, William, *Dearest Lily* (London: Salvation Army, 1985)

_____, *Samuel Logan Brengle* (London: Hodder & Stoughton, 1980)

Delaney, John, "Teresa of Avila (1515–82)." *Dictionary of Saints* (Garden City: Doubleday, 1980): 542

Douglas, Brig. Eileen, *Red Flowers of Martyrdom,* 2nd enlarged edn., ed. by Bramwell Booth, Red–Hot Library (London: Simpkin, Marshall, Hamilton, Kent, & Salvation Army Book Dept., 1907) [sent to "S F Swift from Lil"]

Hall, Clarence W., *Samuel Logan Brengle* (New York: Salvation Army, 1933)

Life of Teresa, 1878

Loomis, "From a Study Window," *The New World* (Chicago: Catholic Press, 13 Oct. 1916)

"Major Swift in US for 2 Months: to work in England with 'Waifs & Strays,'" *War Cry* (July 1895): 80

McCarty, Sr. Eva, *The Sinsinawa Dominicans* (Dubuque: The Hoermann Press, 1982): 282–3, ref. to Susie Swift by Fr. John T. McNicholas, O.C.S., her spiritual advisor, 21 April 1916

"Oversight of Auxiliary Department, U.S." *War Cry* (Dec. 1895)

Rightmire, R. David, *Sanctified Sanity: The Life & Teaching of Samuel Logan Brengle* (Alexandria, VA: Crest Books)

Sandall, Robert, *History of The Salvation Army*, vol. 2 (London: Thomas Nelson & sons, 1947): 69, 76–77

"Sister Imelda Theresa Swift, O.S.D.," *The Missionary*, Washington, D.C., June 1916

"Susie Swift," Harringshaw's *American Blue Book of Biography: Men of 1913* (Chicago: Lakeside Building, 1913

"Susie Swift," Personal Sketch at The Salvation Army Archives (London)

Walsh, James J., M.D., Ph.D., "Twenty Years of Converts," *The Missionary*, 39, Dec. 1925, 356–58

_____, "Sermon Delivered by Rev. Father John Walsh of Troy at the Profession of Sister M. Imelda Teresa," Apr. 30th, 1900.

Archival Research Correspondence

"Susie Forrest Swift (Sr. Imelda Mary Theresa Swift, O.P.), notes from the Sinsinawa Dominican Convent, Sinsinawa, Wisc., Sr. Marjorie Buttner, O.P., Archivist

Dominican Sisters, St. Catherine's Hall, Ashbourne Rd. & Juniper Ave., Elkins Park, PA, 19117, Sr. Martha Marie Kelly, O.P., Archivist

Sr. Mary Bergin, Pres., Congregation of St. Catherine de Ricci, 2350 N. Providence Rd., Media, PA 19063

"Susie Swift File," Salvation Army Archives, London

"Susie Swift File," Salvation Army Archives, Alexandria, VA

Index—Susie F. Swift Biography

Bibliography

Works & Lives of David Crichton Lamb and Minnie Clinton Lamb in Chronological Order

*There is no biography of either David or Minnie Lamb.

"Staff Captain Lamb & Captain Minnie Clinton," *War Cry* (Nov. 10, 1888): p. 4.

"Staff Captain Lamb," *The War Cry* (April 13, 1889)

1892–95—David Lamb presented Salvation Army views before Royal Commissioners studying Prison Reform (Herbert Gladston); Unemployment (Sir Henry Campbell Bannerman), served Bramwell Booth as Private Secretary for Social Affairs and visited the continent.

Lamb, David C., "The Salvation Army in Co–operation with Governing Authorities," *The Officer* [n.d.], pp. 669–75, a paper read at an International Staff Councils

_____, "Lecture on Emigration and Population Problems," *The Herald of Stars,* Jan. 10, 1915, p. 10; also George Lansbury, "Life and Life More Abundant: Two Great Moments," Feb. 3, 1914, p. 97

_____, "Memorandum on Empire Migration and Settlement," Trades Union Congress and London County Council, 1924, 1930

_____, "A Spiritual Jubilee," Commissioner Lamb's Speech at Goldsmith's Hall, London, 24 Oct. 1932, for private circulation. A testimonial to Lamb's 50 years as a Salvation Army officer.

_____, "How Was I Converted? *War Cry,* New York (Oct. 7, 1933): 13 (also Feb. 6, 1932, p. 10)

_____, *Forty Years of Social Change* (reprint of a Broadcast Address of Jan. 13, 1933)–biographical, Jan. 1892–1933, published by D. C. Lamb, 23 Canonbury Sq., London, N1

_____, "Message to Friends," Oct. 21, 1932.

"Population Problems," *The Empire Club of Canada Speeches, 1937–1938,"* Toronto, Canada: The Empire Club of Canada, 1938): 111–123

_____, Letter to G. B. Shaw, of Ayot, St. Lawrence, Wellyn, Herts., from 23 Canonbury Square, N1, July 1941, British Library, G. B. Shaw Papers, 50522 f.393.

_____, *War of Ideas*–the "Jury"–50 Prominent British Commercial Leaders, November 1942, 16 pp., distributed by D. C. Lamb, C.M.G., LL.D., O.F., from Strathmoor Ave. Detroit, Michigan, USA.

_____, "Security from Aggression; The National Unit in Peace and War; & Co–operation in Commerce" After Lamb's 1941 retirement, he took two extended goodwill tours of Canada and the US.

Letter, Gladstone Murray (Victory Building, Toronto) to Rt. Hon. Clement Atlee, P.C., M.P., Secretary of State for the Dominions, Whitehall, London, August 11, 1943.

Lamb, David C., "The Next General," *The Spectator* (Apr. 12, 1946): 4 pp.

_____, "Rhodesia's Soul," *Rhodesia Herald* (June 10 1947)—he spent "recent months" there.

_____, "My Search for the Soul of Rhodesia: The Quality that Shows Itself in Crisis," *Rhodesia Herald*, p. 4 [1947].

_____, "My Search for the Soul of Rhodesia: Gradual Emergence from the Embargo," *Rhodesia Herald* [1947].

The Lamb's 50th wedding anniversary, Nov. 1948.

Lamb's connection to the Otago Settlers Centenary, 1948.

_____, "Family Newsletter," Goodwill tour of North America, Dec. 1948–Apr. 1949 (May 14, 1949), 23 Canonbury Sq., London, N1.

_____, "Sixteen Week Unofficial Goodwill Tour of Australia/New Zealand," *War Cry* (May 19, 1951).

"Memorial Service to the Late Commissioner David Lamb, F.R.E.S. (Fellow, Royal Economic Society), LL.D. (Doctor of Letters, honorary), C.M.G. (Company of the Order of St. Michael and St. George), O.F. (Order of the Founder), led by Commissioner Frank Barrett, at the Southend–on–Sea Salvation Army Citadel, July 22, 1951."

Obituary: "Helper of Humanity," *The War Cry* (July 21, 1951), David Lamb had been a member of the Empire Settlement Committee for ex-Servicemen. In 1941 he had begun "goodwill tours of the USA and four round–the–world voyages—the last in the spring of 1951.

Obituary: "David C. Lamb, Promoted to Glory," *The War Cry* (July 14, 1951), at the home of his daughter at Tytherton Lucas, Wilts.

Kirkham, John C., Deposed but not Despised: A Reflection on the 1929 Deposition of Bramwell Booth as General of The Salvation Army (Victoria, Australia: Citadel Press, 1999).

Secondary Sources

All the World, Nov. 1884–Aug. 1929, vols. 1–49:8, and 1938–40, a monthly record of Salvation Army operations in all lands.

Primary Sources

Estate papers: "David Crichton Lamb," 23 Cannnonbury Square, London N1, died 7 July 1951 at the Cogswells Tytherton Lucas Chippenham, Wiltshire.
Probate, London, 12 Oct. 1951, Harold William Martin, Solicitor, Effects, £4,988 9/3d, at Probate Court Records, High Holborn, London, 1951, Wills and Admons.

Minnie Clinton Lamb, J.P., Governor at Lock Hospital

"Captain Minnie Clinton of Marylebone," *War Cry* (January 14, 1888)
"Mrs. Commissioner Lamb, Her First Corps, Lt. Minnie Clinton," *All the World* (Jan. 1, 1897 & Feb. 1, 1897)
"Mrs. Commissioner Lamb," *Social Officer* (May 1899): 250–51
A Local Social Problem and Its Solution (St. Albans: The Salvation Army, c. 1911) Rochford Hundred, Poor Law Administration
"An Army Advocate: Mrs. Colonel Lamb's Experiences of Probation and Police Court Work," *Salvation Army Slum Brochure 102*, [n.d.]
Mrs. Commissioner Lamb, articles in *The Sunday Post:*

- "Broken Lives," (Sept. 1, 1935): 12
- "Strangest Job I Ever Tackled," (Sept. 8, 1935): 14
- "Secret I Could Not Tell Wealthy Heiress," Sept. 15, 1935): 14
- "Strange Story of Two Wives," (Sept. 22, 1935): 14
- "Her Confession Took My Breath Away," (Sept. 29, 1935): 14
- "Widow's Vow Never to Speak Again," (Oct. 6, 1935): 14
- "Mother Who Chose the Hard Road," (Oct. 13, 1935): 14
- "I Fight for a Girl's Freedom," (Oct. 20, 1935): 14
- "Three Women in a Strange Affair," (Oct. 27, 1935): 14
- "The Men from Devil's Island," Nov. 3, 1935): 14

Obituaries

She was born at Cambourne, Cornwell, of an Irish father and Cornish mother, but moved to County Durham while a baby. She died at Trebetherick, Cornwall at age 75
"An Indomitable Fighter: Mrs. Lamb 57 Years an Aggressive Army Officer, Called to Her Reward," *War Cry* (Apr. 22, 1939)
See *Officer Review* (Spring 1939)
Major Winifred Leal, IHQ, "Minnie (Clinton) Lamb," *The Officer* (Sept. 1939): 411–14.
The Times, Apr. 18, 1939

Sunday Times, June 3, 1932

Sunday Standard, Apr. 20, 1939

"Sudden Death of Mrs. Lamb: Salvation Army Officer for 57 Years: Life of Public Service," *Barking Advertiser* (Apr. 22, 1939)—Mrs. Minnie Lamb, of Kirkden, Chalkwell Ave., Westcliff, was 75, died at Daymer Bay, near Wadsbridge. Her father was a miner.

- Feb. 13, 1882, she became a lieutenant at South Shields.
- At Perth "she was chased through the streets by a mob, and had to be sheltered by the police."
- At Southend she was a Probation Officer and Justice of the Peace.

Minnie Lamb was a:

- Police Court Missionary
- Probation Officer
- Poor Law Guardian
- Chairman and Secretary of the Boarding–out Committee
- Justice of the Peace
- President of the Samaritan League
- Council Member of the National Lunacy Society
- First Visitor for the Board under the Infant Life Protection Act (unpaid)
- Member of the Board of Management, London Lock Hospital
- Member of the Council of the Lunacy Law Reform Society
- Participant at the International Prison Conference at Prague

Nov. 2, 1948, the London Angus Assn. sponsored a 50th wedding anniversary celebration for the Lambs. The Royal Scottish Corp., of Fetter Lane, E.C. gave Mrs. Lamb a check "for her charitable fund." Many letters—including the London Council of Social Services. Mrs. Lamb biography discussion lasted from Sept. 19, 1944 to 1955 and included:

- Correspondence from D. C. Lamb to S. Gauntlett and Chief of Staff Charles Baugh, at the Salvation Army International Heritage Centre.
- Letter: F. L. Coutts to Mrs. Brauen, (Lambs' daughter) Hill Lodge, Harmer Green, nr. Welwyn, Apr. 1947
- Letter: F. L. Coutts to Mrs. H. Day, 39 Heathville Rd., Crouch Hill, No. 19
- Letter: F. L. Coutts to the Chief of Staff, asking why Lamb has not written a "history" of the Army's social work.
- Nov. 13, 1948, Coutts returned 6 sets of papers that included: 1) "Her First Corps;" "The Greatest Sinner I Ever Knew;" and

"Forty Years of Social Change;" that "will be required for the life of Mrs. Commissioner Lamb if this is ever handled." Coutts had met with Miss Catherine Lamb, a daughter who had been a Salvation Army officer and received the Lamb papers when David died in 1951. Catherine lived at Trebetherick, North Cornwall in Sept. 1955.

Index—David C. Lamb Biography

Norman H. Murdoch, B.A., M.Div., M.Th., M.A., Ph.D., is Emeritus Professor of History at the University of Cincinnati. Born in DuBois, Pennsylvania to Salvation Army officer parents in 1939, he was educated at Asbury College, Asbury Theological Seminary, and the University of Cincinnati. He joined the faculty of the University of Cincinnati in 1968, first as an instructor in history, psychology, and sociology, then solely history after 1972.

He has published *A Centennial History of The Salvation Army in Cincinnati* (1985), *Origins of the Salvation Army* (1994); and *Frank Smith: Salvationist Socialist* (2003). He also wrote booklets and made a videotaped debate on the 1787 U.S. Constitution. Five of his essays have been published in books, 13 in scholarly journals, 11 as encyclopedia entries. He has prepared 59 book reviews for history journals and popular publications, and written articles for popular magazines. In 1990 he was managing editor of "William & Catherine Booth," published by *Christian History* magazine. He has given and/or critiqued papers on 44 occasions. With 22 research grants he has made 16 trips to study The Salvation Army in Canada, Britain, Switzerland, Zimbabwe, South Africa, India, Chile, Australia, and New Zealand.

He has also been a member of the Milford, Ohio Board of Education (1976–83) and the chief negotiator (1989) and president of the University of Cincinnati chapter of the American Association of University Professors (1989–95), during which time he was also a member of the AAUP's National Council.

His wife Grace is Emerita Professor of Psychology at the University of Cincinnati. They have moved to a small ranch outside the village of Jacksonville in southern Oregon where Grace raises horses and Norman writes and teaches occasionally.

CREST BOOKS
The Salvation Army National Publications

Shaw Clifton, *Never the Same Again: Encouragement for new and not-so-new Christians*, 1997

Compilation, *Christmas Through the Years: A War Cry Treasury*, 1997

William Francis, *Celebrate the Feasts of the Lord: The Christian Heritage of the Sacred Jewish Festivals*, 1998

Marlene Chase, *Pictures from the Word*, 1998

Joe Noland, *A Little Greatness*, 1998

Lyell M. Rader, *Romance & Dynamite: Essays on Science & the Nature of Faith*, 1998

Shaw Clifton, *Who Are These Salvationists? An Analysis for the 21st Century*, 1999

Compilation, *Easter Through the Years: A War Cry Treasury*, 1999

Terry Camsey, *Slightly Off Center! Growth Principles to Thaw Frozen Paradigms*, 2000

Philip Needham, *He Who Laughed First: Delighting in a Holy God*, (in collaboration with Beacon Hill Press, Kansas City), 2000

Henry Gariepy, ed., *A Salvationist Treasury: 365 Devotional Meditations from the Classics to the Contemporary*, 2000

Marlene Chase, *Our God Comes: And Will Not Be Silent*, 2001

A. Kenneth Wilson, *Fractured Parables: And Other Tales to Lighten the Heart and Quicken the Spirit*, 2001

Carroll Ferguson Hunt, *If Two Shall Agree* (in collaboration with Beacon Hill Press, Kansas City), 2001

John C. Izzard, *Pen of Flame: The Life and Poetry of Catherine Baird*, 2002

Henry Gariepy, *Andy Miller: A Legend and a Legacy*, 2002

Compilation, *A Word in Season: A Collection of Short Stories*, 2002

R. David Rightmire, *Sanctified Sanity: The Life and Teaching of Samuel Logan Brengle*, 2003

Chick Yuill, *Leadership on the Axis of Change*, 2003

Compilation, *Living Portraits Speaking Still: A Collection of Bible Studies*, 2004

A. Kenneth Wilson, *The First Dysfunctional Family: A Modern Guide to the Book of Genesis*, 2004

Allen Satterlee, *Turning Points: How The Salvation Army Found a Different Path*, 2004

David Laeger, *Shadow and Substance: The Tabernacle of the Human Heart,* 2005

Check Yee, *Good Morning China,* 2005

Marlene Chase, *Beside Still Waters: Great Prayers of the Bible for Today,* 2005

Roger J. Green, *The Life & Ministry of William Booth* (in collaboration with Abingdon Press, Nashville), 2006

Norman H. Murdoch, *Soldiers of the Cross: Pioneers of Social Change,* 2006

All titles by Crest Books can be purchased through your
nearest Salvation Army Supplies and Purchasing Department

Atlanta, GA—(800) 786-7372
Des Plaines, IL—(847) 294-2012
Long Beach, CA—(800) 937-8896
West Nyack, NY—(888) 488-4882